GARDENING
through the YEAR

GARDENING
through the YEAR

JONATHAN EDWARDS
& PETER McHOY

HERMES
HOUSE

This edition is published by Hermes House

Hermes House is an imprint of Anness Publishing Ltd

Hermes House
88–89 Blackfriars Road
London SE1 8HA
tel. 020 7401 2077
fax 020 7633 9499
info@anness.com

A CIP catalogue record for this book is available from the
British Library.

Publisher: Joanna Lorenz
Editorial Director: Judith Simons
Project Editor: Sarah Uttridge
Production Controller: Pedro Nelson
Designer: Nigel Partridge
Jacket Designer: Adelle Morris
Editorial Reader: Penelope Goodare

1 3 5 7 9 10 8 6 4 2

Contents

Introduction

Two of the keys to successful gardening are to carry out tasks in the right way and at the correct time. Whether it's sowing or planting, training or feeding, harvesting or storing, each needs to be carried out at a particular time according to the types of plants you are growing and their stage of development. The weather patterns have changed in recent years so that seasons seem less distinct than they used to be, which makes getting the timing right more difficult. Divided into twelve sections, three per season, this book sets out the most important gardening tasks during each season. Using step-by-step photographs, each technique is illustrated in detail so they are straightforward to carry out even for a gardening novice.

Planning ahead

Having all the main garden tasks mapped out through the seasons enables you to plan ahead so that you can make the most of your garden and available time. This is particularly important during the mad spring rush when it seems that everything needs to be done at once. But don't be guided by the calendar alone, since the exact timing for each task will vary from year to year depending on the prevailing weather conditions as well as the local climate and soil in your garden. For example, if your soil is heavy it can be difficult to work and often remains colder for longer in spring, so that cultivation, sowing and planting will have to be delayed until the soil conditions improve.

Spring-flowering bulbs, like the popular Narcissus 'February Gold', are an uplifting sight in any garden as they herald the start of a new season.

Plentiful harvests of vegetable and fruit crops bring the successful growing season to a close, while late-summer flowers linger to provide a continuing splash of colour.

Similarly, if your garden is exposed to cold winds or receives little sun, or perhaps lies in a frost pocket, you may have to adjust your timings by several weeks during spring and autumn to ensure success – putting off jobs during the early part of the year and advancing them at the end. Even if your garden has an average soil with moderate local climate you would be well advised to keep a close eye on how the seasons develop through the year and use this book as a general guide for timing – making adjustments as necessary.

Taking action

During critical times such as early spring and autumn it's worth checking the local weather forecast each day so that you can take action if required. Simple but effective remedies, such as protecting vulnerable early sowings or newly planted tender plants from an unseasonally late frost in spring by covering them with a double layer of garden fleece or sheets of newspaper, might be all that's required to save the day. It's also worth keeping a notebook or diary of your own, so that you can fine-tune your timings

Magnolias make a stunning seasonal focal point during spring when their perfect, waxy flowers are starkly displayed on bare branches.

Combine the spring-flowering tulip 'Warbler' with early bedding like these forget-me-nots for a reliable and colourful display.

in future years to best suit the conditions in your own garden. Last frost dates in spring and first frost dates in autumn are especially useful records to keep.

If you have the time, and are keen to get the earliest possible crops, there are a number of extra techniques you can use. Covering an area of ground with fleece or plastic for a few weeks at the end of winter will help the soil to warm up, enabling you to start sowing vegetables sooner – use an impermeable material if you also want to keep rain off. Other

equipment, such as cloches and heated propagators, can also extend the growing – and harvesting – season, at both the beginning and the end. A greenhouse, especially a heated one, will obviously increase your scope much further. Even without any special equipment, though, you can successfully grow a wonderful range of vegetables, fruit and flowers, simply by following the seasonal advice in this book. To make it easy to follow, each season is divided into the three main elements of greenhouse, ornamental garden and kitchen garden.

Spring is an ideal time to plan new herbaceous borders and improve existing displays by lifting and dividing exhausted or overgrown plants.

Gardening under cover

If you have a protected area such as a greenhouse, you can start gardening earlier in the year and have a convenient and comfortable place to work during inclement weather at any time. By early spring, the greenhouse will already be a hive of activity with early sowings of bedding plants and vegetables. It is easy to get carried away with the first few sowings, so bear in mind how much protected space you have available. For example, a single tray of seedlings could provide more than enough plants to fill the entire greenhouse once they've been pricked out and grown on. Early spring is also a time to wake permanent plants and tender perennials overwintered under cover from their winter slumbers and take cuttings to increase your stock. The greenhouse is at its busiest during mid-spring with a succession of sowings and cuttings taking up every available space. Tender flowers and vegetables can be sown at this time but, like all greenhouse-raised plants, will need careful acclimatizing to the harsher conditions outdoors before they are planted out.

By late spring, the greenhouse will be more difficult to manage because vulnerable plants will still need protection at night during cold spells, while on sunny days the temperatures will soar unless preventative action is taken. However, the pressure for space will be reduced as plants are moved out into the garden, making way for greenhouse crops such as tomatoes and cucumbers inside. Keeping the greenhouse cool by judicious ventilation, shading and damping down is a crucial task in summer, along with watering, feeding and training greenhouse crops to keep them growing well. It is also essential to protect them from pests and diseases at all times.

With early autumn, the greenhouse can either be wound down for winter hibernation or kept in use throughout the coldest months by installing insulation and heating. Autumn is also the best time of year to clean out your greenhouse to help prevent pests and diseases overwintering and attacking crops the following year. Late sowings of winter crops and flowers for early spring colour can be made in early autumn and you can make use of the greenhouse to overwinter tender perennials and container plants. A heated greenhouse can be kept productive throughout the winter, too.

A greenhouse becomes a hive of activity during spring and enables you to grow a wide range of crops that would not thrive outside.

You can keep herbs in production all year round if you have somewhere frost-free to keep them growing during the winter.

Flowers and foliage

As soon as the weather and soil conditions allow, you can take action to improve your border displays. Early spring is an ideal time to tackle any remodelling of existing features or creating new beds and borders from scratch. It's the perfect time for planting, and existing herbaceous perennials can be lifted and divided at this time of the year, too. If you simply want to fill gaps, sow hardy annuals now for a cheap and cheerful display later in the year. By mid-spring, lawns will need their first cut in most areas and you should be thinking about providing support for taller perennials that are liable to flop over when in full flower later in the year. Plant tender bedding and patio containers with summer flowers as soon as the threat of frost has passed. It's also the time to improve your patio by repotting permanent container plants and making the most of any other planting pockets, cracks and crevices around paved areas. Ponds will benefit from a spring clean, and many will need emptying completely every few years for a thorough clear-out. Now is a good time to create new water features, too.

Though strawberries can be grown very successfully outdoors, if grown under glass they will provide an early harvest.

Turn summer baskets into an autumn showcase by replanting them with winter-flowering pansies at the end of summer.

Early summer is a time for preening and pruning to make the most of your garden plants. Removing the fading flowers from many repeat-flowering specimens will not only improve their appearance but will also help encourage further flushes of flowers later on. Many early-flowering shrubs will need to be pruned to keep them within bounds and flowering well. Most hedges also need trimming as the summer progresses. On the patio, container plants will require regular watering and feeding – especially during hot, sunny spells. You can also propagate a wide range of popular ornamental plants during summer. Many trees and shrubs can be increased from semi-ripe cuttings taken in midsummer, while others are easy to root as layers. You can raise many popular flowers from seed that is saved from the garden, while others are easy to propagate by division, layering and cuttings. By late summer, spring-flowering bulbs become available in the shops, and these can be planted straight away.

Great displays can be created even in the smallest of spaces by combining a long-flowering showgirl with a colourful container.

Autumn is another opportunity to add new plants to your garden while the soil is still warm, so that they are well established before winter sets in. All deciduous trees and shrubs can be planted, but wait until spring for evergreens, such as conifers. Winter and spring bedding can be planted as soon as the summer bedding has lost its appeal, and there's also still time to plant spring-flowering bulbs in borders, containers and naturalized in grass. Make the most of patio containers and hanging baskets, too, by planting them with winter-flowering plants as soon as the summer displays are over.

Lawns often look the worse for wear after a long, hard summer's pounding, but you can take steps in autumn to make improvements, such as sharpening edges. Ponds and other water features should be tidied up at this time of the year: removing tender aquatic plants and in colder areas protecting fish over the winter months by installing a pond heater.

A well-planned herbaceous border will be overflowing with a succession of brilliant colours throughout summer and into autumn.

Herbs are ideal for growing in containers because they will thrive on the well-drained conditions and can be moved to the most convenient position. They can also be brought indoors to provide fresh pickings during the winter months.

Summer is the time to prune many fruit bushes as well as plums and cherries to help prevent the spread of disease. Trained forms of fruit tree will also need pruning. Harvesting and storing of fruit, vegetables and herbs starts in earnest during the middle of the summer and continues right into the autumn in a well-planned garden.

As the dormant season closes in, you can extend the harvest period by protecting outdoor crops. Herbs can also be potted up for use during the winter months. And it's the best time to tackle many pruning jobs in the fruit garden as well as carrying out planned improvements and planting new specimens. The dormant season is also an ideal time to take stock of your successes and failures over the past year, as well as ordering new plants and seeds — making your choices according to how well the plants have performed so far in your garden.

As the weather gets colder, not-so-hardy plants will also need protecting, either by wrapping them in some form of insulating material, or by bringing them under cover. Tender bulbs and perennials will need to be lifted and kept frost free over the winter, while container plants can be moved under cover.

The kitchen garden

Preparation starts in early spring for the sowing and planting season ahead. Early crops will need protecting for best results, especially in colder areas. By mid-spring a wide range of vegetables and herbs can be sown and planted if the weather and soil conditions allow. Further sowings of vegetables can be made as required over the coming months and by late spring tender crops can be planted out once the threat of frost has passed. The earliest salad crops will be ready for harvest at the end of the spring along with early potatoes.

By early summer, the main tasks are weeding and watering. You can also take steps to prevent pests by putting up barriers and traps.

Watering, weeding and pest and disease control are the main summer tasks in a productive vegetable garden.

Spring

The spring garden is full of hope and promise. Early bulbs, including crocuses, daffodils and hyacinths, stud beds and borders with extravagant explosions of colour all over the garden, augmented by breathtaking displays from early flowering shrubs, such as camellias, forsythia and rhododendrons. Bulbs in particular can be used to transform the overall appearance of a garden at this time of year. Whether planted in pockets around the garden, massed in containers or scattered in natural swathes across lawns or under trees they'll draw the eye and be the focus of attention. As the season progresses, colourful spring bedding such as violas, double daisies and the ever-reliable wallflower rub shoulders with serene displays of tulips and irises accompanied by popular spring-flowering shrubs, including lilacs, and magnolias. Then ornamental cherries, climbers and the first of the herbaceous plants take on the colour mantle, carrying the display seamlessly into early summer.

A spring carpet of red and yellow polyanthus, bordered by dark blue forget-me-nots, provides the perfect backdrop for the striking blooms of the 'West Point' tulip.

Early Spring

This is a time when gardeners need no encouragement. With lengthening days, the air less chilly, and plump buds and birdsong to stir the imagination, it is the time when gardeners cannot wait to start propagating and planting. Early spring is a time for caution, however, as winter seldom comes to a convenient end as spring approaches. One of the most common causes of disappointment for novice gardeners is sowing or planting too early – especially outdoors. Often, plants and seeds put out several weeks later in the season overtake ones planted earlier because they do not receive a check to growth. If you have the facilities you can make sowings indoors in pots and trays and then plant the young plants out when conditions are favourable a few weeks later. Some vegetables, and bedding plants such as alyssum and French marigolds, are not worth sowing early, because they mature quickly and later sowings will flower or be ready for harvest at practically the same time as the riskier early sowings. On the other hand, a few popular plants, such as pelargoniums, need to be sown early, otherwise displays will be delayed or reduced. If you need only a few specimens, you may be better off buying these as young plants rather than running the risk of raising them from seed yourself.

In cold regions the weather can still be wintry at this time of the year, but in milder areas you can make a start on many outdoor jobs. If sowing or planting outdoors, bear in mind that soil temperature as well as air temperature is important. Working soil when it is too wet can be damaging, too. As a rule of thumb, avoid working and walking on soil if it sticks to your boots or tools. Think ahead and take steps to improve soil conditions if your soil is heavy – cover seedbeds with plastic or cloches a few weeks before you intend to sow or plant to warm the soil up and help dry it out, and work from planks of wood rather than treading directly on the soil to help spread your weight. Choose a warm spot in the garden to prepare a seedbed for early sowings, raising the soil level with boards on wet soils to help dry it out and angling the surface to catch as much sun as possible in colder areas.

Always watch the weather forecast, and take any necessary action if frost is predicted. For example, you could cover newly planted specimens with layers of garden fleece or old newspapers at night and remove it again in the day. And don't be in a hurry to remove winter protection from less-than-hardy plants. During mild spells unwrap them during the day, but cover them again at night if temperatures are forecast to plummet. Any plants that were covered with garden fleece or other insulating material over the winter will need to be unwrapped as the weather improves, but be prepared to cover them up again if another cold snap is forecast.

Colour up the ground under deciduous trees and shrubs by planting low-growing, shade-tolerant flowering plants such as this *Anemone ranunculoides* 'Pleniflora'.

Spring-flowering bulbs, available grown in pots from garden centres, are ideal for adding a seasonal colour boost to lacklustre borders or patio containers at this time of year.

Sowing and planting summer flowers

Hardy annuals are among the easiest plants to grow from seed – they are undemanding of soil and can be simply sown where they are to grow. They are a cheap and easy alternative to the tender bedding plants that will be sold in garden centres later in the spring. You can either sow them in pots and seed trays for planting out around the garden as established plants, or you can sow them direct where you want them to flower.

Sowing the seed

Starting seeds off in pots or trays enables you to provide the best possible germination and growing conditions, with the seedlings safe from slugs and other pests, and you have greater control of the final

Love-in-a-mist (*Nigella*) is a wonderful airy hardy annual that is easily raised from seed sown in early spring.

effect. Sowing direct in the soil, on the other hand, means you can cover large areas easily without the cost or hassle of raising plants in pots. This works particularly well with large-seeded varieties of hardy annuals, such as pot marigold and poached egg plant. Don't be put off by the

thought of preparing a seedbed – this requires no more work than getting beds and borders ready for planting tender bedding later in the season. As long as you choose a sunny position, weed and water, and thin overcrowded seedlings, the results are almost always good. Bear in mind the final height of each variety, sowing the tallest at the back and the shortest at the front.

Sowing in rows makes thinning and weeding much easier – especially if you don't know what the seedlings look like and find it difficult to distinguish between desirable seedlings and weeds. If, however, you want to create a more natural patch of flowers, broadcast sowing (where the seed is scattered randomly) would be more appropriate. This is

SOWING HARDY ANNUALS

1 You will get best results if you prepare the ground thoroughly by digging it over and clearing it of weeds and other debris. Break up any clods and rake the surface to a fine, crumbly structure.

2 If you are growing just for cutting, sow in rows in a spare piece of ground, but if you want to make a bright border of hardy annuals, 'draw' your design on the ground with sand and grit.

3 Use the corner of a hoe or rake to draw shallow drills, but change the direction of the drills from one block to the next to avoid a regimented appearance. Check the packet for spacing between rows.

4 Sprinkle the seeds as evenly as possible. If the soil is very dry, run water into the bottom of each drill first and allow it to soak in.

5 Write and insert a label, then cover the seeds by raking the soil back over the drills. Try not to disturb the seeds unnecessarily.

6 Water thoroughly if the soil is dry. Thereafter, continue to water during dry weather until the seedlings have emerged.

PLANTING OUT SWEET PEAS

1 For general garden display and a mass of flowers, a wigwam of canes is ideal. Incline the canes inwards and tie at the top, or use a proprietary cane holder.

2 Wire or plastic netting fixed to canes to form a circular tower is another efficient way to support tall sweet peas for general garden decoration at the back of a border.

3 Excavate a hole that is large enough to accommodate the rootball with minimal disturbance, at the base of each cane, or about 23cm (9in) apart.

4 Sweet pea plants are sometimes sold with a cluster of seedlings in one pot. Always separate these and plant individually. Spread the roots out, cover, then water thoroughly.

5 Introduce the plants to their supports at an early stage. The pliable stems can be wound in and out of netting, or attached to canes with string or with metal split rings.

6 If sowing directly into the soil, sow two or three seeds at each position, and thin to one later if more germinate.

particularly useful if you have a packet of mixed annuals, for example, where you might want to create the appearance of a wild garden. After preparing the soil thoroughly, scatter the seeds as evenly as possible before raking them into the surface of the soil – first in one direction and then at right angles.

Planting or sowing sweet peas

Early spring is a good time to sow sweet peas direct outside if weather and your soil conditions allow. Sow two or three seeds at each position, and thin to one plant later if more germinate. In colder areas or on heavy soils it is not too late to sow

now indoors. Sweet pea seeds can also be sown in the autumn and overwintered in a coldframe, or sown in a greenhouse in mid- or late winter. These will now have made sturdy plants ready to be planted out. It is a good idea to try both methods, as the seedlings often succumb to slugs but they also dislike root disturbance.

Planting tender bulbs

Gladioli and most other summer-flowering bulbs, corms and tubers can be planted now, though in cold districts it is too early to plant any very frost-sensitive plants because the shoots may emerge and be killed

by a late frost. Consider growing them in rows in a spare piece of ground if you want them for cutting, but they look best planted in blocks or clusters when grown in beds and borders. As a guide to planting depth, most bulbs should be covered with twice their own depth of soil. For example, if the bulb is 2.5cm (1in) deep, cover it with 5cm (2in) of soil, though there are a few exceptions (check the packaging for details). Some tubers and corms, such as those of anemones, tend to become very dry and shrivelled after a long period in store. You can usually plump them up by soaking in water for a day before you plant.

Creating new borders

Early spring is an ideal time to make garden improvements. Simple changes, such as extending an existing border or creating a new one from scratch, can have an enormous impact on the overall design. Borders along the edge of a garden can help disguise the boundary, creating the illusion of space. Rather than having a narrow strip border along a fence, introduce gentle curves that are pleasing to look at and help lead the eye away from the edge of your plot. An island bed is another option. It has the advantage that it can be viewed from all sides, but tends to work less well if space is restricted.

Design matters

You will also need to consider the style of your garden and the type of plants you wish to grow so that they are in harmony with existing features in the overall design. Simple shapes work best in most situations, with regular circles, squares and rectangles tending to produce a more formal effect while irregular shapes enhance an informal atmosphere. The size of the border should depend on its scale when compared to other features and the overall size of the plot. It's also a good idea to bear in

You can transform the appearance and atmosphere of a garden by creating new borders or improving existing ones. Borders along the boundary can be used to help disguise unattractive fences and walls and to create the illusion of space.

CREATING A CIRCULAR BED

1 Insert a post in the centre of the proposed bed. Attach one end of a piece of string, the length of the radius, to the post and the other end to a bottle filled with sand or soil.

2 Walk slowly around the post, keeping the string taut and the bottle tilted, so the sand or soil trickles out as you walk and marks the outline of the circle.

3 View the circle from all angles to make sure that it is in proportion to the rest of the garden. Then you can remove the turf within the circle to produce a perfectly round bed.

Techniques for creating different shapes

Perfect oval Place two posts in the ground and loosely tie a piece of string around them. Experiment with the distance between the two posts and the length of the string to get the size and shape of the bed you require. Place a bottle filled with sand or soil inside the loop of string and walk around the posts, keeping the string taut. The sand or soil will trickle out, creating the outline of a perfect oval.

Kidney shape Use a flexible garden hose to work out the size and shape of an irregular or kidney-shaped bed. Then remove a line of turf around the inside edge to mark it out.

Straight lines Using a straight-edged board or plank as a guide, cut a straight edge with a spade or half-moon edging iron. Or stretch a length of garden twine between two pegs to provide a guide.

mind how much time you can spend maintaining the border. Deep borders might look dramatic, but they will be more difficult to maintain.

When you come to choosing plants, make sure they are suitable for the site and soil. Space them to accommodate their ultimate height and spread, positioning the largest at the back (the centre of an island bed) and progressively smaller growing varieties towards the edge. Choose plants with an upright habit for the back of a boundary border so that they provide sufficient cover without taking up too much ground space. In a mixed border, choose shrubs to form the backbone of the border that are interesting in their own right and will provide a useful foil for other plants. Fill the gaps with perennials, bulbs and groundcover plants. Try to use a mixture of evergreen and deciduous plants so that the display looks good and ever-changing throughout the year.

Preparing the ground

Because flowerbeds and borders are likely to be left undisturbed for many years it is important to clear the area of weeds completely and prepare the soil well. If it is cut into a lawn, you should skim off the turf with a spade. Elsewhere, you can dig out the weeds by hand, spray with a suitable herbicide or cover the area with black plastic sheeting for several months to kill the weeds. Dig the soil thoroughly and incorporate well-rotted organic matter. Digging is best carried out in late autumn on heavy soils, so that the large clods can be exposed to the weathering effects of frost. Dig the first trench to one spade's depth across the plot, and transfer the soil you have removed in a wheelbarrow to the other end of the plot, where it will be used to fill the final trench. Fork a layer of well-rotted compost or manure into the bottom of the trench to improve the soil structure and to provide nutrients for the plants. Dig the next trench across the plot, turning the soil on to the compost in the first trench. Add compost to the new trench and then dig the next.

Continue down the border until the whole of the surface has been turned. Add compost to the final trench and then fill it with the soil from the first trench. Allow the soil to settle and then rake level, removing any new weeds or other debris that come to the surface.

In a formal garden, straight borders can be used to reinforce the overall appearance. Here, standard roses have been underplanted by spring-flowering bulbs to extend the period of interest.

Dividing and planting perennials

If they are left undisturbed, most perennials eventually become congested at the roots, which reduces vigour and flowering. You can improve your displays by lifting and dividing overgrown clumps every few years. Not only will you get bigger and better flowers, but the plants will remain healthier and you will also get hundreds of free plants that you can use elsewhere in the garden, sell for charity or give away. Regular lifting and dividing also enables you to clear established borders of troublesome perennial weeds, such as couch grass.

Dividing perennials

Perennials can be divided in spring or autumn, but spring is best for plants of borderline hardiness as well as for those perennials that flower late in the season. Some perennials, such as astilbe, liriope and solidago, respond to frequent division. Others, such as agapanthus, alstroemeria, eryngium and hellebores, do not like being disturbed and can take several

Anemone ranunculoides 'Pleniflora' will spread, forming a carpet of cheerful yellow flowers each spring.

SIMPLE DIVISION

1 The day before you plan to divide it, water the plant thoroughly. Dig up a clump of the plant, in this case Michaelmas daisy (*Aster novi-belgii*).

3 You can replant a few of the most vigorous pieces in the bed, but dig over the soil first, removing any weeds and adding some well-rotted organic material.

2 Insert two forks back to back into the plant and lever apart by gently pushing the handles to and fro. Keep on dividing the rootball until the pieces are of the desired size. Discard any exhausted, woody sections.

4 Alternatively, small pieces of the plant can be potted up individually. After watering, place these in a closed coldframe until well established, then plant out after hardening off.

years to recover from the process. Perennials that have not been divided for a long time tend to produce all their most vigorous shoots towards the edge of the clump, with weaker growth in the older, central portion.

How you divide a perennial will depend on the type of roots it produces and how long it has been since it was last divided. For most perennials you should be able to ease the crown apart using two border forks held back to back and pushed and pulled against each other. Looser rootballs can be teased apart by hand, while a few might need slicing into sections using an old kitchen knife. Really tough, woody clumps are more easily sliced into sections with a sharp spade. No matter what

method you use, lift the clump out of the border and into an open space such as on a lawn, path or patio, so that you can move around it easily without damaging other plants. If the clump is very large, slice it into sections that are small enough to carry out of the border. Discard the least vigorous central sections of each clump and replant only healthy divisions, each with plenty of shoots and roots, that are free of perennial weed roots. Clear the border of weeds and improve the soil by adding well-rotted organic matter and a handful of slow-release fertilizer before replanting. Water well after planting and keep well watered during dry spells throughout summer and autumn.

Planting herbaceous borders

Herbaceous border plants can be planted at any time from containers, but most gardeners prefer to get them planted in spring so that they contribute to the summer show. If you buy plants by mail order they may arrive as small root-wrapped plants, and these should be planted before the new shoots emerge or while they are still very short.

If your herbaceous plants are root-wrapped, keep them in a cool, shady place until you are ready to plant. Make sure that the plants are kept moist at all times. Remove the wrapping only just before you are ready to plant. Spread out the roots widely within the planting hole before

You can create a striking effect in a large, informal herbaceous border by restricting the colour scheme to just two colours. Red and yellow look particularly good in bright sunshine.

PLANTING HERBACEOUS PLANTS

1 If planting a border, lay the plants out first so that you can visualize the result, spacing them to allow for growth. Adjust them until you are satisfied with the arrangement.

2 Water the plants about an hour before you start and knock them out of their pots only when you are ready to plant. Tease out any roots that circle the rootball before planting.

3 Make sure that the ground is clear of weeds before planting, and work methodically from the back of the border or from one end. You will be able to plant most herbaceous perennials with a trowel or hand fork, but you may need a spade for large plants.

4 Return the soil, making sure that the plant is at its original depth, and firm well to eliminate any pockets of air around the roots, which could cause them to dry out. Water well both after planting and during any dry spells until established.

returning the soil. Root-wrapped plants are more vulnerable than container-grown plants until they become established, so take extra care and keep them well watered.

Planting container plants

Container-grown perennials can be planted at any time of the year provided the soil is not too wet or frozen. However, planting in early spring allows you to enjoy their flowering display in their first year. Water the plants before planting. Prepare the ground thoroughly, removing weeds and any other debris. Perennial weeds should be removed complete with their roots. Make a hole for each plant and set them at the same level as they were in the pot. Firm the soil around each plant and level the soil after planting, before watering well. Mulch around new plants with a loose organic material, such as well-rotted garden compost or manure, to help reduce water loss and prevent competition from weeds.

Planting trees and shrubs

Spring is an ideal time to plant shrubs and trees because the soil is moist and is beginning to warm up so that new root growth will help the plant become established quickly. You can plant container-grown specimens any time provided the ground is not too wet or frozen. You can plant bare-rooted specimens during winter or early spring.

Planting distance

An important consideration when planting shrubs and trees is the distance that should be left between them. A common error is to place new specimens far too close together, so that within a few years the difficult decision of which to remove has to be made. You can avoid unbalancing the overall design in this way by checking how big the shrubs are likely to grow in a good gardening encyclopedia and then calculating your plant spacing to accommodate them. You may find that initially the newly planted border can appear rather stark, especially if you have bought small specimens. However, this can be overcome by filling the gaps in the early years with a scattering of hardy annuals, short-lived perennials or groundcover plants that can be removed as the shrubs and trees take up more space.

If you want to achieve instant results, choose a range of quick-growing shrubs, such as butterfly bush (*Buddleja*), lavatera, sambucus and ceanothus, mixed with a selection of specimen evergreens and groundcover plants. If they are watered and fed well, the border should fill out in just a couple of years.

Preparing the site

The most important task is to prepare the planting site thoroughly by removing perennial weed roots and incorporating well-rotted manure or garden compost. Always plant the specimen at the same depth as it was in the pot and water well before planting. Dig a hole slightly larger than the pot or rootball and then check the depth by placing the specimen in the hole and laying a cane across it. Add or take away soil as necessary, then position the specimen again. Bare-rooted trees should be inspected for damaged roots, which should be trimmed using a pair of secateurs (pruners). Check the rootball of container-grown shrubs and trees and unwind any roots circling the base of the rootball.

Staking trees

Taller trees will need staking to keep them upright and help them to establish quickly. All trees in an exposed garden should be staked at planting time, with the stake put on the windward side. Bare-rooted trees can be secured using a short vertical stake hammered into the hole at this stage. Container-grown trees are best staked after planting using an angled stake that does not interfere with the rootball. Attach the tree to the stake using an adjustable tree tie, which can be loosened as the tree grows, so that its stem is not constricted as it expands.

To make sure there are no air pockets around the roots, trickle a little soil around the roots, shake the plant gently and add more soil. Firm lightly as you go. Use your heel to firm the soil around all trees and shrubs after planting and water well. Cover the surface with a mulch to keep down weed germination and help prevent the soil from drying out. Organic mulches will slowly become incorporated into the soil by worms and other soil-borne organisms, improving its texture and providing nutrients, so top them up each spring to maintain their effectiveness.

Quick-growing shrubs, such as this semi-evergreen lavatera, are ideal for filling gaps in borders, helping a new garden to appear lush and well-established.

PLANTING A SHRUB

1 Always clear the area of weeds, especially any deep-rooted perennials, which will be difficult to eradicate if they grow within the root system of the shrub. Dig in plenty of garden compost or rotted manure.

2 Water the plant well an hour before planting. Dig a hole about twice the width of the pot or rootball. Position the plant and place a stick across the hole to make sure it will be at its original depth.

3 Remove the shrub from its container, taking care not to damage the roots. If roots are wound tightly around the inside of the pot, tease some of them out to encourage them to grow out into the surrounding soil.

4 Place the rootball in the hole. Holding the plant upright, fill the hole around the rootball and firm the soil down well to eliminate any air pockets.

5 To get your shrub off to a good start, apply a general garden fertilizer at the recommended rate around the plant. Keep away from the stem. Water well.

6 'Balled' or 'root-wrapped' shrubs are sold with their roots wrapped in hessian, a plastic or metal cage or some other material. Check the depth of the planting hole as before.

7 When the plant is in position, untie the wrapping and slide it into the hole. Avoid disturbing the ball of soil around the roots.

8 Replace the soil, and firm well to eliminate pockets of air. Apply fertilizer and water as described for container-grown plants.

9 It is worth mulching the ground after planting to conserve moisture and suppress weeds, which will compete for nutrients.

Pruning trees and shrubs

Most trees and shrubs do not need regular pruning, other than to remove dead, damaged or diseased material. If space is restricted, however, you may have to prune annually to keep them within bounds. A few trees and shrubs will produce better displays if they are cut back at the right time and in the right way. How you prune will depend largely on the plant you are dealing with and the type of growth you are trying to promote.

Pruning strategies

If you are pruning to improve flowering you will need to know whether the shrub blooms on wood produced during the previous season or on new wood produced during the current season. However, if you do not know anything about the shrub you could use the fail-safe one-in-three method. Prune one-third of the shrub back each year, choosing the oldest stems – so after three years, no stem is more than three years old. The one-in-three method is also a good way of rejuvenating old shrubs, such as you might find in a neglected garden filled with overgrown, unfamiliar plants.

Many popular shrubs can be improved by regular pruning in early spring. Only prune shrubs that you

Pruning *Spiraea japonica* 'Goldflame' during early spring will produce more compact shrubs with brighter and bigger foliage.

know require spring pruning, otherwise you may cut out the shoots that will bear this year's flowers. If in doubt, consult an encyclopedia that gives pruning information. You can get improved flowering from quick-growing shrubs that flower on the current season's growth, such as *Buddleja davidii*, *Hydrangea paniculata* and lavatera, by pruning them before new growth starts. Similarly, shrubs such as dogwood (*Cornus*) and *Spiraea japonica* 'Goldflame', that are mainly grown for their decorative stems and colourful foliage, can be pruned now to enhance the display the following

winter. Another example, the whitewash bramble (*Rubus cockburnianus*), is cut back to the ground annually in early spring because of the appeal of the white bloom on the new growth. New shoots will soon grow and the plant will be just as attractive next winter. Indeed, the colour on young stems is more pronounced and the plant is more attractive if all the canes have been produced in the current year.

On the other hand, grey-leaved plants (such as lavenders, *Santolina chamaecyparissus* and senecio) can be pruned lightly in early spring to keep them compact and the foliage dense. Do not cut back into old wood because this is unlikely to re-shoot.

Deadheading heathers

The removal of fading flowers, known as deadheading, is a quick and easy technique that will help keep heathers looking neat. In early spring, trim them with shears. Cut just below faded flowers but avoid cutting into the old wood because it will not re-shoot.

PRUNING WHITEWASH BRAMBLES

1 Cut old canes of *Rubus cockburnianus* to just above the ground using secateurs (pruners). New shoots will appear from below ground.

2 You might find it easier to use long-handled pruners (loppers) to cut back the oldest and thickest stems, which will be tough and woody.

SPRING PRUNING SHRUBS

1 Prune shrubs grown for coloured winter stems shortly before new growth starts. These include *Cornus alba* and *Cornus stolonifera* cultivars and *Salix alba* subsp. *vitellina* 'Britzensis'. Only prune plants that have been established for a few years.

2 Cut back all the stems to an outward-facing bud about 5cm (2in) from the ground or from the stump of old, hard wood.

3 Although the pruning seems drastic, new, more vigorous and brightly coloured shoots will soon appear and by next winter will make a splendid sight. Prune annually if you feed and mulch the plants, otherwise prune back established plants every second spring.

4 Trim over grey-leaved shrubs, such as the popular *Santolina chamaecyparissus* and *Helichrysum angustifolium*, to keep them neat and compact. Take care not to cut into old, woody stems, which will not re-shoot.

5 If you prune the plant regularly from a young age, prune back close to the base to a point where you can see new shoots developing. This may be as low as 10cm (4in) from the ground on some plants.

6 The plant will look bare and sparse after pruning, but within a month should be well clothed again. Lightly fork in some slow-release fertilizer around the shrub to encourage new stems.

7 *Buddleja davidii* produces its flowers at the tops of tall, lanky stems if left unpruned. Each spring, cut back all the shoots to within about two buds of the previous year's growth.

8 Again, this type of pruning looks drastic but it will greatly enhance the look of the plant later in the year by encouraging vigorous, productive stems.

Pollarding

Pollarded shrubs and trees are grown on a short trunk with their main stems pruned back to a framework each spring. The previous season's growth is almost completely removed in early spring by pruning back to within 5cm (2in) of the established framework, leaving one or two buds on each stem to regrow. *Eucalyptus gunnii*, *Sambucus nigra* and cotinus all benefit from this sort of treatment and will produce more colourful leaves.

Pruning roses and climbers

Roses and clematis have both developed an undeserved reputation for being difficult to prune. Until fairly recently rose enthusiasts would have you believe that the only way to get a decent display from your bushes was to follow an intensive care programme of pruning, feeding and disease control. Recent research, however, has shown that rose pruning needn't be an exact science and that it can be done quickly and easily by anyone.

Pruning roses

Trials have shown that you can achieve very good results from hybrid tea (large-flowered) and floribunda (cluster-flowered) roses simply by cutting them roughly to an even height with secateurs or even a hedgetrimmer without worrying about the detailed pruning. The conventional method is still practised by most rose enthusiasts, however. Don't worry if you make one or two wrong cuts – the roses will probably still bloom prolifically. Given a moist, fertile soil, regularly enriched with organic material, roses should grow strongly enough to withstand most pest and disease attacks.

To get the most from your climbing rose, such as this deliciously scented, double pink 'Madame Grégoire Staechelin', prune it in early spring so that you can enjoy a bumper crop of delightful early-summer flowers followed by large, round, bright red hips in autumn.

PRUNING BUSH AND SHRUB ROSES

1 Moderate pruning is the most appropriate for established hybrid tea roses. Cut back the stems by about half, to an outward-facing bud to keep the centre of the bush open.

2 You can treat floribundas in the same way, but if you prune the oldest shoots severely and others lightly, flowering may be spread over a longer period.

3 Whichever type of rose you are pruning, cut back any dead, damaged or diseased shoots to healthy wood, making a clean, slanting cut.

Roses do need to be pruned regularly, however. This is because rose stems will continue to grow and flower well only for a few years before they become exhausted. You can reinvigorate the plant by pruning back exhausted stems to a healthy bud lower down that will grow into a vigorous, free-flowering new shoot. In nature old stems wither and die back, allowing newer stems to take over. By pruning you are simply speeding up this recycling process and you'll also help to keep the shrub compact and healthy. Early spring is the ideal time to prune all bush and shrub roses, including miniatures.

Pruning clematis

The mystique surrounding clematis pruning has probably developed because they are not all pruned in the same way. However, as long as you know when your clematis flowers and whether it flowers on the current season's growth or stems produced during the previous season, you won't go far wrong. Clematis are divided into three groups: early-flowering forms that produce blooms on last year's stems only (known as Group 1); those that flower during late spring and early summer on last year's stems and again during late summer on growth produced in the current season (known as Group 2); and those that flower during late

Pruning standard roses

It's essential to maintain an even shape to the head of a standard rose. Prune ordinary standard roses now using secateurs (pruners), cutting out broken or damaged stems and then reducing the remaining stems by about two-thirds. Weeping standards should be pruned like ramblers in autumn.

Repeat-flowering climbing roses that bear blooms in a series of flushes throughout the summer can be pruned in early spring. Remove any weak and old stems entirely. Also, cut back stems that flowered during the previous year by one-third to a half and trim any sideshoots on the remaining stems to two or three buds. Tie in the pruned stems using soft string or plant ties.

summer only on new growth (known as Group 3). All types of clematis can be pruned in early spring if necessary.

• **Group 1** Spring-flowering clematis, such as cultivars of *C. alpina*, *C. armandii*, *C. cirrhosa*, *C. macropetala* and *C. montana*, need pruning only when they have to be restrained. Cut out sufficient branches to reduce congestion and cut those that encroach beyond their space back to their point of origin or to a pair of plump buds.

• **Group 2** Includes late-spring-flowering and early summer varieties, such as 'Barbara Jackman', 'Daniel Deronda', 'Lasurstern', 'Marie Boisselot', 'Nelly Moser', 'Richard Pennell', 'The President' and 'Vyvyan Pennell'. After cutting out all the dead, damaged or weak growth, remove any wood that is making the clematis congested, cutting back to a pair of strong buds. Leave strong, healthy stems unpruned, or trim back only lightly (these will carry the first flush of flowers).

• **Group 3** Includes late-summer-flowering clematis, such as 'Bill Mackenzie', 'Ernest Markham', 'Etiole Violette', 'Jackmanii', 'Perle d'Azur' and 'Ville de Lyon'. These are perhaps the easiest of all to prune since all stems should be cut back during early spring to the lowest pair of plump buds.

Pruning honeysuckles

These popular climbers either flower on the current season's growth or on stems produced during the previous season. Honeysuckles that flower on new shoots do not need regular pruning unless they get out of hand. Forms that flower on the previous year's growth should have stems that have flowered cut back to a newer shoot lower down on the stem.

Prune honeysuckles only if the flowers are too high or the growth too thick and tangled. If you don't know the variety, cut the oldest stems that have flowered the previous season back to a newer shoot lower down.

Lawn improvements

If you have a patchy area of grass that needs improving, you can either oversow it with grass seed or create a new lawn from scratch. If you want to oversow an existing lawn, rake the area thoroughly to remove thatch (the dead moss and grass that collects at the base of the grass blades in the lawn), prick over any bare areas with a fork and sow seed at half the rate per square metre/yard you would for a new lawn. Rake the seed into the bare patches, water well and use black cotton to protect the area from birds.

Making a new lawn

Before you create a new lawn, you will have to decide whether to raise it from seed or to lay turf. The main advantages of a lawn from seed are that it is cheaper and easier than laying turf and you can choose from a range of grass seed mixtures, including formulations for hot or shady and dry sites. You can even get specially hard-wearing grass mixtures for a family lawn. Some turf specialists also offer seed mixtures to suit your specific requirements, but these can be expensive. Even ordinary turf may cost four times as much per square metre/yard as seed, and it is the less flexible option because it has to be laid as soon as it arrives, no matter what the weather or soil conditions. Turfing large areas is also hard work, but turf gives near instant results, whereas a lawn grown from seed can take up to six months before it's usable.

Whichever method you choose it is important that you prepare the ground thoroughly if you want to achieve a quality lawn. You will need to begin work several weeks before sowing or planned delivery of the

PREPARING THE GROUND

1 Dig the ground thoroughly, and make every effort to eliminate difficult or deep-rooted perennial weeds. Then rake the soil level. Use a system of pegs, levelled with a spirit level on a straight-edge, to set the height.

2 Allow the soil to settle for a week, then consolidate it further by treading it evenly to remove large air pockets. If you do not have a roller, the best way to do this is to shuffle your feet over the area, first in one direction, then in the other.

3 Rake the consolidated soil to produce a fine crumbly structure suitable for sowing seeds. If you can, leave the area for a couple of weeks to allow weed seeds to germinate. Hoe them off or use a weedkiller that leaves the ground safe for replanting within days.

LAWNS FROM SEED

1 Choose a windless day and sow grass seed as evenly as possible. You will get better results by being more systematic about your approach. Use string and canes to divide the area into 1m (1yd) strips, and divide these into 1m (1yd) squares.

2 Use a small container that holds enough seed for a square metre/yard (make a mark on it if the amount only partly fills the container). Scatter the seeds as evenly as possible with a sweeping motion of the hand, first in one direction and then at right angles.

3 If you have to sow a large area it might be worth hiring a seed/fertilizer distributor that you can simply wheel over the area. Always check the delivery rate over sheets of paper or plastic first. Lightly rake the seed into the surface. Water if necessary to keep the soil moist.

You can improve the appearance of established lawns by oversowing threadbare patches at this time of the year. Use a suitable seed mixture to match the existing lawn.

seed should germinate about a week after sowing if the soil and weather conditions are favourable. Wait until the grass blades are 8cm (3in) long before making your first cut, setting the blade height to trim just the tips. This will encourage the grass seedlings to shoot from the base and create a thicker lawn more quickly. Thereafter, reduce the cutting height and trim when the grass gets to 5–8cm (2–3in) for the first season. It is essential that you keep the mower blade sharp so that the seedlings are not ripped out of the ground as you mow. Wait until next spring before you feed your lawn with a spring feed.

If you don't have time to prepare the ground properly this spring, delay sowing seed or laying turf until the autumn instead.

turf. On heavy soils it is often easier to prepare the site in autumn, ready for a new lawn in spring. Choose a fine day when the soil is workable and clear it of all existing grass, perennial weeds and other debris. Dig the area thoroughly and leave large clods to be broken down by frost action over the winter. In early spring, rake the area level and remove any debris that has worked its way to the surface. Mark out the site with pegs and use a spirit level to check the level. Once the site is level, firm it by treading — using tiny shuffling steps with the weight on your heels. Repeat this process until you have created a firm, level bed. Finally, rake the soil carefully from different directions to produce an even surface with a fine breadcrumb-like texture — perfect for both sowing and laying turf (see left and right).

Keep your new lawn well watered until it is established. Turves must receive sufficient water to dampen the soil beneath or the roots will not grow down into the ground. Grass

LAWNS FROM TURF

1 Use a plank to stand on while you lay the next row, since this will help to avoid damaging the turf you have just laid. Stagger the joints between rows to create a bond like brickwork. Make sure these do not align.

2 Tamp down each row of turf (you can use the head of a rake as shown), then move the plank forwards to lay the next row. The turf will be firmed by your weight as you work off the plank laying subsequent rows.

3 Brush sieved sandy soil, or a mixture of peat and sand, into the joints. This will help to bind the turves together.

4 Shape edges when the lawn is laid. Lay a hose as a guide for a curved edge, or use a plank of wood for a straight edge.

Preparing the vegetable plot

Before sowing and planting start in earnest, the vegetable plot needs to be carefully prepared. As soon as weather and soil conditions allow, areas that were dug over in autumn can be cleared of weeds and raked level. Light, sandy soils can be cultivated from scratch now, but heavier soils will need to have large clods broken down by frost–thaw action over the winter months. You could work from short boards or planks laid on the surface to spread your weight and prevent damage to the structure of heavy soils. Wait until the soil is dry enough not to stick to your tools and boots.

Improving the soil

Break down any remaining clods of soil, removing large stones and other debris as you go. If you are creating a seedbed, the surface needs to be as flat and even as possible, with the surface layer of soil having a fine, breadcrumb-like structure. If the soil is too wet to prepare, cover an area to be used for early sowings with a

It is essential to improve the soil before sowing or planting. Not only will you get bigger yields, but the crops will be less susceptible to pest and disease attacks too.

piece of clear plastic sheeting. This will help to warm it up and dry it out by protecting it from further rains as well as encouraging surface weed seeds to germinate so they can be hoed off before sowing starts. Once the seedbed has been prepared, cover it with cloches or a sheet of clear plastic until you are ready to sow. The plastic will act like a mini-greenhouse – warming the soil and so speeding germination and seedling establishment. If cats are a problem in your area but you don't want to keep the rain off, cover the prepared vegetable plot with netting to prevent them from digging and fouling the seedbed.

The vegetable plot also needs regular feeding if yields are not to suffer. Unlike beds and borders in the ornamental garden, little natural recycling occurs. The crops are removed and leaves do not naturally fall and decay. Bulky organic manures

APPLYING FERTILIZER MANUALLY

1 If you are applying by hand, measure out the amount of fertilizer required for a square metre/yard, so that you can visualize how much you need, or pour it into a container as a measure and mark how full it is.

2 Mark out metre/yard widths with strings, then use a couple of canes to divide these into squares. When one square has been applied, move the back cane forwards to mark out the next area.

3 Use your measure to scoop up the appropriate amount of fertilizer, then scatter it evenly. It is a good idea to wear gloves when handling the fertilizer. Hold your hand about 15–23cm (6–9in) above the soil.

4 Always rake the fertilizer into the surface. This spreads it more evenly and helps it to penetrate more rapidly. Remove any stones or other debris brought to the surface by raking to leave the surface as even as possible.

1 Sow the seeds and cover the area with the fleece. It will help warm the soil, and protect seedlings from a degree or two of frost and from flying insect pests. Anchor it down loosely with bricks while you secure the edges.

2 You can secure the edges by burying them in a slit cut into the ground or just heaping soil over them. Water will soak through the fleece, and it will also stretch as the seedlings emerge and develop into sturdy plants.

3 You can buy various types of proprietary pegs to hold the fleece in position, and these are preferable to soil because they make it easier to lift and replace the fleece for weeding and other cultivation tasks.

do much to improve soil structure and increase the nutrient-holding capabilities of the soil, but unless you follow an intensive organic approach and apply sufficient manures and garden compost, some chemical fertilizers are necessary if you want a heavy crop. The quickest way to apply a general fertilizer to the whole vegetable plot is with a wheeled spreader that you can adjust to deliver the appropriate amount. Calculate and test the delivery rate first over polythene laid on the patio or lawn.

Protecting early crops

Horticultural fleece was unknown to a previous generation of gardeners, but the fact that it is now widely used commercially is evidence of its usefulness. The fleece warms up the soil like a cloche, while allowing rain to penetrate, and should provide protection from a degree or two of frost. It also acts as a barrier against flying insect pests that are now beginning to be active. You can use it just to start off your seeds or as protection for a growing crop.

Other types of protective covers can also be used. Insect-proof mesh

is a very fine, long-lasting net, which effectively keeps out flying insect pests. Although it doesn't provide frost protection, it can be used to protect crops from late spring onwards when garden fleece holds in too much heat and cannot be used. Perforated plastic films, known as

floating cloches, let through rain and 'give' enough to rise with the growing crop.

Whichever crop protection you use, you will have to pull it back to weed and thin plants. You will find that weeds thrive under the protection as well as the crops!

Broad (fava) beans, like most vegetables, need an open sunny site which is protected from strong winds, and a reasonably fertile soil.

Early planting and sowing

Sowing early can be a gamble. If the weather is cold the seeds may rot before they germinate, and some vegetables tend to run to seed if they are subject to very cold conditions after germinating. The exact timing will vary from year to year, depending on the prevailing soil and weather conditions. In some years, in some gardens, the soil temperature may not rise high enough until mid- or late spring.

Making a start

If you intend to make a lot of early sowings or your soil is cold and heavy, consider investing in a soil thermometer to check the temperature. Insert the thermometer to a depth of 5–7.5cm (2–3in) each day and record the temperature. Wait until it has risen above 5°C (41°F) for a week before you sow broad (fava) beans and peas, and above 7°C (45°F) for most other early crops. You can help to boost the soil temperature by covering the seedbed with cloches or a sheet of plastic.

If you are sowing early for the first time, concentrate on hardy crops, such as broad beans and early peas.

Sowing planner

Crop	Temperature	Timing
Bean, broad	5°C (41°F)	late winter – early spring
Bean, French	10°C (50°F)	mid-spring – early summer
Bean, runner	10°C (50°F)	mid-spring – early summer
Beetroot	7°C (45°F)	late winter – early summer
Broccoli	5°C (41°F)	mid-spring – late spring
Brussels sprout	5°C (41°F)	late winter – mid-spring
Cabbage	5°C (41°F)	early spring – late spring
Calabrese	5°C (41°F)	late winter – late spring
Carrot	7°C (45°F)	early spring – early summer
Cauliflower	5°C (41°F)	late winter – mid-spring
Celery	10°C (50°F)	early spring – mid-spring
Courgette (zucchini)	15°C (59°F)	mid-spring – late spring
Cucumber	15°C (59°F)	early spring – mid-spring
Leek	7°C (45°F)	late winter – mid-spring
Lettuce	5°C (41°F)	late winter – early summer
Marrow	15°C (59°F)	mid spring – late spring
Onion	7°C (45°F)	late winter – early spring
Parsnip	7°C (45°F)	late winter – mid-spring
Pea	5°C (41°F)	late winter – late spring
Pepper	15°C (59°F)	early spring – mid-spring
Radish	5°C (41°F)	midwinter – late summer
Spinach	10°C (50°F)	early spring – early summer
Swede (rutabaga)	5°C (41°F)	early spring – early summer
Sweet corn	10°C (50°F)	mid-spring – late spring
Tomato	15°C (59°F)	early spring – mid-spring
Turnip	5°C (41°F)	early spring – early summer

SOWING EARLY VEGETABLES OUTDOORS

1 Peas and broad (fava) beans are best sown in multiple rows so that they can support each other as they grow, with walking space between the double or triple rows. Take out a flat-bottomed drill 5–8cm (2–3in) deep.

2 Space the seeds by hand. Peas should be planted 4–8cm (1½–3in) apart in three staggered rows, and broad beans should be 23cm (9in) apart in a double staggered row.

3 Pull the soil back over the drill to cover the seeds. If the ground is dry, water well, and keep watering as they grow. If seed-eaters, such as mice or birds, are a problem, netting or traps may be necessary.

PLANTING ONION SETS

1 Take out a shallow drill with the corner of a hoe or rake. To keep the drill straight, use a garden line held on pegs driven into the ground at each end of the row. The sets should be about 15cm (6in) apart.

2 Pull the soil back over the drill, but leave the tips of the onions protruding. If birds are a problem – they may try to pull the onions out by the wispy old stems – protect them with netting.

You could also try a few short rows of a wider range of vegetables, but be prepared to resow if they don't do well. In unfavourable conditions peas and beans can be sown in containers in a coldframe to plant out as seedlings. Alternatively, sow seed in a piece of guttering filled with compost (soil mix) that can be transferred to the garden as a complete row of seedlings. Early crops of brassicas, beetroot (beets) and carrots can also be started off in pots – sow thinly and thin seedlings to leave six of the strongest in each pot. Plant out when the soil and weather conditions improve, spacing the plants about 15cm (6in) apart.

Hardy vegetables, such as broad beans and brassicas, that were sown in the greenhouse or coldframe during late winter should be growing well and forming sturdy plants by early spring. When soil and weather conditions allow these can be planted out, after they have been hardened off and acclimatized to the harsher conditions outdoors. Position cloches over the planting site to warm the soil while the plants are being hardened off. Plant out at the correct planting distance and water well before re-covering with the cloches.

Onions and shallots can also be planted now. The biggest onions are usually grown from seed, but the results can be disappointing. Sets (small onion bulbs) are an almost foolproof way to grow onions and shallots, and you should be rewarded with a reasonable crop for very little effort. Shallots are spaced about 15cm (6in) apart, so that the tip of the bulb is just protruding. Pull the soil back round them with a hoe or rake. Shallots are useful for an early crop, and you can usually plant them outdoors in late winter, except in very cold regions. If you missed the winter planting, start them off in individual pots now. Keep the pots in a coldframe or greenhouse until the shoots are 2.5–5cm (1–2in) high. Then plant the sprouted shallots in the garden, spacing them about 15cm (6in) apart in the row.

Dividing chives

Herbaceous herbs, such as chives, are best divided in early spring or autumn. Use a fork to loosen the soil under the clump and break it up into suitable sized pieces for replanting.

1 When dividing in early spring, cut down the tops to leave 2.5cm (1in) so that you can see what you are doing and to make the clump easy to divide.

2 Having cut off the tops, tease the clump apart carefully with your hands, avoiding root damage as far as possible. Divide the pieces until each division has 10–20 stems. Make sure each has a generous root system.

3 Replant the divisions in prepared ground, spacing them 25cm (10in) apart. Water well and keep well watered until they are established.

Sowing bedding plants and early vegetables

Most bedding plants and vegetables can be sown now under cover in most areas, as long as you can provide the right conditions for germination and growing them on. Wait until mid-spring before you sow Canterbury bells, godetia, French marigold, verbascum and zinnias as well as courgettes (zucchini) and French and runner beans. Flowers to sow in late spring include eryngium, forget-me-not, Brompton stock, honesty, polyanthus, sweet William, teasel and wallflowers.

Conditions for germination

All seeds need air, warmth and moisture to germinate and some need light too. How quickly and evenly they germinate will depend on how well you can control these conditions as well as the type and condition of the seed you use. Seeds will not germinate if the temperature is too high or too low, but the ideal temperature varies from species to species (see below). How old the seed is as well as the conditions in which it was stored will also affect its viability to germinate. A few seeds have an in-built chemical inhibitor that prevents germination

By raising your own plants from seed you will save money. Plants grown in cellular trays will suffer less root damage when transplanted than those sown in blocks.

unless the seed is given a special treatment, such as soaking or chilling. Many shrubs and alpines, for example, have to be given a period of cold before they will germinate. You can do this the natural way by placing the sown seeds outside over the winter, or you can short-cut the process by placing them in the refrigerator, set at 1–5°C (34–41°F), for a few weeks. Bedding plants that need light to germinate include ageratum, begonia, cineraria, lobelia and nicotiana; mimulus, petunia, salvia and stocks, on the other hand, will germinate in

SOWING IN TRAYS

1 Fill the seed tray with a good quality seed compost (soil mix), spread it evenly and remove any lumps. Tamp down the compost lightly to produce a level surface. Sow the seed thinly across the compost.

2 Cover with a thin layer of compost (unless the seeds are very fine or need light to germinate), lightly firm down and label the tray. Labelling is very important because many seedlings look the same.

USING A PROPAGATOR

1 Place the sown seeds in a propagator. Adjust the temperature of heated propagators as required. You should find the optimum temperature indicated on the back of the packet, but you may need to compromise if different seeds need different temperatures.

2 If the propagator is unheated, it should be kept in a warm position in a greenhouse or even somewhere well lit within the house. Start opening the vents once the seeds have germinated to start the hardening-off process.

Multiple sowing

Many root crops, including beetroot (beets) and turnips as well as onions, shallots and leeks, can be sown in pots and planted out in clusters. Sow six to eight seeds in an 8cm (3in) pot filled with fresh compost and reduce the number of seedlings to six by removing the weakest. Grow on and harden off as normal and plant out at double the recommended spacing for individual plants. The plants will naturally push apart as they grow and produce a good crop of roots or bulbs. This method not only reduces the amount of space they take up in the greenhouse and coldframe but also cuts down on the time it takes to grow them and plant them out, as well as minimizing the cost by using fewer pots and less compost. Since the whole potful of plants is set out as one, there is less root disturbance which helps to avoid a check in growth. This is a useful way of growing mini-vegetables, which have become popular.

the dark but do better in light. Always check the seed packets for the recommended sowing temperature and sowing depth before you sow.

When sowing indoors, there are a few golden rules you should follow:
• Use fresh, well-sterilized sowing compost (soil mix). Don't use ordinary potting compost because this contains too many nutrients, which will damage the emerging roots.
• Sieve the compost to remove lumps. This is particularly important for small-seeded varieties.
• Firm the compost lightly with a special tamper or the bottom of another container to remove air pockets and level the compost.
• Water the compost before sowing by standing the pot or seedtray in a shallow tray of water until the surface of the compost darkens with moisture. Continue watering by this method as the seedlings emerge.
• Sow the seed evenly over the surface, with plenty of space between each seed. This will make pricking out and potting on a lot easier later.
• Cover the pots or seed trays with a clear plastic lid and put them in a warm position out of direct sunlight, or place them in a propagator.

Alternatively, you can cover the pots loosely with clear plastic bags. Those that require dark can be put into an airing cupboard until they show the first signs of germination.
• Move seedlings to a well-lit spot away from draughts and shaded from strong direct sunlight after they have germinated and prick them out once they produce their true leaves.

Sowing small seed

Very fine seed is much more difficult to sow evenly than larger seed. You can overcome this by mixing it with a small amount of dry silver sand

before you sow. Not only will the sand effectively 'dilute' the fine seed, allowing you to spread it more evenly, but you can also see where you have already sown because the light-coloured sand stands out against the dark-coloured compost.

SOWING IN CELLULAR TRAYS

Fill the blocks with compost (soil mix) and tap on the table to settle it down. Sow one or two seeds in each cell. Cover lightly with compost. Remove the weaker seedling from each cell if both germinate.

SOWING IN DEGRADABLE POTS

For plants that dislike root disturbance, it may be worthwhile sowing them in pots made of peat or some other degradable material. The entire pot can then be planted directly into the ground.

Aftercare of seedlings

When you are growing your own plants from seed it is essential to have the space and facilities to grow them on. Pricking out and potting on are critical stages of development that can affect how the plants grow thereafter. Ideally you need to maintain a temperature of 15–19°C (60–66°F) for most seedlings – lower temperatures will slow establishment and growth. The aim is to provide the best possible growing environment in which the plants can grow and develop without suffering a check in growth.

After germination

Prick out seedlings as soon as they are large enough to handle. The exact timing isn't critical because seedlings will prick out successfully any time between seed-leaf stage and when the seedling has got a couple of pairs of true leaves. However, if you leave them in their original trays or pots too long, they will quickly become overcrowded and difficult to separate without damaging them.

Bedding geraniums (pelargoniums) are expensive to buy as plants but are easy to raise from seed if you can provide the right temperature for germination and space to grow them on.

PRICKING OUT SEEDLINGS

1 Choose a module that suits the size of the plants. A small seedling, such as ageratum, will not need such a large cell as, say, a dahlia. Fill the individual cells loosely with compost (soil mix) suitable for seedlings. Level with a straight-edge, but do not compress it. It will settle lower in the cells once the seedlings have been inserted and watered.

2 Loosen the seedlings in the tray or pot before pricking out, and if possible lift them one at a time by their seed leaves, supporting the roots with the end of a pencil or dibber. The seed leaves are the first ones to open when the seed germinates and they are usually smaller and a different shape from the true leaves. Do not handle the stem or roots.

3 Use a tool designed for the purpose, or improvise with something like a pencil or plant label, to make a hole large enough to take the roots. Gently firm the compost around the roots, being careful not to press too hard. Water thoroughly through a fine rose, then keep the plants out of direct sunlight for a couple of days.

If the seedlings are germinated in a propagator or under a plastic cover, they will need to be hardened off slightly before they can be pricked out. Do this by gradually increasing the ventilation around them over a few days by opening the ventilators or propping up the lid or cover, but avoid cold draughts Make sure you remove the lid before the seedlings come into contact with it, or they will be distorted and may even die.

Pricking out

Some plants, such as bedding pelargoniums and pot-plants for the greenhouse and home, are best pricked out into individual pots (see right), but this takes up a lot of space and compost (soil mix), so most bedding plants are pricked out into trays. Instead of using ordinary trays, you can use a modular or cell system, like the one shown left, where each plant has its own pocket of soil, separated from the others. The benefit of this method is that there will be less root disturbance when the plants are transplanted into pots or their final position out in the garden.

Water the fresh compost a few hours before you intend to prick out. If possible, gently lift out each seedling individually, holding it by a leaf – never by the stem or roots. Support the roots with a pencil, dibber or plant label and position the seedling in a hole in the surface of the compost so that it is at the correct spacing and at the same depth it was before. After pricking out, place the seedlings in a well-lit position out of direct sunlight and keep them moist with a mist sprayer.

Tiny seedlings, such as those produced by begonia and lobelia, are easier to prick out in small clumps. Prick out about half-a-dozen seedlings at a time, though the number is not critical. You can either prick them out again into individual pots after two or three weeks, or leave them as a clump to grow on together, when they will look like one substantial plant.

Potting on

Once seedlings have filled their allotted space they will need potting on into small pots of fresh compost.

All young plants will eventually have to be planted outside in their final position. However, if the prevailing conditions outside are not suitable you may have to delay planting out. Because the compost contains feed for only a few weeks of growth, you may have to give delayed plants a boost by applying a suitable dilute liquid feed. Before planting out, harden the plants off gradually, either using a coldframe and opening it by increasing stages each day, or by putting the plants outside during the day and bringing them in at night.

PRICKING OUT INTO POTS

1 Fill small pots with compost (soil mix) and firm it lightly to eliminate air pockets, using the base of another pot.

2 Loosen the compost with a small dibber or transplanting tool. Hold the seedling by its leaves, not the stem.

3 Make a small hole in the centre of the pot, deep enough to take the roots. While still holding the seedling by a leaf, very gently firm the compost around the roots, using a small dibber or your finger. Don't press too hard because watering will also settle the compost around the roots.

4 Water carefully to settle the compost around the roots and keep the seedlings in a warm, humid place out of direct sunlight for a few days. Instead of writing labels for individual pots, it is more convenient to group individual varieties into trays and use just one label.

Bringing on permanent plants

Any permanent greenhouse plant that has outgrown its pot should be repotted before the season gets too busy. Plants you wish to increase in size should be moved into a pot one size larger. Use fresh potting compost (soil mix) that has been placed inside the greenhouse for a few days to warm up. Take care to firm compost right down the sides of the rootball using a short piece of cane or dibber. If you want to keep the plant the same size, repot it into

its original pot by teasing compost away from the roots of the plant to reduce the overall size of the rootball before repotting.

Routine care

Container-grown citrus plants that have been overwintered in the greenhouse can also be repotted if necessary. Either pot up into a larger pot or simply replace the top 2.5–5cm (1–2in) of compost: carefully scrape away any loose

material without damaging the roots and replace with fresh compost.

Permanent greenhouse plants, such as aeoniums and echeverias, which have been kept touch-dry through the winter months, can be watered in early spring to revive them. It's also a good time to increase your stock by propagating. Other plants, such as orchids and container-grown bougainvilleas, will need to be watered. Climbers, such as passion flower and plumbago, can be pruned back to within a couple of buds of the previous year's growth to keep them within bounds.

Cacti and succulents can be repotted too. Although most succulents do not present any special handling problems, prickly cacti have to be treated with respect. If possible, choose a compost formulated for cacti, because this will be well drained and have the right sort of structure and nutrient level. A soil-based compost is a practical alternative. Some commercial growers use peat-based composts, but these are best avoided. Apart from the difficulty of keeping the water balance right, peat-based

REPOTTING CACTI AND SUCCULENTS

1 To handle a prickly cactus without injury, fold a strip of newspaper, thick paper or thin card to make a flexible band that you can wrap around the plant and use as a handle. Carefully wrap it around the plant and hold it firmly.

2 Tap the pot on a hard surface to loosen the rootball. You can then often lift the plant using the paper band. If it refuses to move, try pushing a pencil through the drainage hole to break the bond.

3 If the plant has been in the same compost (soil mix) for a long time, crumble away a little of it from the base and around the sides of the rootball. Do this with care to minimize damage to the roots. You can also remove loose compost from the top of the rootball.

4 Hold the plant in its new pot using the improvised handle, and trickle a suitable compost around the old rootball. The shape of some cacti can make this difficult to do without your hand touching the spines, in which case you can use a spoon.

5 Tap the bottom of the pot on a hard surface to settle the soil around the roots. This is especially important because it is often difficult to firm the soil with your fingers if the cactus is prickly. Wait for a couple of days before watering.

PLANTING A CACTUS BOWL

1 Select the plants that you intend to use. Plants that require similar conditions are best grown together. For example, most desert plants are compatible and most rainforest ones will grow together but not the two groups mixed together. Separate the winter-flowering Christmas cactus.

2 Stand the container in its eventual home and then place the plants you intend to use in it. Arrange them for the best effect. Do not overcrowd the plants. Putting too many in the same container will detract from its overall appearance and it will soon look overgrown. Arrange for shape, style and colour.

3 Put plenty of drainage material in the base of the container, then fill with cactus compost (soil mix) and plant the specimens, firming in well. Add pieces of rock, if you like, then top-dress with fine gravel. A paintbrush is useful for levelling the gravel and pushing it around the plants.

composts do not have the weight and structure to support large cacti and succulents.

Large specimens do not need regular repotting. Simply remove about 2.5 cm (1 in) of soil from the top and replace with fresh cactus compost. The majority of cacti and succulents are best in pots that are quite small in proportion to the size of the top growth. When potting on, it is usually best to move the plant into a pot only one size larger. Make sure you use plenty of drainage material in the bottom of the pot.

Cacti and succulents are generally slow growers and require only occasional repotting. As long as they are given a suitable free-draining compost (soil mix) and plenty of light and warmth, they should provide year-round interest with very little routine care.

Using flower supports

There are few things more disappointing than seeing herbaceous borders collapse just as they're coming into flower. Blustery winds, heavy rain or just the sheer weight of the developing flowerheads can be to blame. It is, therefore, worthwhile taking steps to support vulnerable plants before they topple. Fortunately, not all herbaceous plants require staking (see below for varieties that usually do not), but those that do should be tackled now before they have put on too much growth. Always keep a supply of canes and string in reserve for emergency repairs after a storm.

Methods of support

First of all, you can reduce the need for plant supports by growing the right plants in the right place and encouraging them to produce strong,

Most delphiniums, except the dwarf varieties, need staking to ensure they do not fall over. It is well worth the effort when they produce their beautiful tall spikes of flowers. They come in many colours – this white variety is 'Sandpiper'.

Well-behaved perennials

Acanthus	Hosta
Agapanthus	Iris
Alchemilla	Kniphofia
Alstroemeria	Liatris
Anchusa	Limonium
Anemone ×	Liriope
hybrida	Lychnis
Astilbe	Lysimachia
Begonia	Lythrum
Brunnera	Nepeta
Centaurea	Oenothera
Crocosmia	Penstemon
Dianthus	Polemonium
Dicentra	Potentilla
Dictamnus	erecta
Digitalis	Pulmonaria
Echinops	Salvia
Euphorbia	Scabiosa
Filipendula	Schizostylis
Gaillardia	Sedum
Geranium	Senecio
Geum	Stachys
Helleborus	Trollius
Hemerocallis	Verbascum
Heuchera	Veronica

self-supporting growth. Most herbaceous plants (unless of course they are shade-loving varieties) should be grown in a sunny, well-drained spot. If grown in the shade they will become drawn and weak, so will be much more likely to collapse. For this reason, herbaceous plants grown in a border next to a fence are less able to support themselves than the same plants grown in an island bed where they get much more light from all sides. Giving a high-potash fertilizer without a lot of nitrogen will also encourage smaller, sturdier plants which will need less staking.

There are several types of support you can use. The style you choose will depend on the type of plants you are growing and your attitude to gardening. If you are well organized and do not mind the sight of wiry supports in your borders, you can position hoops, stakes and canes early in the season before the plants have had time to grow. If, however, you have a just-in-time approach to

gardening or prefer to keep your garden free of wiry clutter you may prefer to opt for supports that can be carefully positioned much later in the season. In an informal garden or a prominent border traditional twiggy sticks are the least obtrusive supports. If they are carefully entwined, they can bring a rustic charm to borders as well as acting as an effective support when the plants grow up through them. You can buy such material from garden centres in early spring, but the cheapest option is to recycle twiggy prunings from hedges and shrubs. Bamboo canes and string are the next cheapest option but are time-consuming to erect if you've got a lot of plants to support. You can also buy purpose-made wire hoops and linking stakes, which are easy to use and very effective.

Choosing your support

Which type of support you choose should also depend on the type of

STAKING BORDER PLANTS

1 Proprietary hoops with adjustable legs can be placed over a clump-forming perennial. The new shoots grow through the grid, gaining support from the frame and eventually hiding it.

2 Tall flowering stems can be staked individually by tying them to a cane that is shorter than the eventual height of the plant and hidden from sight behind the stem.

3 Wire netting can be used vertically, creating cylinders, held firmly in place with posts. The plant grows up through the centre, with the leaves coming through and covering the sides.

plant you are supporting. Those that produce sprawling growth could be supported with unobtrusive twiggy sticks, while those that form multi-stemmed clumps would be best supported using proprietary wire stakes or a circle of bamboo canes linked with string. If you are growing a whole border of such plants, you could save a lot of time by using large-mesh plastic netting. If it is supported on large stakes either end of the bed, it can be held taut over the plants and gradually raised as they grow. Herbaceous plants that produce large flowerspikes, such as delphiniums, gladioli and hollyhocks, are generally best supported individually, using a single bamboo cane and split-ring ties. Stakes should be pushed 15–30cm (6–12in) into the ground.

Stay safe

Eye injuries caused by the sharp ends of supporting stakes when weeding and working around herbaceous plants are among the most common injuries in the garden. The best way to avoid such problems is to carry out any maintenance work before staking and use supports that are easily seen. Very short supports (less than your arm's length) and taller supports (a lot longer than your arm's length) are far less likely to cause injuries, so bear this in mind when you choose supports for your plants. Clearly marking the ends of canes using decorative cane tops or colourful ends that can be easily seen is another option. An alternative way of protecting your eyes is to wear a pair of protective goggles.

Lupins do not always need support, especially in a sheltered position, but it is usually safer to stake the tall varieties. They should quickly grow up to hide the stakes.

Making a new pond

To look good a pond needs to be positioned in a natural-looking setting within the garden. Ideally, it should be sited in full sun, well away from overhanging trees. A nearby tree, even if not close enough to create heavy shade, can cause problems by dropping leaves into the pond. Although it will look natural if it is at the lowest point in a garden, this is not necessarily the best place. Experiment with a garden hose in several positions before you start to dig. The size and shape will depend on personal taste, but it should reflect the overall design of the garden. Check there

are no hidden underground obstructions, such as pipes and cables, before you excavate the hole.

Practical matters

To be self-sustaining, make your pond as big as possible, with a surface area of at least 5 square metres (over 50 square feet). Make the deepest areas at least 60cm (24in) so that the water does not get too warm in summer. Smaller ponds will also require more maintenance, clearing overgrown plants and topping up the water level during hot spells. If you want to grow marginal plants, the pond will

need a shallow shelf along at least one edge about 23cm (9in) below the surface. Make the shelf at least 23cm (9in) wide so that there is plenty of room for the plants.

There are various ways to line a pond. Concrete is very durable, but requires more skill and expertise than using bought pond liners. In most circumstances it is easiest to construct a pond using either a pre-formed rigid shell or a flexible liner. The main advantage of a rigid pond liner is that you don't have to worry about designing the shape. They are available in both formal and informal designs in a range of

INSTALLING A FLEXIBLE LINER

1 Mark out the pond shape. Use garden hose or rope for an irregular shape and pegs and string for straight edges. Remove any turf and start to excavate the pond. Redistribute topsoil to other parts of the garden.

2 Dig the whole area to about 23cm (9in) deep, then mark the positions of the marginal shelves to about 23cm (9in) wide. Dig deeper areas to at least 60cm (24in) deep. Angle all vertical sides so they slope slightly inwards.

3 Check the levels as you work. Correct discrepancies using sieved garden soil. Make sure there are no sharp stones on the base and sides that might damage the liner, then line the hole with builders' sand.

4 On stony soil you may need to line the hole further with loft insulation, old carpet or a special pond liner underlay (which is expensive). Trim the liner underlay so that it fits neatly into the hole.

5 Ease the liner into position without stretching it unduly. Choose a warm day, as it will be more flexible. Weigh down the edges with stones, then fill the pond slowly with water. Ease the liner into position so that it follows the contours as the pool fills.

6 Once the pond is full, trim back the excess liner to leave an overlap of at least 15cm (6in) around the edge. Cover the overlapping liner with paving or other edging. To disguise the liner, overlap the edging at the water's edge by 2.5cm (1in).

MAKING A POND USING A RIGID LINER

1 Place the pre-formed unit on the ground and transfer the shape to the ground by inserting canes around the edge of the unit. Use a garden hose, rope or sand to mark the outline on the ground.

2 Remove the unit and canes and excavate the hole to approximately the depth of the unit plus at least 5cm (2in), following the profile of the shelves as accurately as possible.

3 Use a spirit level and straight-edged board, laid across the rim, to check that the hole is level. Measure down from the board to check that it is the required depth.

4 Remove any large stones and pad a layer of fine soil or sand in the bottom of the hole. Put the pond in the hole, then add or remove soil to ensure a snug and level fit. Check with a spirit level that the pond is level.

5 Remove the pond and line the hole with damp sand if the soil is stony. With the pond in position and the levels checked again, backfill with sand or fine soil, being careful not to push the pond out of level.

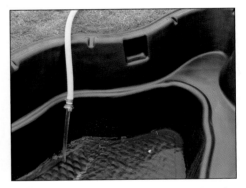

6 Fill with fresh water and backfill further if necessary as the water level rises, checking the level frequently to make sure the unit has not moved. Allow to stand for a few days before stocking with plants.

sizes. However, they do not come in very large sizes, and they tend to be more difficult to install than flexible liners. If you want to create an unusual shaped pond you'll have to choose a flexible liner, but it can be difficult to get the shape that you want on very light soils. Rigid liners are made from either fibreglass or plastic, while flexible liners are available in PVC, butyl rubber, LDPE or polythene. The latter is the cheapest but will only last for a few years before it will need to be replaced. To calculate the size of flexible liner use this formula:

- Length = 2 × maximum depth + maximum length of the pond.

- Width = 2 × maximum depth + maximum width of the pond.

For example, for a pond that is 3 × 2m (10 × 6ft) with a maximum depth of 50cm (20in), you will need a flexible liner that is 4 × 3m (14 × 10ft).

Edging your pond

The material you choose to edge your pond should reflect the formality of the pond. The clean straight lines of paving slabs are an ideal choice for formal ponds. Lay the slabs on top of the edge of the liner so that there is at least 15cm (6in) of liner under the edging stones. The edging stones should

overhang the surface of the pond by 2.5cm (1in) and be clear of the pond's water level. Make sure they are well-secured on a bed of mortar. For more informal settings, you can use plants to soften the paving edge or use broken or small-unit paving, which can be laid to follow gentle curves. In a wildlife garden, you could lay the turf right up to the water's edge or create a beach effect with large pebbles so that birds and other wild creatures can bathe and drink with ease. Turfing to the edge of ordinary ponds is not recommended because soil and clippings will inevitably fall in and foul the water.

Creating a bog garden

A bog garden contains permanently moist soil and enables you to grow plants that are well-adapted to such conditions. Bog gardens associate well with water features such as ponds and streams, helping to integrate them into the wider garden. They can also make an attractively lush feature in their own right. Mid-spring is an ideal time to make a new bog garden.

Making a bog garden

If you are making a garden pond using a flexible liner it is easy to extend the excavation to create a depression 45cm (18in) deep for the bog garden. All you need to do is buy a liner that is large enough to cover both areas and lay it on a bed of sand. The liner covering the bottom of the bog garden needs to be perforated with a few holes and lined with a layer of gravel 5cm (2in) deep for drainage. Build a low wall of stones to separate the pond from the bog area, and lay some fine-mesh netting along the bog garden side of the stones to prevent the soil washing into the pond. Half-fill the bog garden with soil mixture made from 75 per cent

Bog gardens work particularly well alongside water features such as this gurgle pond, but can make attractive features in their own right too.

loam and 25 per cent well-rotted organic matter. Lay some decorative pebbles to conceal the netting, then top up the bog garden with soil mix that's had a little balanced slow-release fertilizer mixed in. Trim the edge of the liner to leave a 15cm (6in) overlap all the way around, and cover this with pebbles or with a layer of soil or turf. If you don't have a pond, you can create a bog garden in the same way using perforated pond liner. You can also create a bog garden adjacent to an existing water feature, but take care not to undermine the feature.

PLANTING A BOG GARDEN

1 Adjust the position of the bog plants while they are still in their pots until you are satisfied with the arrangement. Cultivate the soil carefully, avoiding any subterranean liner, and remove any perennial weeds complete with roots.

2 Water each container well and allow to drain before planting the centre of the bog garden first. Make a planting hole and set the plant as it was in the container.

3 Firm the soil carefully around each plant. Level the soil over the bog garden after planting is complete and cover the surface with a layer of loose organic mulch to help prevent moisture loss and keep down weeds.

Good bog garden plants

Aruncus	Ligularia
Astilbe	Lobelia
Caltha	cardinalis
Cardamine	Lysichiton
Filipendula	Lythrum
Hemerocallis	Matteuccia
Hosta	Primula
Houttuynia	Rodgersia
Iris ensata	Schizostylis
Iris sibirica	Trollius
Juncus effusus	Zantedeschia

Planting boggy ground

If you have a naturally boggy garden, you can grow bog garden plants throughout. Because bog gardens over 1.8m (6ft) wide are difficult to maintain, consider running a pathway through the area. On a small scale, stepping-stone logs would be adequate, but over larger areas consider installing a raised walkway made from timber decking materials. If pressure-treated with preservative to prevent rotting, they'll last many years even with their supports in soggy soil. Along the edges of your bog garden, grow moisture-loving shrubs or make a backdrop from willow canes, which will root to form a living screen.

All bog gardens need regular watering in dry spells, so it is always worth laying a seep hose on the soil surface before you plant. Once planting has been completed, cover the seep hose with a layer of mulch so that it is out of sight.

MAKING A PEBBLE FOUNTAIN

1 Mark out the diameter of the reservoir and dig a hole slightly wider and deeper than its dimensions. Place a shallow layer of sand at the bottom. Make sure that the reservoir rim is slightly below the level of the surrounding soil so that water will drain naturally into it.

2 Backfill the gap between the reservoir and the sides of the hole with soil. Firm in. Create a catchment area by sloping the surrounding soil slightly towards the rim of the reservoir. Place two bricks at the bottom to act as a plinth for the pump. Then position the pump.

3 Ensure the pipe used for the fountain spout will be 5–8cm (2–3in) higher than the sides of the reservoir. Line the catchment area with a plastic sheet and either cut it so the plastic drapes into the reservoir or cut a hole in the centre for the fountain pipe. Fill with water.

4 Check that the pump works, then position the plastic sheet over the reservoir, with the fountain pipe protruding through the hole. Fit the fountain spout. Weigh down the edges of the sheet to keep it in place as you work.

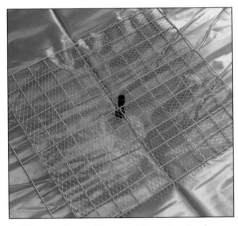

5 Place a piece of heavy-duty galvanized mesh (large enough to rest on the rim of the reservoir) on top to support the weight of large cobbles. Place a finer mesh on top of the larger one to prevent smaller stones falling through.

6 Cover the area around the pump with a layer of cobbles. Check the height of the spout is satisfactory. When you are happy with the fountain, finish arranging the cobbles so that the spout is hidden.

Planting a hanging basket

The best hanging baskets are those planted with fairly small plants that are then grown on in a light, frost-free place until it is safe to put them outdoors – perhaps in late spring or early summer. A greenhouse is ideal, but you might also be able to use an enclosed or protected porch. Giving the baskets protection for a few weeks enables the plants to recover from being transplanted before they have to contend with the more exposed conditions outdoors.

Practical matters

Larger hanging baskets are easier to look after and produce far better displays, so choose the largest your hanging basket bracket can hold – ideally 45cm (18in) in diameter. There are basically two types of basket: those made from open wire mesh and those with solid plastic sides. Traditionally, baskets were made from plastic-coated wire mesh that was lined with sphagnum moss with plants poking through holes in the mesh and cascading over the rim.

Reliable basket plants

Foliage	Petunia
Cineraria	Portulaca
Glechoma	Scaevola
Hedera	Tagetes
Helichrysum	Verbena
petiolare	Viola
Lysimachia	
Plectranthus	Trailers
	Anagallis
Flowers	Convolvulus
Begonia	sabatius
Bidens	Diascia
Brachyscome	Fuchsia
Felicia	Lotus
Gazania	Pelargonium
Heliotrope	(ivy-leaved)
Impatiens	Sanvitalia
Osteospermum	Sutera
Pelargonium	Tropaeolum

PLANTING A HANGING BASKET

1 Stand the basket on a large pot or a bucket to keep it stable while you are filling the basket. Carefully place the liner in position so that it fills the basket. Pierce a few holes in the bottom.

2 Half-fill the liner with compost (soil mix), then mix in some hydrated water-retaining granules to help prevent the basket from drying out. Add some slow-release fertilizer to feed plants throughout the summer.

3 Cut holes 4cm (1½in) across in the sides of the liner. Wrap the plant in a small piece of plastic and carefully poke it through the hole. Remove the plastic, loosen the rootball and add more compost mixture.

4 Plant up the rest of the basket, packing the plants much more tightly together than you would in the open ground. Top up with compost and water well. Keep the basket under cover until all risk of frost has passed.

Solid-sided baskets are planted only in the top so that the container is never completely hidden from view.

Watering hanging baskets is the critical maintenance task through the summer months. Wire-mesh baskets are more difficult to keep moist because water is lost through the sides, although this can be partially overcome by lining the bottom of the basket with plastic or placing a saucer in the basket (to act as a water reservoir) before adding the compost (soil mix). Some solid-sided plastic baskets also have a special reservoir built into the base, making them even easier to keep moist. Another option is to add water-retaining granules to the compost before you plant or to use a special hanging basket formula that has enhanced water-holding capacity. Either will mean you can leave more time between waterings. Don't be tempted to use more than the recommended amount, and check first that the compost does not already contain a water-retaining substance, since excessive amounts can cause the compost to froth up.

Wire-mesh hanging baskets need to be lined before the compost is added. Traditionally, a 5cm (2in) layer of sphagnum moss was used, but today this is rejected by many gardeners on environmental grounds. Consequently, recycled materials, such as wool, cotton and coconut fibre, have become popular, or you could opt for pre-formed liners made from other materials, including compressed paper and polystyrene foam. Make sure you choose one that looks attractive so that it doesn't detract from your basket displays early in the season. Most man-made liners can be reused for more than one season if you do not damage them when you empty the basket in the autumn. Another option is to use materials from your garden. For example, moss raked from the lawn can be used as long as you haven't treated the grass with chemicals recently, and trimmings from conifer hedges make attractive, long-lasting evergreen liners for winter baskets.

Planting a wire basket takes more time and skill than a solid plastic

Orange pansies planted with daisy-like *Brachyscome* and trailing convolvulus make a delightful combination, and if watered and fed regularly should provide a display that lasts all summer.

USING WATER-RETAINING GRANULES

1 For those that need pre-hydrating, pour the recommended amount of water into a bowl. Add the granules, stirring occasionally until they have absorbed the water.

2 Add the hydrated granules to compost (soil mix) at the recommended rate. Mix the hydrated granules thoroughly with the compost before using the mixture for planting.

one to get right. Use trailing plants in the sides and around the rim, with more upright plants in the top. When planting the sides, you may find it best to push the plants out from the inside so that the rootball is not damaged. Alternatively, roll up the rootball in a small piece of plastic before sliding it carefully through the hole. Once the plant is in the right position, simply pull off the plastic. To make watering easier, push a small, empty pot into the top of the basket after planting and fill it with stones. Then, apply water into the pot so that the water can gradually soak into the compost.

Growing vegetables from seed

Vegetable sowing begins in earnest now, with crops like beetroot (beets), spinach beet, summer cabbages, salad and pickling onions, scorzonera and turnips, as well as further sowings of lettuces, peas, radishes, spinach, carrots and cauliflowers. Dwarf beans can be sown in mild areas. There are several ways in which you can grow vegetables in the garden: in rows or beds, among other plants or as part of a formal but decorative potager.

Designing the plot

Traditionally, vegetables have been grown in straight rows in a dedicated area of the garden with paths between rows. This arrangement means that you can choose the most suitable part of the garden to grow your crops and you can prepare the soil to benefit the crops you are growing. Moreover, by growing in straight rows it is easier to tell your plants from weeds – which is particularly important when they are at the seedling stage. The main drawbacks are that there is a lot of competition among plants in the row when they reach maturity and a lot of space is wasted between the rows.

By growing in dedicated beds, the middle of which is just within reach from permanent paths that run along the sides, you can grow crops in shorter straight rows. Because there are fewer paths, this system is more space efficient, and the closer spacing between rows means there is less room for weeds to get established. You do not have to walk on the soil,

which means it is not compacted and so remains in better condition. Resulting crops are of better quality and grow more quickly than in the traditional row system. You can improve growing conditions further by making raised beds.

Not everyone has the space for a vegetable plot, and you can also grow vegetables among ornamental plants. The main disadvantages to this are that the vegetables suffer from more competition for light, nutrients and moisture, they are more difficult to look after, and they leave gaps in the display when they are harvested. However, because the plants are not all growing in one place, pest and disease outbreaks are likely to be less common. You can either hide your crops away at the back of ornamental borders or make a display of the more decorative vegetables, such as frilly-leaved lettuce and brightly coloured chard, which make an edible alternative to summer bedding. In a formal garden you could grow vegetables in beds edged with low-growing box in the style of a traditional French potager.

Perennial vegetables, such as asparagus, rhubarb and artichokes, are normally grown in an area away from the annual crops where they can be left undisturbed and cropped at appropriate times of the year.

Using sowing strips

Take out a drill as usual and place the strip on edge in the drill. Return the soil to the drill, and keep the ground moist. Because the seeds receive protection from the material in which they are embedded, and this sometimes also contains nutrients to give the seedlings a boost, you may find it an easy way to achieve a row of well-spaced seedlings.

FLUID SOWING

1 Sow the seeds thickly on damp kitchen paper and keep them in a warm place to germinate. Make sure that they remain moist and check daily to monitor germination.

3 Mark a straight line using a length of garden twine held on pegs driven into the ground, then take out the drill in the normal way, with the corner of a hoe or rake.

2 Once the roots emerge, and before the leaves open, wash the seeds into a sieve and mix them into prepared wallpaper paste (without fungicide) or a special sowing gel.

4 Fill a plastic bag with the paste and cut off one corner (rather like an icing bag). Twist the top of the bag to prevent the paste oozing out, then move along the row as you squeeze out the seeds in the paste.

SOWING MAINCROP VEGETABLES OUTDOORS

1 Rake the seedbed level and remove any stones or other debris that comes to the surface. Make sure that all perennial weeds are removed.

2 Most vegetables grown in rows, such as beetroots and carrots, are best sown in drills. Always use a garden line to make sure the drills – and therefore the rows – are straight.

3 Take out a shallow drill with the corner of a hoe or rake. Always refer to the seed packet for the recommended sowing depth of the seed, which varies considerably.

4 Flood the drills with water a few minutes before sowing if the weather is dry. Watering after sowing is likely to wash the seeds away or into clumps.

5 Sprinkle the seeds thinly and evenly along the drill. Do this carefully now and you will save time later: you will have to thin the seedlings if they have been sown too close.

6 Use a rake to return soil to the drills by raking in the direction of the row and not across it, otherwise you might spread the seeds and produce an uneven row.

Seed types

Most vegetable seed is bought in packets that contain a foil sachet. You can also get pelleted seed that has been coated in clay. This is easier to sow evenly and at the correct depth. The clay simply falls away when it becomes moist. A few types of popular vegetables are supplied embedded at the correct spacing on a strip of degradable material (see left). A few difficult-to-germinate varieties can be bought 'primed': in these cases the first germination stage has been reached. All these preparations are an expensive way to buy seeds, but save much time and disappointment.

Alternatively, you could improve your chances of success with difficult seeds by fluid sowing, which involves germinating the seeds before sowing. Parsnips, early carrots, onions and parsley are sometimes sown this way.

Stony soil

If the soil is very stony, it is worth making an effort to remove stones from small areas of ground before planting certain crops. Rootcrops, such as carrots and parsnips in particular, need a clear root-run, otherwise they will produce poor-quality, forked and stunted roots that are less useful in the kitchen.

SOWING ROOTCROPS IN STONY SOIL

1 To create the perfect root-run in stony ground use a crowbar to make conical holes at the required planting distance.

2 Fill each hole with potting compost (soil mix). Sow the seed in the centre before covering with more soil.

Planting vegetables

Cabbages and cauliflowers are not normally sown in their final positions. Instead, they are started off in a seedbed, or sown in late winter and spring in pots or modules in the greenhouse, then transplanted to their growing positions. If you are unable to grow your own plants from seed, you can order a limited number of cultivars by mail order from seed companies. Alternatively, buy young plants from garden centres from mid-spring, which can be a useful way of replacing losses or filling gaps.

Dealing with young plants

It is always best to raise your own plants from seed. Buying plants is more expensive than buying seed, and inevitably you will have far less choice of varieties. If you do buy plants from a garden centre, check to find out when they are going to have their next delivery and buy as soon as they arrive. Look for named varieties that are stocky and well

TRANSPLANTING CABBAGES AND CAULIFLOWERS

1 If you have your own seedlings to transplant into the vegetable patch – perhaps growing in a coldframe – water thoroughly an hour before you lift them if the soil is dry.

2 Loosen the soil with a fork or trowel. It is best to lift each one individually with a trowel if possible, but if they have not been thinned sufficiently this may be difficult.

3 Plant with a trowel and firm the soil well. A convenient way to firm soil around the roots is to insert the blade of the trowel about 5cm (2in) away from the plant and press it firmly towards the roots.

4 You can also firm the soil with the handle of the trowel if you don't want to use your hands, but this is not a good idea if the soil is wet as it will dirty the handle. Always water in thoroughly after transplanting.

Planting planner

Crop	Planting distances		Crop	Planting distances	
	Between rows	In the row		Between rows	In the row
Bean, broad (fava)	45cm (18in)	10cm (4in)	Lettuce, hearting	30cm (12in)	30cm (12in)
Bean, French	45cm (18in)	10cm (4in)	Lettuce, loose leaf	23cm (9in)	5cm (2in)
Bean, runner	60cm (24in)	15cm (6in)	Marrow	90cm (36in)	90cm (36in)
Broccoli	60cm (24in)	60cm (24in)	Onion, maincrop	23cm (9in)	5cm (2in)
Brussels sprouts	90cm (36in)	90cm (36in)	Onion, salad	15cm (6in)	1cm (½in)
Calabrese	30cm (12in)	15cm (6in)	Parsnip	23cm (9in)	15cm (6in)
Cabbage, Chinese	45cm (18in)	30cm (12in)	Pea	60cm (24in)	5cm (2in) in 15cm (6in) drill
Cabbage, spring	30cm (12in)	15cm (6in)	Pepper	45cm (18in)	45cm (18in)
Cabbage, summer	30cm (12in)	30cm (12in)	Potato, early	60cm (24in)	50cm (20in)
Cabbage, winter	45cm (18in)	45cm (18in)	Potato, maincrop	75cm (30in)	40cm (16in)
Carrot, early	15cm (6in)	5cm (2in)	Shallot	30cm (12in)	23cm (9in)
Cauliflower, summer	45cm (18in)	45cm (18in)	Spinach	30cm (12in)	15cm (6in)
Cauliflower, autumn	60cm (24in)	60cm (24in)	Swede (rutabaga)	30cm (12in)	23cm (9in)
Courgette (zucchini)	90cm (36in)	90cm (36in)	Sweet corn	35cm (14in)	35cm (14in)
Garlic	23cm (9in)	10cm (4in)	Tomato	45cm (18in)	45cm (18in)
Leek	30cm (12in)	15cm (6in)	Turnip	15cm (6in)	15cm (6in)

grown and that have dark leaves (where appropriate). Avoid any that look lanky or damaged or that are suffering from stress.

Transplanting inevitably causes a check in growth because the roots are disturbed and the plant has to acclimatize to its new, more exposed environment. However, there are a number of things you can do to minimize the disruption. Always transplant when the young plant has reached the right stage of growth and when weather and soil conditions allow. Carefully harden off plants raised under cover before transplanting them into the open. Ideally, water the plants before and after transplanting on a day when the weather is overcast and the soil is moist. On sunny days, shade the transplants and keep them well watered until they are established. In general, younger plants transplant better than older ones do.

Prepare and mark out the planting site before you start, and transplant only a few plants at a time. Do not lift a whole row at once because delays in replanting will increase stress. Transplant only those young plants that look healthy and vigorous, discarding any weak and spindly ones. Use a measuring stick laid along the row with the planting distances marked on it as a guide to ensure correct spacing and speed up the transplanting process. Most transplants are planted at the same depth as they were growing in the seedbed or container and gently firmed in. Leeks are the main exception to this rule and should be planted in 15cm (6in) deep holes and watered in instead of firming.

Plant potatoes

It is safe to plant potatoes in most areas, since it will take several weeks before the frost-sensitive shoots emerge from the soil, and these can be protected by earthing (hilling) up the plants. In cold areas, however, it is best to chit your potatoes and delay planting for a couple of weeks. Place the tubers in a tray in a light position, perhaps by a window, where there is no risk of frost. Chitting is useful if you want the tubers to get off to a quick start.

PLANTING POTATOES

1 Use a draw hoe, spade or a rake head to make wide, flat-bottomed or V-shaped drills 10–13cm (4–5in) deep. Space the rows about 60cm (24in) apart for early varieties, and 75cm (30in) for the maincrop.

2 Space the tubers about 40–50cm (16–20in) apart in the rows. Make sure that the shoots or 'eyes' (buds about to grow into shoots) face upwards. For larger tubers, leave only three sprouts per plant and rub off the others.

3 Cover the tubers by pulling the excavated soil back into the drill. Do this carefully to avoid moving or damaging the tubers. Firm the soil with the back of the rake and water well.

4 If you don't want the effort of earthing up your potatoes, plant under a black plastic sheet. Bury the edges in slits in the soil and cover with soil to anchor the sheet.

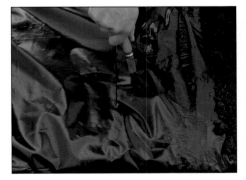

5 Make cross-shaped slits in the plastic with a knife where each tuber is to be planted. To make sure you get the correct spacing cut a piece of cane to use as a guide.

6 Plant through the slit, using a trowel. Make sure that the tuber is covered with 2.5–5cm (1–2in) of soil. The shoots will be able to find their way through the slits.

75cm (30in). Other crops can be protected from flying pests using special crop covers. Cabbage butterflies, for example, can be kept off susceptible crops by covering rows with garden fleece. Lay the fabric loosely over the row so there is plenty of room for the plants to develop, and bury the edges to keep it safely in place.

3 Fleece and insect-proof mesh can be used to protect growing crops from flying pests, such as cabbage white butterflies. Use insect-proof mesh for summer crops.

4 Cabbage root fly can be kept at bay by placing a felt or plastic collar around the base of the brassica plant in order to stop the fly laying its eggs.

Protecting your crops

You will get bigger and better crops earlier in the year if you protect them from the worst of the weather, especially late frosts. A range of techniques is available that will help you protect vulnerable young plants from the weather as well as from

Growing herbs

Every garden has the space to grow herbs. Many make ideal container plants because they are fairly drought tolerant, and you can even grow them in hanging baskets. Growing them in containers also means you can position the herbs in a convenient spot near to the kitchen. If you want to grow a lot of herbs, however, you will need to grow them in the garden either among other plants in mixed beds and borders or in a dedicated herb garden. If you are new to growing herbs, choose types that you use most often in the kitchen.

Siting a herb garden

Most herbs prefer a sunny site protected from cold winds, although a few, including chives, lovage and mint, can tolerate shadier conditions.

Position the herb garden as near to the kitchen as possible, so that it is convenient to collect herbs as and when they are needed. Herb gardens can make very decorative features if they are well planned (see below). Traditional herb wheels always look effective in any garden, but in a contemporary setting you might wish to consider one based on a chequer-board design with paving slabs as the 'white' squares and planting pockets filled with herbs as the 'black' squares.

The soil should be well-drained for most of the Mediterranean herbs. Prepare the site by digging it thoroughly and removing all weeds and other debris. Rake it level before you mark out the design that you want on the surface with sand trickled from a bottle or cup.

Stocking a herb garden

You can raise herbs from seeds or buy them as plants. Once you have a few plants established, you can also propagate your own from cuttings, division or layering, so a herb garden needn't cost a lot to create. Many herbs, once established, will spread themselves prolifically by seed or runners without any help from you. Indeed, mint is so invasive that most gardeners grow it in pots buried in the ground, to prevent it taking over. However, some herbs, such as parsley and basil, will prove expensive if you use a lot of them, unless grown from seed. On the other hand, some herbs, including golden and variegated forms of marjoram, mint, sage and thyme, do not come true from seed, so you will need to buy these as plants. Also bear in mind that annual

MAKING A HERB WHEEL

1 Use string and canes to mark a circle, then measure off a series of equal points on the circumference for the spokes. Sink a length of earthenware pipe in the centre.

2 Trace over the whole design with fine sand or line-marker paint. Although you can have as many sections as you like, more than six or eight will look fussy.

3 Excavate a trench for the bricks and fill it with dry concrete mix to form a firm footing. Remember that you want the top level of bricks to be level with the top of the earthenware pipe.

4 Build the outer circle and spokes with one or two courses of bricks, set in mortar. A herb wheel does not have to be very high; two or three courses of bricks should be sufficient.

5 Fill in the sections of the wheel and the earthenware pipe with a layer of rubble and gravel to provide drainage. Then add good-quality topsoil mixed with fine grit.

6 Plant up the herb wheel with a selection of culinary herbs, such as sage, thyme, rosemary and lemon verbena. Water in thoroughly and add an organic mulch.

PLANTING A HERB GARDEN

1 First prepare the site by thoroughly weeding and forking over to break up the soil, then rake the ground level. Box trees have been used to line this wooden-edged herb bed.

2 To help plan the planting, mark out the design with sand trickled out of a pot. If you make a mistake or change your mind you can easily replace the lines.

3 Remove the herbs from their pots and plant them carefully, making sure that they are at the same level as they were in the container and loosening the rootball.

4 Water the plants thoroughly and keep them watered in dry weather until they are established. Avoid planting on a hot day; if possible, do it when rain is forecast.

5 The newly planted herb garden will look rather bare at first, but it won't be long before the plants begin to fill out and grow to fit their allocated space.

herbs will need to be replaced each year, and some perennial herbs will thrive for only a few years.

There are many herb specialists that stock a huge range of different cultivars, but for most circumstances you'll find a good range of basic (and most useful) herbs at your local garden centre. Look for stocky, well-grown plants with fresh foliage and no signs of pests or diseases. Some herbs are particularly prone to certain pests and diseases, so inspect the plants for symptoms. Mints, for example, often suffer from rust disease, which shows itself as tiny orange spots on the undersides of the leaves. Watch out for the tell-tale pale lines in the leaves of parsley that are an indication of celery fly attack, and inspect bay trees carefully for scale insects. Also check that the herbs have been hardened off properly before you buy. If not, you will have to do it yourself before you plant.

Grow herbs with similar requirements together, as this will make them easier to look after. Plant them at the same depth they were in their pots and don't forget to label them. It's also worth noting down the names of the herbs on your planting plan just in case the labels get mislaid. Water well until they are established.

You can grow herbs in almost any container from plastic pots to large tubs. For convenience, keep them near to the kitchen door.

Sowing and taking spring cuttings

The greenhouse is at its busiest during mid-spring with early sowings of hardy annuals and vegetables that need to be hardened off before planting out and new sowings of tender plants to be made. It is also a good time to propagate many popular shrubs and overwintered tender perennials from softwood, or spring, cuttings. But beware: it is easy to get carried away when propagating plants, especially if you are raising plants from seed. The secret to making the best use of available space is careful planning. You can ease the pressure on space to some extent by erecting temporary staging and shelves.

Planning and scheduling

First, work out exactly how many plants you think you will need in your garden and use this to calculate how many seeds to sow. A good general guide is to sow twice as many seeds as you need plants. This will then accommodate any losses and allow for a 70 per cent germination rate – the minimum standard for commercially produced vegetable seed and a reasonable expectation for commercial flower seed.

Because most seed packets contain hundreds if not thousands of seeds, a single packet will contain sufficient for several seasons. However, once the foil pouch inside the seed packet has been opened, the viability of the seed deteriorates with time. Therefore, provided the seed is stored well, in the second year you could expect around 50 per cent germination and in the third as little as 30 per cent. Before you sow, take sufficient seed out of the foil packet for the sowing and seal it immediately, place it in an airtight container, such as an old lunchbox, and keep it somewhere cool, such as the crisper drawer in a refrigerator. The best way to buy and use seed is to club together with friends and neighbours so that you can share the seed in a single packet and buy fresh each season. Of course, packets of larger seed and new cultivars will contain fewer seeds.

Don't sow all your seed at once. The seedlings will all need pricking out and potting on at the same time (both of which take a lot longer than sowing) and will require more space to grow at the same time – putting pressure on your possibly over-stretched bench and shelving space. You would be far better off sowing in small batches over a few weeks. This method gives you much greater flexibility too, so you can respond more effectively to sowing successes and failures by subsequently sowing more or less seed as required. If you have a lot of seed to deal with or have had problems sowing at the right time in the past, consider making yourself a seed organizer out of a card-index box, or similar, divided up into weeks throughout spring and summer. Then, slot each packet of seed into the week you plan to start sowing it. Seed that you intend to sow in succession can be moved on to the next sowing date after you have made the first sowing of that particular type.

SOWING TENDER VEGETABLES

1 Sow runner beans about six to eight weeks before the last frost is likely. Fill a 15–20cm (6–8in) pot with sowing compost to within 2.5cm (1in) of the rim. Put three seeds in the pot, cover with compost and water gently.

2 Keep the pots in a warm place, and give them good light as soon as the seeds have germinated. If all the seeds germinate, pull out the weakest seedlings to leave just one or two of the strongest to grow on.

3 Outdoor and greenhouse cucumbers can be sown now. Use small pots and fill with a seed-sowing compost to within 2.5cm (1in) of the rim. Position two or three seeds in each pot, placing them on their narrow edge. Cover with compost and water.

4 Sweet corn is best raised in pots to plant out after the threat of frost has passed, except in very mild regions. You can use ordinary pots, but many gardeners prefer to use fibre pots. The roots will grow through these once they are planted out.

HARDENING OFF BEDDING PLANTS

1 Place the plants in a coldframe a week or two before planting-out time. Close the top at night and on cold days, otherwise ventilate freely. If frost threatens, cover the frame with insulation material or take the plants into a greenhouse or indoors again.

2 If you don't have a coldframe, you can cover groups of plants with cloches. Ventilate them whenever possible so that the plants become acclimatized to the cooler temperature while they are still receiving protection from the worst winds and cold.

3 If you don't have frames or cloches, group the trays or pots together in a sheltered spot outside and cover them with garden fleece or a perforated plastic floating cloche. However, you will need to take them under cover again if frost is forecast.

If you end up with too many seedlings, it is wiser to give them away rather than growing them on yourself because they will take up valuable space and cost extra in pots and compost (soil mix). After germinating the seed you should pick the strongest seedlings for pricking out, because they will perform better in the long run.

For a bumper crop from midsummer, sow runner beans in containers now, ready for planting out after the threat of frost has passed.

However, if you have sown a mixture, prick out a range of sizes, or you may select only the most vigorous cultivar from the mixture.

Cuttings

Softwood cuttings, which are taken from the new shoots produced in the current year, root quickly and easily, and you can multiply many of your plants this way. Caryopteris, clematis, forsythia, fuchsia, helichrysum, kolkwitzia, lavender, pelargonium and shrubby types of sage are all worth trying now. Prepare pots of a suitable rooting medium before you take the cuttings.

Hardening off

All plants raised indoors or in a greenhouse need hardening off before planting out. If this is done properly the plants will remain sturdy and healthy, but losses could be high if you move tender plants straight out into cold biting winds or hot, dry conditions outdoors after a cosseted life on the windowsill or in the greenhouse. Plants that you buy from shops and garden centres should have been hardened off before you buy them.

TAKING SOFTWOOD CUTTINGS

1 Trim or pull off the lowest pair of leaves (if the plant has scale-like stipules, such as on a pelargonium, pull off these as well). Trim the base of the stem with a sharp knife, cutting just below a leaf joint.

2 Make a hole in the compost, then insert the cutting, firming the compost gently around it. Water carefully. Do not force the cutting into the compost as this may damage it. You can plant several cuttings around the edge of each pot to save space – but don't let the leaves touch.

Late Spring

The end of spring can be deceptive. It often seems as though summer has already arrived, yet in cold areas there can be severe late frosts. Take local climate into account before planting any frost-tender plants outdoors. Even with experience it can be a gamble as an untypical season might produce surprises. Judging when frosts are no longer likely is mainly a matter of assessing risk. A good guide is to watch when summer bedding is put out in the local parks. These gardeners will have amassed generations of local knowledge of your area, which is by far the best guide.

Late spring is often the busiest time in the gardening year. Early sowings will have been pricked out and potted on ready for hardening off and planting out in the garden. Further sowings will still need to be made, so that the pressure for greenhouse and coldframe space will be at its most intense. The weather will be improving throughout late spring and so it will be safe to plant out tender plants in all except the most exposed gardens by the end of spring.

All new plants need regular care to avoid checks in growth. Young plants in pots may need to be fed with a dilute liquid feed if the weather delays planting for more than a couple of weeks. Once planted, all new additions should be kept well watered until established. Keep weeds under control at all times, ensuring they are not allowed to flower and set seed. A mulch applied between plants will help to prevent weed seeds germinating and retain soil moisture.

Pests and diseases can also be troublesome by this time, so inspect all plants regularly and take the appropriate action as soon as symptoms are noticed. Slugs and snails are the primary pest to watch out for if the weather is wet, while aphids can multiply alarmingly as temperatures rise. All can be controlled effectively by hand if you catch them early enough, although you may prefer to take preventative action, such as using barriers, chemicals or biological controls, to protect the most vulnerable plants as well as any prized specimens.

In the greenhouse, it is essential to keep control of the environment so that plants grow unhindered. If the weather is hot, the main challenge now will be keeping the greenhouse cool by careful ventilation, shading and damping down. Greenhouse crops, such as tomatoes and cucumbers, will be growing fast and require regular watering and feeding as well as training. It is now safe to move not-so-hardy permanent container plants outside for the summer in most areas. But keep an eye on weather forecasts for an unseasonably cold night during the first few weeks and take action to protect any tender plants.

Many vegetables, including lettuces, peas, spring onions (scallions), early carrots and radishes, will need to be sown in small batches several times over the coming weeks to ensure there is a continuous supply of mature crops during the summer months. Tender crops, such as tomatoes, aubergines (eggplant), marrows and courgettes (zucchini), can be planted out as soon as the threat of frost has passed in your area.

The thornless climbing rose 'Zéphirine Drouhin' produces an abundance of colourful blooms, and fills the air with its sweet perfume.

Growing herbs in pots means you can keep them close to the kitchen door so they are easy to pick when needed.

Sowing flowers

Biennials, such as wallflowers and forget-me-nots, are easy to raise from seed, and because they can be sown direct outdoors they need very little attention. Border perennials, such as lupins and aquilegias, are also easily raised from seed sown now, and many of them will flower next summer. Others may take another year or so to become established before flowering.

What is a biennial?

Biennials are plants that grow and establish in the first year, then flower, set seed and die in the second year. There are many good and popular flowering biennials that can be sown in late spring or early summer. Now is the time to sow double daisies, forget-me-nots, wallflowers, polyanthus, sweet Williams, Iceland poppies and sweet rocket (see right). One of the main advantages of growing hardy biennials is that they are sown after the spring rush is over and you don't need to provide any expensive equipment. Biennials also flower at useful times. Early types, such as polyanthus and winter pansies, can be in bloom during late winter if weather conditions are kind, while the double daisies and forget-me-nots add much to the spring displays. But plants such as

Biennial selector

Name	sowing time	flowering period
Anchusa	early summer	late winter – late summer
Brompton stock	early summer	late spring – midsummer
Canterbury bell	mid-spring	late spring – midsummer
Double daisy	late spring	early spring – midsummer
Evening primrose	early summer	early summer – mid-autumn
Forget-me-not	late spring	early spring – early summer
Foxglove	early summer	early summer – midsummer
Honesty	early summer	mid-spring – early summer
Iceland poppy	late spring	early summer – late summer
Pansies, winter	early summer	late winter – midsummer
Polyanthus	late spring	late winter – early summer
Sweet rocket	mid-spring	early summer
Sweet William	late spring	early summer – midsummer
Verbascum	mid-spring	early summer – late summer
Wallflower	late spring	mid-spring – early summer

SOWING BIENNIALS AND HARDY PERENNIALS

1 Prepare the ground thoroughly, and make sure that you remove all traces of perennial weeds and their roots. Break the soil down into a fine, crumbly structure once it has been cleared of weeds.

2 Take out drills with the corner of a hoe or rake to the recommended depth (this varies with the seed, so check the packet). The drills can be quite close together, because the seedlings will be transplanted later.

3 Run water into the drill before sowing if the soil is dry. Space the seeds thinly, and as evenly as you can. This makes thinning and later transplanting much easier.

4 Cover the seeds carefully by easing the soil back with the back of a rake, taking care that you do not disturb the seeds. Remember to add a label.

5 Thin the seedlings as soon as they are large enough to handle easily so that they do not become overcrowded. Remove the weakest seedlings without uprooting those left behind.

the late-spring-flowering Brompton stocks and sweet Williams are the most useful, because they can be used as gap fillers – they can cover any spaces that are left behind by spring-flowering bulbs as well as provide temporary cover between new shrubs and perennials in a recently planted bed.

Raising from seedlings

If you need to raise a lot of plants, sow directly into a prepared seedbed (see opposite). Thin out the seedlings as soon as they are large enough to separate, and plant out into their final positions during mid-autumn. For just a few plants, or if your soil is very heavy, you can also raise biennials in seed trays and pots – just like bedding plants. This method is particularly worthwhile for late-winter-flowering biennials, such as winter pansies and polyanthus, which need optimum growing conditions to develop into sturdy plants. Prick out and pot up the seedlings into individual containers and stand them outside, making sure they get plenty of water during the summer. Feed every couple of weeks with a dilute liquid fertilizer. Plant out in mid-autumn, spacing plants about 15–45cm (6–18in) apart, depending on how big the plants grow.

Make sure the beds are weed-free before planting out – if any perennial weed roots remain, it will be difficult to dig them out without disturbing the plants. It is best to remove new weeds by hand as they appear – avoid using a hoe as it is likely to damage the plants. Covering the soil with a mulch of organic material will help prevent weeds germinating, and will also improve soil structure and fertility as it is incorporated.

Sweet Williams (*Dianthus barbatus*) are a short-lived perennial, grown as a biennial. They come in a range of pinks, white and bicoloured, and as the name suggests, they are sweetly scented.

BETTER FLOWERING DISPLAYS

1 Deadheading Regularly remove fading flowerheads to encourage repeat-flowering plants to produce a succession of new blooms over a longer period.

2 Feeding An application of high-potash fertilizer during the growing season will help promote better flowering. If using a granular feed, take care not to get any on the leaves.

3 Mulching A layer of composted bark or garden compost will help suppress weeds and conserve moisture. As the worms take it down, it will also improve the soil.

4 Pinching out Keep plants compact by pinching or cutting out the central growing tip to encourage sideshoots to develop, making for more bushy growth.

Caring for trees and shrubs

Late spring is a good time to take stock of your shrubs and trees and check that they are providing good value for money when you consider the space they occupy. Those that have outgrown their allotted space can be earmarked for pruning back in autumn, although a few can be tackled now using the one-in-three pruning method. Once flowering is over, shrubs such as ceanothus, olearia and philadelphus that may have become overgrown can be cut back by removing the oldest and thickest stems. By repeating the process after flowering each year for three years, you will have completely rejuvenated the shrub without losing the entire flowering display.

Improving trees and shrubs

You can also improve the display of an established tree or shrub by planting a suitable climber next to it and training the climber to scramble through the canopy of foliage. For best results, choose a complementary climber that matches the vigour of its host and produces its flowers at a time when the host does not, in order to extend the overall display. The host should have a framework that is strong enough to bear the weight of the climber and should not be too young or too old. Do not try to brighten the display of an old and exhausted host because you will simply hasten its demise.

Position the climber on the side of the prevailing wind, so that its stems will be blown against the supporting host and not away from it. Plant the climber in the 'drip zone' just under the edge of the canopy of the host so that any water that runs off the foliage during downpours falls where the climber can make use of it. If the host is very large and well established with lots of roots near the surface, you will need to protect the climber from competition with its host. Dig a large hole, removing any perennial weeds and tree or shrub roots as you go, add plenty of well-rotted organic matter, and plant the climber. You can line the sides of the planting hole with sheets of strong plastic to allow the climber a free root-run. With a shrub host, drive in a cane next to the climber, angled towards the shrub, tie the top to the shrub and train the climber along it. With

A large rhododendron like this can have its season of interest extended by growing a climber through it. A good choice might be an early-flowering clematis, such as *Clematis alpina*, which will flower before the (deciduous) rhododendron is in full leaf, and is not so vigorous as to overwhelm its host.

'Zephirine Drouhin' is a beautiful, repeat-flowering climbing Bourbon rose that's excellent for covering a wall (whether sunny or not) or growing through an established large shrub or tree.

a tree, it is best to tie the climber to a secure stake, and tie a rope from the stake to the canopy of the tree. This will greatly reduce the danger of the climber being pulled out of the ground whenever the tree sways in a strong gust of wind.

Adding groundcover

The space underneath established trees and shrubs can also be improved using climbers as groundcover. Again choose a complementary partner that will enhance the existing display. Between trees you can use fast-growing climbers such as some types of clematis and honeysuckle or large-leaved, variegated ivies, such as *Hedera colchica* 'Dentata Variegata'. The area between shrubs could be improved with less vigorous clematis or with small-leaved decorative ivies. Ivies are particularly useful because they are evergreen and because it is easy to remove unwanted stems. Add spring-flowering bulbs to come up through the ground-covering climbers to extend the flowering interest into another season.

PLANTING A CLIMBER NEXT TO AN ESTABLISHED SHRUB

1 Improve the appearance of a dull shrub by adding a climbing companion. Choose one that does not flower at the same time as the shrub.

2 Dig a hole at the edge of the supporting shrub so that the climber will receive rain. Improve the soil if necessary, and plant the climber, angled towards the shrub

3 Using a cane, train the climber, such as this clematis, into the shrub. Spread out the shoots so that it grows evenly throughout the shrub.

4 Water the new plant thoroughly and mulch around the plant to conserve moisture in the soil. Continue to water, especially in dry weather, until the climber is established.

Stocking your pond

This is a good time to plant up your pond, whether you are establishing a new one or just adding some new plants to an existing one. For a pond to look good for much of the year and to remain largely self-reliant you need to choose the plants carefully, selecting the right combination of well-behaved species that will suit your size of pond.

Planting a pool

Pond plants are categorized according to the position they occupy in the pond.

• Deep-water plants, such as waterlilies, help to cover the surface with foliage, providing much-needed shade for fish and discouraging the growth of algae.

• Decorative marginal plants are positioned in the shallows, at the edge of a pond, with their roots in water and their topgrowth above it.

• Submerged aquatics, such as elodea, are efficient at releasing oxygen into the water, which helps to keep it healthy for fish and other wildlife.

PLANTING MARGINAL AQUATICS

1 If you are using a planting basket that does not have micro-mesh lining, line it with hessian sacking before filling it with aquatic compost (soil mix).

2 Remove the plant from its container and plant it in the basket at its original depth, using a trowel to add or remove compost as necessary. Firm it in well.

3 Cover with gravel to help keep the soil in place when you position the container in the pond, and to reduce the risk of it being disturbed by fish.

4 Soak the planted basket before placing it on the shelf at the edge of the pool. The top of the basket should be 2.5–5cm (1–2in) below the water surface.

One of the best-loved pond plants, waterlilies, not only produce a succession of beautiful flowers, but their leaves provide shade that discourages the formation of algae.

Some oxygenating or submerged plants are sold as cuttings bundled together, perhaps weighted so that they sink. Some are very decorative, such as water crowfoot, which produces feathery submerged growth and occasional cup-shaped, golden-centred, white flowers on the surface, or water violet, which bears upright spikes of lilac flowers in summer. Simply throw them into the pond.

Deep-water plants are easiest to grow in specially designed planting baskets. The baskets are often square, so that they fit neatly together, and are flat-bottomed to make them stable. Traditional lattice-sided baskets must be lined with hessian sacking before planting to

PLANTING A WATERLILY

1 Planting baskets are the best option, but for deep-water plants such as waterlilies you can use a washing-up bowl. Make holes in the bottom and line it with sacking before adding aquatic compost (soil mix).

2 Never add ordinary fertilizers as these are likely to encourage a proliferation of algae that will turn the water green. Instead, use a special fertilizer, sold specifically for aquatic plants.

3 Remove the waterlily from its container, and plant in the bowl at its original depth. Top up with aquatic compost as necessary, gently firming the compost as you do so.

4 Add a layer of gravel to prevent the compost washing out or being disturbed by fish as they search for food. The gravel also weighs down the container.

5 Soak the container by standing it in a bucket or bowl and flooding it from the top. This will help to prevent compost from washing out later.

6 Place the bowl in a shallow part of the pond initially, especially if new leaves are just developing. Alternatively, raise it up on bricks in deeper water.

prevent the compost (soil mix) from washing out, but modern aquatic containers have micro-mesh sides. Growing your pond plants in aquatic baskets allows you to move the plants around and take them out easily when necessary.

It is important to use aquatic compost that has been specially formulated for pond plants. The plant nutrients in ordinary compost are too easily leached out into the surrounding water, which encourages algal growth. After planting, top up the basket with a 2cm (¾in) layer of pea gravel to prevent the compost from washing out of the basket and making the water muddy. Soak each planted basket thoroughly in a

bucket of water to remove any air bubbles before carefully lowering it into the pond.

If your pond has very narrow marginal shelves that cannot accommodate standard containers, try making a planting container from an old pair of tights (pantyhose). Insert one leg inside the other to form a tube that has double sides. Fill this with aquatic compost and tie at the end. Make small holes in the top to plant through and tie up the holes afterwards so that the compost cannot escape. Then mould the planting sausage to the shape of your pond.

When you buy waterlilies, they will have been raised in shallow water

so the leaves (or lily pads) will have short stems. This means that the plant will need to be raised up on an up-turned pot or, depending on the depth of your pond, bricks for a couple of weeks so that the leaves float on the surface. Lower the container in the pond week by week until it is resting on the bottom.

Introducing fish

First, acclimatize the fish to their new environment by floating the plastic bag that you transported them in on the surface of the water for an hour. This will allow the water temperatures to equalize gradually, then the fish can swim out of the bag. Never put fish directly into the pond.

Planting permanent containers

You don't have to spend a lot of money each year filling containers with bedding plants and tender perennials to get a colourful display. There are many hardy plants that will do the job for you year after year with the minimum of maintenance. Containers also give you the opportunity to try out plant combinations on a small scale before using them in the open garden.

Practical matters

Although many perennials are not well suited to growing in containers, there is a good selection that will thrive and make attractive easy-care patio plants. Because perennials are generally deeper rooted and more vigorous than bedding plants, they will need larger containers if you want a long-term, trouble-free display. To prevent the most vigorous plants overwhelming the others, grow the plants in individual pots that can be grouped together to form an attractive display on the patio. This is a good way of growing invasive perennials, such as variegated ground elder, which would otherwise run riot in beds and borders. Include plants with attractive foliage in your collection to extend the period of interest, and

Perennials for containers

Small containers	Pulmonaria
Ajuga	Sempervivum
Alchemilla	**Large containers**
Aquilegia	Acanthus
Bellis	Agapanthus
Bergenia	Astilbe
Diascia	Dicentra
Erigeron	Euphorbia
Ferns (hardy)	Geranium
Festuca	Hemerocallis
Hakonechloa	Hosta
Lamium	Leucanthemum
Ophiopogon	Sedum

combine plants that flower at different times, because hardy perennials do not flower for as long as traditional bedding plants.

Any type of container will do provided it is at least 30cm (12in) across, ideally 45cm (18in), with several drainage holes. To reduce watering, use plastic pots that do not lose moisture through their sides, or line porous containers, such as terracotta pots, with plastic sheeting before you plant (taking care not to cover the drainage holes). Cover the drainage holes with crocks or stones to prevent the compost (soil mix) washing out and fill the container with a loam-based formula, such as John Innes No. 2. Unlike peat-based composts, loam-based types maintain their structure over many years, and being heavier, they also make the container more stable.

Shrubs in tubs

Many shrubs can be grown more or less permanently in large containers. Choose types that can tolerate a restricted root-run and that grow relatively slowly. Many conifers are ideal because they provide year-round appeal, but you can also grow other evergreens, such as bay, box, lavender,

PLANTING A SHRUB IN A TUB

1 Choose a large tub or pot with an inside diameter of at least 45cm (18in), unless you are planting a very small shrub. A heavy clay or stone container will be more stable than plastic for top-heavy plants. Cover the drainage holes with pieces of broken pots.

2 Part-fill the tub or pot with a loam-based compost (soil mix). Knock the plant from its pot, and if the roots are tightly wound around the rootball tease some of them out so they will grow into the surrounding compost more readily.

3 Add or remove compost as necessary, so that the top of the rootball and soil level will be 2.5–5cm (1–2in) below the rim of the pot to allow for watering. Make sure the shrub is upright before adding compost around the sides.

4 Backfill the compost around the roots firmly, because trees and shrubs offer a great deal of wind resistance. Water thoroughly after planting. Thereafter, water as necessary, including during the winter months.

rosemary and spotted laurel. Flowering shrubs are a better choice if you want to make a splash at a particular time of year. Dwarf rhododendrons and deciduous azaleas light up the spring patio, as do colourful camellias. These plants must be grown in acid conditions, so choose an ericaceous formula and water with saved rainwater. Growing these shrubs in tubs means that you can even grow them successfully in a garden with chalky (alkaline) soil. However, for an ever-changing, attractive display you need look no further than the coral bark maple (*Acer palmatum* 'Sango-kaku'), which has attractive foliage all summer, fiery autumn colour and stunning winter bark.

If you have somewhere you can keep your container plants protected in winter, you can extend the range of shrubs you grow in your garden by choosing tender exotics for your containers. Try the ferny-leaved mimosa (*Acacia dealbata*), which bears clouds of yellow flowers, or a member of the citrus family for a crop of oranges, lemons or limes.

Fuchsias will grow very successfully in containers, producing their beautiful flowers over a long period. Hardy varieties can stay outside all year in most gardens.

PLANTING A CLIMBER IN A HALF-BARREL

1 Fill a half-barrel with a loam-based compost (soil mix). You need a large, deep container and heavy compost, which will hold the canes securely as well as the plants.

2 Choose a climber to suit the size of the container. For instance, in a barrel of this size, you could grow three or four non-vigorous clematis. Angle the plants together.

3 Tie the canes together with string or use a proprietary plastic cane holder. When the growth reaches the top, it will tumble down again and make the planting look even denser.

Planting your patio

Pots and tubs can make superb displays on the patio, but there are other opportunities in and around the patio you can take advantage of. If your paving looks a bit stark there are a number of ways you can soften the edges and break up the harsh-looking appearance. This is especially desirable if you want to create an informal, cottage garden feel in the patio.

Introducing plant material

Around the edges you could create planting pockets by removing one or two paving stones and replacing the hardcore with soil before planting (see below). Choose an area that is not much used and that is well away from the points of access. Some species are so well adapted to growing in the harsh conditions found on a sun-drenched patio that even quite small cracks and crevices can be planted successfully.

Planting cracks

Look out for cracks between paving that are colonized by weeds, because these will provide ideal conditions for growing drought-tolerant, low-growing plants that are tough

enough to be walked on occasionally. Filling cracks with plants prevents them being recolonized by weeds and eliminates the need to spend time on weeding. Choose plants that produce ground-hugging, dense growth that doesn't get too woody, so that they do not become a safety hazard for anyone using the patio. Most thymes are ideal because they also fill the air with a pleasing aroma when they are gently crushed underfoot.

Prepare the cracks by removing or killing the existing crop of weeds. The easiest way with firmly-lodged perennial weeds is to use a spot weedkiller that will kill the roots. Clear out as much debris as you can from the crack using a patio weed hook or an old screwdriver. The deeper you can go the better so that any new plant will have more rooting space to become established. Trickle a loam-based compost (soil mix) into the crack, poking it in to remove any air pockets.

The easiest way to plant a crack is to sow seeds thinly, then dust with sieved compost before watering with a fine spray that doesn't wash away the seed. When the seedlings are large enough to handle, they need to

Plants for paving

Cracks
Aubrieta deltoidea
Dianthus deltoides
Erinus alpinus
Mentha requienii
Scabiosa graminifolia
Thymus serpyllum
Crevices
Globularia cordifolia
Lewisia tweedyi
Saxifraga callosa
Sedum spathulifolium
Sempervivum
Thymus
Planting pockets
Armeria juniperifolia
Campanula carpatica
Cerastium tomentosum
Chamaemelum nobile
Erica carnea
Iberis sempervirens
Origanum dictamnus
Sedum telephium
Veronica prostrata

be thinned, leaving the strongest seedlings at their final spacing. In wider cracks you can plant with small plug plants that have a wedge-shaped rootball that will slot easily into the crack. If the rootball is too wide, gently compress it between the

PLANTING THE PATIO

1 Lift one or two paving slabs, depending on their size. If they have been mortared into position, loosen the slabs with a cold chisel and club hammer, then lever them up with a chisel or crowbar.

2 If the paving slab has been bedded on concrete, break this up with a cold chisel and club hammer. Remove the rubble and fork over the soil, adding well-rotted garden compost or manure and a slow-release fertilizer.

3 Plant the shrub or climber, firming it in well and watering thoroughly. Arrange decorative pebbles or gravel over the soil to make the feature more attractive and reduce the chance of the soil splashing on to the paving.

palms of your hands until it is narrow enough to slot in.

Planting crevices

Crevices in walls can be tackled in a similar way. You may have to enlarge the hole to take the rootball and compost by drilling or chipping at the edges with a club hammer and cold chisel. Fill the prepared hole with loam-based compost. Ideally, the crevice should be angled downwards so that the compost is not washed out by rain. If necessary, lodge a stone at the entrance to prevent the compost falling out. Sow or plant the crevice in the same way as cracks in paving (see above).

Once the cracks and crevices have been planted (or seedlings thinned), cover the surface of the compost with a layer of stone chippings or

PLANTING CRACKS AND CREVICES

1 Chisel out spaces in your paving at least 5cm (2in) deep and remove as much of the rubble as possible. Add loam-based compost (soil mix) and sow or plant as appropriate. Water regularly, using a fine mist sprayer to avoid washing the compost away.

2 Press moist loam-based compost into a crevice using a small dibber or your fingers. Firm in to avoid air pockets. Insert the plant and add more compost. Keep the compost moist by spraying with a fine mist until the plants become established.

grit to prevent the compost being colonized by weeds before the plants become established. The grit mulch will also help maintain soil moisture

around the roots of the plants. Water well after planting and keep watering until the plants are well established.

Soften the harsh outline of your patio by planting up pockets, cracks and crevices with suitable plants. Here, herbs such as thyme are used to good effect, as they are allowed to form neat mats of fragrant foliage and flowers.

Topiary and alpine troughs

There is a growing fashion for topiary these days, and ready-clipped shrubs are sold in every conceivable shape, from simple spheres and cones to sculptured racing cars and patio sets. Because topiary is usually created using very slow-growing plants, such as box (*Buxus*), the finished article is not cheap, especially if you choose one of the larger, more complex shapes.

Going it alone

Topiary needn't cost the earth if you are prepared to do it yourself – and it can be highly rewarding. It needn't take forever, either, since you can use faster-growing plants, such as some species of conifers, if you don't mind clipping them frequently, or make a mock-topiary using a quick-growing evergreen climber, such as small-leaved ivy, trained over a wire frame (see below).

Traditional topiary is easy to create if you have the patience. A young box plant can be clipped into shape over a number of years to create almost any form you like. Formal shapes such as spheres and cones are the easiest because you can use canes and wires to provide accurate guides when you trim. More elaborate designs will require an artistic eye and a good deal of creative skill if they are to look

Topiary has a long tradition in Japan, with highly stylized shapes that can take many years to perfect.

MAKING AN IVY STANDARD

1 Choose an ivy that has pliable stems, such as *Hedera maroccana* 'Spanish Canary'. Insert a broom handle or cane into a pot filled with loam-based compost (soil mix) and place the plants at even intervals around its base.

2 Working from bottom to top, carefully wrap the stems around the broom handle or cane, tying the stems together with twists or split rings at regular intervals, to create a braided effect around the cane.

3 As you get higher up the broom handle or cane, take care to check that the stems cross each time in a straight line above the previous crossed stems, and that the regular spacing is maintained throughout.

4 Take a 25cm (10in) wire hanging basket and place it upside down on top of the broom handle or cane. Fix it securely in place with staples, wire or nails so that the weight of the plant won't dislodge it.

5 Wind the tops of the shoots through the wire basket and snip off all the lower leaves using scissors. As the ivy continues to grow, train the shoots through the basket, covering the frame completely.

Plants for traditional topiary

Berberis	Ligustrum
Buxus	ovalifolium
Crataegus	Lonicera nitida
Cupressus	Myrtus
sempervirens	communis
Hedera	Osmanthus
Ilex	Prunus lusitanica
Juniperus	Santolina
communis	chamae-
Laurus	cyparissus
nobilis	Taxus

PLANTING A TROUGH

1 Place the trough in its final position before it is filled; otherwise, it will be too heavy to move. It must be in a warm, sunny spot. Troughs look best when they are raised on bricks or concrete blocks. Make sure it is stable and will not tip over.

2 Make sure that the trough is level and has adequate drainage holes. Place coarse drainage material over the drainage holes and over the base of the trough to a depth of about 5cm (2in). Pieces of broken pot, brick or other rubble are all suitable.

3 Top the drainage material with a suitable free-draining alpine compost (soil mix), adding it in layers and making sure that it is firmed in thoroughly, especially in the corners and around the edge. Fill to within 2.5cm (1in) of the top.

4 Decorate the surface with attractive pieces of rock. Angle the pieces into the compost, making sure that about one-third of each piece is buried to create mini-outcrops that will provide various pockets for planting a selection of alpines.

5 Plant the selected alpines in the trough, scooping out holes to take the rootball of each in turn. Firm the plants in but avoid the temptation to over-firm. Place the larger and central plants first, finishing with smaller ones around the edges.

6 Finish off with a top-dressing of coarse grit or rock chippings, pushed well under the topgrowth of each alpine. Keep well watered at first, but avoid wetting the leaves unnecessarily. Once established, the trough should need only occasional watering.

convincing. However, you can make the job easier by growing the plant up through a pre-formed shape made out of chicken wire. It will not be pleasing on the eye until the plant has grown up through the mesh to hide it from view, but the finished topiary will look all the better for it. As shoots grow through the wire mesh, pinch them out between finger and thumb or periodically trim the shoot tips using a pair of secateurs (pruners). This will encourage more bushy growth that will produce a more solid-looking shape. If the shape you have chosen involves developing growth in particular

directions, select a suitable shoot and tie it in to a wire running in that direction. Again, pinch it out to encourage sideshoots to form and pinch these out in turn to cover the wire guide. Remove the ties after a couple of years when the shoot has turned woody and is fixed in position. Repeat this process until the growth meets at the perimeter of the topiary and the whole mesh frame has been covered.

To keep shapes looking neat they will need clipping several times a year, depending on the vigour of the plant used. In late spring give them their first trim and trim again as

necessary throughout the summer, leaving at least four weeks between cuts, with the last trim in early autumn. If you trim later than this the new growth does not have time to ripen properly before winter and is easily damaged, ruining the overall appearance of the topiary.

Damaged topiary can be repaired, however, by training in a new healthy shoot from lower down and tying it into position. Pinch out as before to encourage bushy growth which will soon fill the gap. You can restore the shape of neglected topiary in spring too. Trim it in stages to restore the overall shape and refine the outline.

Successional sowing and intercropping

The biggest challenge when growing your own vegetables is to have them mature at the right time so that you do not have any more gaps or gluts than necessary. Planning is of critical importance: choosing the right combination of crops and varieties, and making repeat sowings when appropriate, should enable you to approach the ideal of providing fresh produce for the kitchen daily.

Maintaining the supply

With some crops, such as peas, Brussels sprouts and cabbages, you can combine cultivars that differ in the time they take to mature. That way you can get a longer period of harvest. Of course, there may be times when you do not want to spread the harvest period. You may, for example, want to freeze a large batch of one type of vegetable for winter use.

Successional sowing

Some crops, such as lettuce, peas, spring onions (scallions), early carrots and radishes, need to be sown several times during the season to ensure a succession for the kitchen table. This is known as successional sowing. Sow these crops in short rows at regular intervals throughout the growing season. Wait until the previous sowing has germinated and started to grow before you make your next sowing.

Intercropping

If space is limited in your garden, you can make additional sowings of quick-growing crops, such as lettuce and radish, between the widely spaced rows of slower-growing types, such as Brussels sprouts and cauliflowers. This is known as intercropping. The quick-growing crops will take advantage of the space between the brassica seedlings and help to suppress weed growth too. The quick-growing crop is harvested before the brassicas need the space to grow to their full sizes.

You can use a similar technique on ground destined for late-sown or planted crops or after early-harvested crops to make the most efficient use of the growing space. And if you are really cunning you can do both. For example, a succession of lettuce crops can be sown and grown on the patch of ground planned to take a later-sown crop of sweet corn. The earliest lettuce harvested will make room for the new sweet corn plants and the later-cropped lettuce will mature between the sweet corn seedlings as they grow. Another trick to try is to sow a few pots of quick-growing crops each time you sow. Grow these on in a coldframe so that they can be planted out to fill any gaps that appear as the result of losses or early harvesting.

Saving space

You can also save space by growing crops closer together than normally recommended. Root crops such as swede (rutabaga), parsnip and beetroot (beets) can be grown in this way, as can leeks, onions and many types of brassica. For example, you can grow mini-cauliflowers from summer cultivars sown in spring or early summer that are grown at much closer spacing than normal. Sow

SOWING SWEET CORN

1 Sow only when there is no risk of frost and the soil temperature has reached 10°C (50°F). In cold areas, warm up the soil with fleece or cloches for a week or two first. Alternatively, sow in pots and plant out later.

2 Sow the seeds 2.5cm (1in) deep and 8cm (3in) apart, and thin plantlets to the final recommended spacing later – typically 30cm (12in) apart each way. Sow in blocks rather than in single rows.

3 Cover with a fine net floating cloche or garden fleece. This can be left on after germination until the plants have pushed the cover up to its limit without damaging them.

4 In areas where outdoor sowing is unreliable, raise the plants in modules or peat pots. Plant them out when there is no danger of frost and after careful hardening off.

several seeds every 15cm (6in) where they are to grow, and thin these to one seedling if more than one germinates. The heads are much smaller than normal, but total yields can still be good. Thinning is a tedious but essential task. The final spacing between plants will determine both the size of the individual vegetables and the total yield. Exact spacing will often depend on whether you are more interested in the total crop or large, well-shaped individual specimens.

Multiple sowing

Some gardeners grow certain vegetables – such as carrots, beetroot, onions and leeks – in small clusters. Four to six seeds are usually sown in each cell of modular trays and planted out without any attempt to separate them. These are not normally thinned. The vegetables are usually smaller and less well shaped than those sown in rows and thinned normally, but the overall weight of crop may be good if the spacing recommended for this type of cultivation is followed.

Sow or plant sweet corn in blocks rather than in rows to ensure a good set, because the plants are wind-pollinated and not insect-pollinated, like most other vegetables.

THINNING SEEDLINGS

1 Follow the spacing advice given on the seed packet when sowing. The packet should also recommend the ideal final spacing between plants after thinning so that all the plants left have room to grow to their optimum size.

2 Thin in stages, pulling up surplus plants between finger and thumb. The first thinning should leave the young plants twice as close as their final recommended spacing, to allow for losses after thinning.

3 Before the plants begin to compete with each other for moisture and nutrients, thin once more to the final spacing. With some crops, the thinnings can be used in the kitchen to add to salads.

Plant tender crops

Tender crops, such as tomatoes, aubergines (eggplants), marrows and courgettes (zucchini), can be planted out as soon as the threat of frost has passed in your area. In milder regions, this can be around mid-spring, but in colder areas you might have to wait until now or even early summer before you can plant tender crops outside. Be prepared to protect vulnerable crops with a cloche or floating mulch if a late frost is forecast.

Growing beans

In mild areas runner and climbing French beans can be sown direct outside at this time of year, but in colder areas you'll have to wait until early summer or start the seeds off indoors. Canes and nets are the main methods of supporting runner and pole beans. If you use a net, choose a large-mesh net sold as a pea and bean net, and stretch it taut between well-secured posts. If you use canes, the most popular methods to use are wigwams and crossed canes. Proprietary supports are also available but, although usually very effective, they can be expensive.

Plant out tender marrows during late spring for a bumper crop of fruit that will start from midsummer and go on until autumn.

Growing tomatoes

Tomatoes are perhaps the most popular of all tender vegetables, partly because they are easy to grow, but also because they have a flavour that cannot be equalled by the commercially grown crops sold by supermarkets. They can be grown in a greenhouse or outside in all but the coldest districts where the summer is not reliably long enough for the fruit to ripen. You'll get the biggest yields from greenhouse-grown crops, while those grown outside are often tastier, especially after a long, hot summer. It is important to

PLANTING OUTDOOR TOMATOES

1 Plant at the spacing recommended for the cultivar – some grow tall and large, others remain small and compact. Always make sure they have been well hardened off.

2 In cold areas, cover plants with cloches for a few weeks, or use garden fleece to protect them on cool nights. Remove the protection on hot days.

3 Once the fleece or protection has been removed, stake the plants immediately, tying them loosely to the cane with soft string. Some dwarf varieties may not require staking.

Planting out marrows and courgettes (zucchini)

This marrow seedling has been raised in a degradable fibre pot. This means that it will suffer less root disturbance when planted out.

choose the right cultivar: outdoors go for 'Golden Sunrise', 'Ida Gold', 'Incas', 'Marmande Super', 'Outdoor Girl', 'Red Alert', 'Sweet 100', 'Tornado', 'Totem' or 'Tumbler'; indoors opt for 'Gemini', 'Sioux' or 'Shirley'. 'Ailsa Craig', 'Alicante', 'Gardener's Delight', 'Mirabelle', 'Sungold' and 'Tigerella' can be grown indoors or out. A few varieties, notably 'Tumbler', have been bred specifically for hanging baskets – these can produce good crops and look very attractive, but they will need frequent watering.

Tomatoes sown in late winter or early spring will have been pricked out and potted up individually into 9cm (3½in) pots. When they are 20–25cm (8–10in) tall and have their first truss of flowers starting to show colour, they are ready to plant out, provided the temperature is at least 13°C (55°F). If you haven't sown your seed yet, there is still time to do so now for a crop in late summer. Alternatively, you can buy a limited selection of named varieties as plants from garden centres. This can be an economical way of obtaining a few plants because tomato seed is expensive and you will avoid the risks and costs involved with early sowings.

The most popular way to grow tomatoes – indoors or out – is in a growing bag. Provided you keep them well fed and watered throughout the growing season, you're more or less guaranteed a good crop. Growing bags are a cheap way to buy compost (soil mix), and because it is sterilized there will be no problems from soil-borne diseases. Pests still need to be controlled, however, otherwise quality and yields will be reduced. Staking can be a problem if you want to grow tomatoes in growing bags on a hard base. There are many proprietary designs of cane supports intended for crops such as tomatoes in growing bags, and most should last for several years. If the growing bag is positioned on soil you can push the cane through the bag into

Growing your own courgettes means you can also enjoy the flowers, which are delicious raw, steamed or fried.

the soil. Prepare the growing bag before planting by plumping it up like a pillow to loosen the growing medium. If it is to be used in a greenhouse, place it inside at least a week before planting to allow time for the compost to warm up.

PLANTING RUNNER AND POLE BEANS

1 Sow two seeds 5cm (2in) deep by each cane or support. Thin to one plant later if both germinate. Wait until the soil temperature is at least 12°C (54°F) before sowing. Use a soil thermometer to check.

2 If you raise the plants in pots, plant them out once there is no reasonable risk of frost. Use a trowel and plant them just to one side of the cane. Tie them to the cane as soon as they are tall enough and continue to tie them in.

Harvesting early crops

The earliest crops will soon be ready for harvest. Early sowings of lettuce and other leafy crops, radish, spring onions (scallions), early peas and carrots will all be reaching maturity. The last of the overwintered crops, including brassicas, leeks and root crops, will also be available for use in the kitchen. Early crops can be picked regularly as they become ready, and eaten deliciously fresh.

Young vegetables

Start pulling early carrots and radish as soon as you can see the roots are starting to swell. Early carrots take about two months from sowing to harvest. Pull them selectively, aiming to remove them when the roots are 1–1.5cm (½–⅔ in) across. Thinnings of carrots can also be used in salads. Spring onions can be pulled, but do so before the bulb starts to swell. Water these crops the day before harvesting to make pulling easier.

Spinach and loose-leaf lettuce can be picked as soon as the leaves are large enough; select the largest individual leaves from each plant. Later you can cut whole plants of

1 Pinching out the tops of the beans is good practice because it discourages blackfly. The tops can then be boiled and eaten.

2 Tall forms of broad bean will need supporting with string tied to canes that are set at intervals along the rows.

loose-leaf lettuce to leave a 2.5cm (1in) stump, which should regrow for a second crop a month or so later. Harvest cut-and-come-again lettuce as seedlings about a month after sowing. Rocket (arugula) and endive can also be harvested in less than two months after sowing. Stagger the cropping to ensure a continuous supply. With early peas, pick the pods as soon as they start to swell and before they are too large and tough. Pick them regularly thereafter to maximize the yield.

Early potatoes

Although the first crop of potatoes will not be available for a few weeks, make sure the developing tubers do not get exposed to light using a technique called earthing (hilling) up (see right). If they are exposed, their skins will turn green and the tubers will be poisonous to eat. By drawing soil into a ridge over the potatoes you will help cover any that are near to the surface and keep weeds under control as you go. Do this regularly until the foliage of adjacent rows touches. Earthing up also encourages formation of new tubers from the newly-covered stems.

You can, however, get new potatoes available for harvest at any time of the year by growing them in large containers. A large plastic wheelie bin (wheeled trash can) is ideal, since it is about the right size and is easy to move around. First drill drainage holes in the base, then half-fill with a 50:50 mix of good garden soil and old potting compost (soil mix) – a useful way of recycling the compost from last year's hanging baskets and patio containers. Mix in a slow-release fertilizer to feed the crop

1 Radishes are harvested simply by pulling them from the ground by hand. They should be harvested when they are large enough to eat. Do not let them get large and woody.

2 Spring onions (scallions) can be harvested by pulling them from the ground by hand, but you may need to loosen the soil gently with a fork as you pull.

throughout its life. Chit the tubers before planting, which means leaving them in a light, frost-free place, such as on a windowsill, until sprouts grow to about 2cm (¾in) long. Plant them in a large pot, and when they are well-established plants with 20cm (8in) of topgrowth, plant them into the half-filled bin. Gradually add more compost as the shoots grow (without covering the leaves) until the bin is full. Keep frost-free at all times. Seed potatoes planted in early summer will be ready for harvest in late autumn, those planted in late winter can be harvested by mid-spring, and a crop planted in early spring will be ready by midsummer. Carefully push your hand into the compost to search and remove any chicken-egg-sized tubers. Lightly firm the soil mix after harvesting and leave the plants to grow on for a couple of weeks before probing again. Alternatively, you can harvest all the tubers in one go by emptying the bin completely. This is a particularly worthwhile method of growing new potatoes for the Christmas table.

Radishes are extremely fast-growing. When harvesting, discard any that have become large or old, as they will be too woody and hot to eat.

PROTECTING AND EARTHING (HILLING) UP POTATOES

1 Potatoes will usually recover from slight frost damage, but if you know that a frost is forecast once the shoots are through the ground, cover the plants with newspaper or garden fleece. Remove the cover the next morning once the frost has gone.

2 Start earthing up the potatoes when the shoots are about 15cm (6in) high. Use a draw hoe to pull up the soil either side of the row. Do this carefully so that you do not damage the stems with the hoe, which will leave the plants susceptible to pests and diseases.

3 Continue to earth up in stages, as the potatoes grow, until the soil creates a mound about 15cm (6in) high. Regular earthing up not only prevents light from reaching the tubers but also prevents weed seedlings getting established.

Herbs in containers

Many herbs make ideal container plants. Not only is this a convenient way of growing them, but there are a number of advantages compared to growing them in the garden border. Most herbs are native to the Mediterranean area and so like the well-drained conditions a container offers. Indeed, if your soil is too heavy to grow herbs, you can still grow these plants successfully in pots on the patio.

A movable feast

Herbs in containers are easy to move around so that you can bring them near to the kitchen door when they are in season and hide them away somewhere less prominent at other times of the year. In addition, when you go away, you can move the containers to a shady spot to reduce the need for watering.

If you are mixing herbs in a larger container, group those with similar requirements to make looking after them easier. Short-lived herbs and those used in large amounts, such as basil and chives, are worth growing in separate pots so that they are easily replaced when they are over or all used up. Vigorous herbs, such as mint, which send spreading and penetrating shoots beneath the soil's surface, can be kept under control by growing in a pot (see opposite). Mints don't like to dry out, so sink the pot nearly rim-deep into a larger container or the ground, or grow them in a glazed pot placed in semi-shade.

The main disadvantage of growing herbs in containers is that they will need watering regularly throughout the growing season. Perennial herbs will also need watering during dry spells at other times of the year, and tender varieties will be more susceptible to frost than those planted in the ground.

Choosing a container

Choose a large container for perennial herbs and medium-sized pots — at least 20cm (8in) diameter

PLANTING UP A HERB POT

1 An ornamental herb pot is best filled in stages. Cover the drainage hole with crocks before adding free-draining compost (soil mix) to the height of the first planting pockets.

2 Using small plants, knock them out of their pots and push the rootballs through the holes in the planting pockets. Reduce the size of the rootball if necessary.

3 Add more of the compost and repeat with the next row of planting holes. Unless the pot is very large, don't try to pack many herbs into the top because there will be too much competition. A single well-grown plant often looks much better.

4 Large earthenware pots can look just as good as herb pots with planting pockets if you plant them imaginatively. If you have a half-barrel use this instead. Place a bold shrubby herb, such as sweet bay (*Laurus nobilis*), in the centre.

5 Until the sweet bay grows to fill the pot, you should be able to fit a collection of smaller herbs around the edge. Avoid mints, however, which are usually too rampant to use with other plants and will quickly outgrow their allotted space.

CONTROLLING MINTS

1 A growing bag is an ideal home for mints. They will be happy for a couple of seasons, and then are easily removed and replanted for a fresh start. Choose small, healthy plants that will establish quickly.

3 If you want to plant your mint in the border (which will avoid the chore of watering it frequently), plant it in an old bucket or a large pot. It is important to make sure that there are drainage holes in the bottom, and fill with soil or compost (soil mix) before you plant the mint.

2 Instead of filling the growing bag with one kind of mint, try planting a collection of perhaps four to six different kinds. There are a surprising number of different mints, and the flavours vary quite widely.

4 Mint spreads quickly, and to prevent its roots growing into the surrounding soil, you should make sure that the rim of the pot is just visible above the surface. Lift, divide and replant annually or every second spring, to maintain vigour. Take a piece of root from the old plant.

Choosing herbs

Hanging baskets	Large containers
Basil	Bay
Marjoram	Hyssop
Rosemary	Lemon verbena
(prostrate)	Rosemary
Sage	Sage
Thyme	
Winter savory	*Growing bags*
	Basil
Small containers	Lemon balm
Basil	Mint
Chamomile	Parsley
Marjoram	Sorrel
Mint	
Summer savory	
Thyme	
Winter savory	

After planting, position Mediterranean herbs in a sunny spot on the patio. Many, including rosemary, lavender, thyme and marjoram, will be most aromatic and flavoursome when grown in full sun, and in poor soil – feeding increases growth, but the flavour will be less intense.

Ornamental herb pots make wonderful garden features. Here, a selection of cascading thymes are used to good effect.

– for the rest. This will make watering less onerous. Porous terracotta is ideal for drought-tolerant Mediterranean herbs, but moisture-loving herbs, such as dill, fennel, lovage and coriander (cilantro), will do better in a glazed or plastic pot. If you choose an ornamental herb pot, like the one right, it is best treated as a short-term home to be replanted annually. Bear in mind that the tapered shape will make it difficult to remove well-established plants. For the best effect, you can create a theme of matching styles or colours, so that the container display looks co-ordinated. A loam-based compost (soil mix) such as John Innes No. 2 usually gives the best results, though an all-purpose compost can also be used.

You can grow herbs in all sorts of containers, from hanging baskets, in which smaller perennial herbs such as golden marjoram and thyme work well, to growing bags, which could accommodate a thriving crop of basil. In a windowbox outside the kitchen window try growing herbs in individual containers that can be easily slotted in and out as they come into season. Larger containers, such as half-barrels, are ideal for shrubby herbs, such as bay and rosemary.

Climate control

It is essential to keep control of the greenhouse environment if you are to achieve the best possible results from greenhouse crops. At this time of the year, temperatures can rocket as soon as the sun comes out, causing plants considerable stress. Ideally, aim to maintain a temperature of 21–26°C (70–79°F) for most plants through the careful use of ventilation, shading and damping down.

Using ventilation

At this time of year, you should be able to control temperatures sufficiently by opening vents in the greenhouse on warm days and closing them again at night. By opening a vent along the ridge of the greenhouse and one at the side, you'll create a 'chimney effect' as the hot, humid air escapes through the roof, drawing in cooler, drier air through the side. You can make the whole job easier by installing automatic vent-openers that will respond to the prevailing conditions. There are devices designed to open both hinged and louvred vents. Look for models that are spring-loaded so you can close the vent tightly during the night. For adequate ventilation on warm days you will need several opening vents in the roof and along the sides of the greenhouse. Ideally, they should be equal to about one-fifth of the floor area of your greenhouse. Most greenhouses are supplied with far fewer vents, so it is worth considering installing extra roof and side vents from the outset.

Providing shading

When the weather warms up in the early summer, opening vents alone will not be sufficient to keep the greenhouse cool. You will need to take steps to reduce the amount of sunlight that enters the greenhouse by applying shading washes to the glass or installing blinds or shading fabric. Washes that are applied to the glass are the cheapest and easiest option, and one application alone will last for the whole of the season. The wash does not vary the amount of shade it provides in response to changing weather conditions, so it can reduce crop growth in bad years. However, there is one type, called Varishade, that turns transparent when it gets wet, which means more light can get through in rainy

You can keep temperatures inside a greenhouse under control from late spring onwards through careful ventilation, shading and damping down. You can also position sun-loving plants such as tomatoes so that they provide shade for other plants.

If you are not at home during the hottest part of the day, automatic vent-openers which respond to temperature can be a great help in regulating the atmosphere inside the greenhouse.

weather, and then it clouds over again when it dries. If you decide to have blinds or fabric to provide shade, then they are best fitted to the outside of the greenhouse where they will most effectively prevent the sun's heat getting through the glass. If they are fitted inside, some of the heat from the sun will penetrate the glass, warming the air inside the greenhouse.

Staying cool

During the hottest weather of the summer even these precautions may not be enough, especially if the weather is still. You can improve ventilation further by installing an electric fan that will move air in and out of the greenhouse. There are solar-powered devices available so you don't need to worry about wiring it into the mains. Damping

down is another option. This involves wetting the floor and staging inside the greenhouse on hot days, so that energy is absorbed as the water evaporates and is carried out of the greenhouse in the form of water vapour. Some greenhouse plants are better adapted than others to the scorching effects of the sun, so you can arrange the greenhouse so that sun-loving crops, such as tomatoes, are grown on the sunniest side and provide shade for more sun-sensitive crops.

KEEPING YOUR GREENHOUSE COOL

1 It is vital not to let greenhouses overheat. A maximum/minimum thermometer is an invaluable piece of equipment, not only showing the current temperature but recording the highest that has been reached during the day, as well as the coolest at night.

2 You need to reduce the amount of sun entering the greenhouse during the hottest part of the year. Shading, in the form of temporary netting, helps to keep the temperature down and also protects the plants from the scorching effects of the sun.

3 Splashing or spraying water over the greenhouse floor helps to create a humid atmosphere and reduce greenhouse temperatures: energy is absorbed as the water evaporates. This traditional technique is known as damping down.

Training crops

Greenhouse crops always used to be grown in the greenhouse border, and the soil changed periodically. This was considered risky, and ring culture became fashionable. In more recent times growing bags have been in favour. All three systems have merits and drawbacks, so you can choose whichever appeals to you most or seems the easiest.

Planting methods

Growing crops in the border soil is the best option if you find regular watering a chore. Because the plants' roots are able to tap into water reserves deep in the ground, they will need less frequent watering. The soil will need to be improved by applying well-rotted organic matter and a general fertilizer before planting. If yields drop after a few years, there may have been a build-up of soil-borne pests and diseases and so you will need to remove the soil and replace with fresh from the garden.

Growing bags contain sterilized compost (soil mix) and so there is no problem with soil-borne pests. You will get very good results provided you can keep the crops well fed and watered. This may mean watering them several times a day in the hot weather, but you can get automatic watering devices that will make the job much easier. Feed fruiting crops with a high-potash liquid feed, such as that sold for tomatoes, every two weeks, once the fruit has started to develop.

Training tomatoes

Plant stocky plants in spring when the first flower truss is starting to show colour. Throw away any very

GROWING METHODS FOR TOMATOES

1 Always dig in as much well-rotted manure or garden compost as you can spare and rake in a general garden fertilizer before you plant your tomatoes. Although they can be planted earlier, most gardeners find this is a good time because the greenhouse usually has more space once the bedding plants have been planted out in the garden.

2 Most greenhouse varieties grow tall and need support. Tall canes are a convenient method if you have just a few plants, but if you have a lot of plants the string method may be more suitable. Tie lengths of string vertically to horizontal wires adjacent to the plants and use these to support the main stem as it grows.

3 With ring culture, the water-absorbing roots grow into a moist aggregate and the feeding roots into special bottomless pots filled with potting compost (soil mix). Take out a trench about 15–23cm (6–9in) deep in the greenhouse border and line it with a waterproof plastic (this minimizes soil-borne disease contamination).

4 Fill the trench with fine gravel, coarse grit or expanded clay granules. Then place the special bottomless ring culture pots on the aggregate base and fill them with a good potting compost. Firm the compost lightly to remove air pockets.

5 Plant into the ring and insert a cane or provide an alternative support. Water only into the ring at first. Once the plant is established and some roots have penetrated into the aggregate, water only the aggregate and feed through the pot.

6 Growing bags are less trouble than ring culture to set up, but you still have to feed plants regularly, and watering can be more difficult to control unless you use an automatic system. Insert a cane through the bag or use a string support.

SUPPORTING TOMATOES

Tie vertical strings between horizontal wires alongside each plant and use these to provide support for the growing main stem.

spindly plants or those with yellowing foliage because they will never recover fully. String is a simple and economical way to support your tomatoes. Fix one wire as high as practicable from one end of the greenhouse to the other, aligning it above the border, and another one just above the ground. Tie lengths of string between the wires, in line with each plant. You don't need to tie the plant to its support – just loop the string around the growing tip so that it forms a spiral.

Training cucumbers

Cucumbers are also best grown as cordons, with a single main stem tied to a vertical cane or string. Try growing cucumbers in growing bags on the greenhouse staging. Insert canes between the growing bags and the eaves, and fix horizontal wires along the length of the roof. You can then train the growth along the roof and the cucumbers will hang down. A standard growing bag should hold about two cucumber plants. Do not overcrowd the plants. Tie the plant in to the support as it grows and pinch out any sideshoots, flowers and tendrils until it reaches the first wire. Then train two sideshoots along each horizontal wire, removing sideshoots only.

Many modern cucumber varieties produce only female flowers, but some greenhouse varieties produce both male and female blooms (the female bloom has a small swelling at its base). Pinch out the male flowers before they pollinate the female ones, because the resulting cucumbers will taste bitter.

Growing peppers

Sweet peppers (*Capsicum*) like the same conditions as tomatoes and so are easy to grow alongside them. Pinch out the tips of the young plants after planting to encourage sideshoots to grow. Provide a single cane support for each plant and tie all the stems loosely to it. Keep the compost moist and mist plants to discourage red spider mite.

Tender sweet peppers are easy to grow in the border soil or, as here, in growing bags supported with canes. They change from green to red or yellow as they ripen, so pick them when they are at the stage you want.

Summer

Although most of the hard work has been completed in the spring rush, the garden is still a hive of intense gardening activity during the first few weeks of summer. With the threat of frost passed in all but the coldest regions, it is a time to relax and enjoy your garden. Everything is growing rapidly, in many areas tender plants can be put out, and weeds seem to grow faster than you ever thought possible. The bulk of the sowing and pricking out will have been completed by now, so the challenge is to keep all your new plants growing strongly, making sure they don't go short of water and protecting them from pest and disease attack. Most gardens look their best in early summer when the grass is still looking fresh and flowering is reaching its peak.

There'll be something new to delight you nearly every day in the ever-changing displays and your garden enjoyment will be extended into long summer evenings with *al fresco* meals and garden parties.

A well-planted garden will be overflowing with colour by summer. Here *Crocosmia* 'Lucifer' stand out against a backdrop of variegated cannas and golden Achillea.

Early Summer

Early summer is a time when you can relax a little and enjoy the results of all your efforts of the last few months. Bedding plants in borders and containers will be growing rapidly, bringing an abundance of colour to prominent areas of the garden, including patios, window boxes and hanging baskets.

However, there are still jobs to be done, and pests and diseases are as active as ever. Vigilance and prompt action now will often stop the trouble from spreading, thus avoiding the need for more drastic control measures later. Weeds too will need to be kept under control, and preventing any from flowering and setting seed should be your main priority. Unexpected late frosts can occur and in colder areas they may be almost inevitable, so keep garden fleece to hand to cover up newly planted tender flowers and vegetables if a cold night is forecast.

Early summer is a good time to top up mulches around the garden. Give the ground a thorough soaking beforehand. It's a good idea to mulch all newly planted specimens, as well as the surface of containers, to help retain soil moisture and prevent competition from weeds. In prominent positions try decorative mulches such as chipped bark or stone chippings and pebbles. Around established plants elsewhere, you can use well-rotted manure, garden compost or lawn clippings. Even old carpet can help reduce the need for watering and weeding, as long as it is water-permeable (to let rain through).

In the greenhouse, watering and feeding are of paramount importance and can take up a lot of time if you have a lot of containers and crops. However, there are steps you can take to reduce the workload such as installing drip or capillary watering aids. Early summer is also an ideal time to renovate overgrown or straggly permanent greenhouse plants as well as propagating new plants from cuttings and division.

Outside, fruit and vegetables will need watering during prolonged dry spells to avoid checks in growth and reduced yields. Many early crops, such as beetroot (beets), broad (fava) beans, cabbages, carrots, early potatoes, peas and spinach, will be reaching maturity and be ready to harvest, as will perennial crops such as asparagus, globe artichokes and rhubarb. Early summer is also the ideal time to prune many fruit trees and bushes.

Although there is always plenty of colour at this time of year, be prepared for a few weeks when the garden is perhaps not looking at its best. Early summer is a transitional period, and there is often an interval between the spring-flowering plants dying back and the peak of colour offered by abundant summer bedding. However, you can get bigger and longer lasting flowering displays from many bedding plants, as well as repeat-flowering roses and annuals, by regularly removing fading flowers. This not only improves the appearance but also encourages further flushes of flowers later in the season.

Summer harvests from the fruit garden start with succulent strawberries which should be picked when fully coloured.

Dahlia 'Bishop of Llandaff' and *Crocosmia* 'Lucifer' join forces in this vibrant combination in a fiery border display.

Deadheading and mulching

This is a lovely time in the garden, when every time you step outdoors you are greeted by masses of fresh flowers and foliage, the first results of all the hard work you put in over spring. A little extra attention now will keep that freshness going throughout the season, but don't let the workload spoil your pleasure in this delightful time of year.

Deadheading

Many annuals and perennials will produce better and longer lasting displays if they are regularly deadheaded. Annuals in particular respond to having their faded flowers trimmed off by producing further flushes of bloom. This is because annuals grow, flower, set seed and die in a single growing season. So if you prevent them from setting seed by removing the flowers as they fade, they try again by producing further flushes of flowers. The effect is less marked with perennials but still worthwhile for some species. Many types of bedding plant produce too many flowers to make deadheading worthwhile, but ageratum, dianthus, erigeron, all types of marigolds,

Hardy geraniums can benefit from a heavy trim if they get tatty, because they will produce a neat mound of new growth and may flower again too.

mesembryanthemums, mimulus, osteospermums, pansies, phlox and poppies do perform better. If you do not have time to deadhead all your plants, concentrate on those that will benefit most, and plants in prominent positions, such as in

containers on the patio and beds and borders next to paths or near the house. Deadheading may seem a laborious process, but it allows you to keep a close eye on your plants so that you will spot problems early. There are several methods of deadheading; the one to choose depends on the type of growth the plant makes.

Pinching out Meticulously pinching out individual fading blooms by hand is the best way of deadheading many large-flowered annuals. Pinching off the stem between finger and thumb just behind the flower is the best method for plants that produce branching flowerheads that don't all mature at the same time.

Cutting with scissors Annuals and perennials that produce single flowers on long stems are best deadheaded by cutting at the bottom of the stem with a sharp pair of garden scissors. Scissors are also

DEADHEADING

Where roses bear their flowers in clusters, which is common to the majority of rambling roses, start deadheading by removing any individual faded flowers within the cluster. Single flowers can be removed as they fade.

Once the whole flower cluster has faded, cut back to a strong bud facing the way you wish the stem to grow. Here the leaves nearest the cluster are showing signs of black spot, so cut back to a bud behind the diseased growth.

useful for trimming compact plants that produce huge numbers of very tiny flowers. In this case, simply shear off all the wiry flower stalks once most of them have passed their best.

Using secateurs A few plants produce very thick stems that cannot be cut with a pair of scissors, they are best cut back with secateurs (pruners). Plants that produce flower spikes, such as lupins, should have the flower spike cut back to a sideshoot lower down once the flower is spent. This will encourage the sideshoots to produce a display of their own later in the season.

Using shears With a few perennials, such as hardy geraniums, you can cut the whole plant back after flowering using a pair of shears. These plants tend to look tatty by the middle of the summer, but will put on neat new growth and even a second flush of flowers if they are cut back to ground level after flowering. If you have a lot of soft-stemmed bedding you could even try deadheading with a nylon-line trimmer, but you must take care not to damage the plants too much.

MULCHING WITH CHIPPED BARK

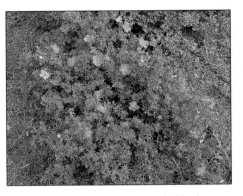

1 Here the potentilla is surrounded by bare earth. Until the bed has been filled with other plants, weeds will be a constant problem, and applying a weed-suppressing mulch will reduce the work needed to keep it clear. The mulch will also make the bed more attractive, as well as conserving moisture in the ground.

After deadheading clear away all of the trimmings and give the plants a thorough watering. If they have been cut back hard, it's also worth giving them a boost by applying a liquid feed. Don't be in a hurry to deadhead all your perennial plants, because some seedheads are worth keeping to provide autumn and winter interest. And if you want to try raising your own plants from seed saved from the garden, you will have to leave some plants to set seed.

2 Chipped or composted bark is a very good mulch. It should be stored for several months to let it release any resin and start to decompose. Some gardeners worry that it introduces fungal diseases, but the spores of these are already in the air and the bark does not appreciably increase the risk.

Mulching

Now is a good time to apply or renew a mulch on the beds to help suppress weeds and conserve moisture. Weed and water the ground first. Composted bark, chipped bark or gravel will set the plants off well. You could also consider using garden compost or leaf mould as a mulch. Other mulches, such as black plastic sheeting, grass clippings and straw, work well but look less attractive.

MULCHING WITH PLASTIC SHEETING

1 Special black plastic, with holes in to allow water to pass through to the soil, is available from garden centres. If you lay the plastic before you plant up the bed, you can cut holes in it and plant through it. Otherwise, you will need to cut it to fit around the existing plants.

2 Plastic would be the perfect mulch were it not so unattractive. However, it can be covered with a layer of gravel or small stones. Make sure the plastic is perfectly flat, with no ridges in it that will poke up through the stones, then pour the gravel on to cover the plastic completely.

3 Gravel makes an ideal background against which to see the plants, and it also looks attractive in its own right. It is easy to maintain and can be simply raked to keep its appearance fresh and level. Make sure that the plastic does not show through, as this can spoil the effect.

Pruning and trimming shrubs

Now that you have more time to stroll around the garden, there is an opportunity to examine and tidy up your permanent plants. Although most shrubs will grow and flower perfectly well without regular pruning, many spring- and early-summer-flowering shrubs benefit from a light trim at this time of the year. It is also not too late to catch up with spring pruning missed through lack of time.

Summer pruning

Without regular attention, some deciduous shrubs will eventually become bare at the base and produce all their flowers out of sight at the top of the plant. Many evergreen shrubs tend to get too big or become lop-sided or mis-shapen. Evergreens grown largely for their ornamental foliage, such as holly and laurel, are usually well-behaved and require little attention. However, low-growing flowering evergreen shrubs, such as lavender, senecio and hebes, can be given a light clipping after flowering to keep them neat and compact. Larger flowering evergreens, such as berberis, escallonia and viburnum, should not need regular trimming but can be clipped after flowering if required.

Signs of winter damage will be easy to spot at this time of year, and all dead and badly damaged stems should be cut out with secateurs (pruners). Similarly, vigorous all-green shoots produced on variegated plants are easy to identify and must be removed, otherwise they will outgrow and eventually swamp the variegated shoots, spoiling the overall appearance of the shrub.

Light trim

Some shrubs should be trimmed annually during the summer because they do not respond to hard pruning. If you cut them back hard they do not produce new shoots from old wood lower down. By giving them a light trim every year you will keep them within bounds and avoid the need for more drastic action. Shrubs such as broom, tamarisk and genista can have up to half of their new growth removed, while evergreen ceanothus, halimium, indigofera and cistus can have all flowered shoots cut back by up to two-thirds.

Routine pruning

Other spring- and early-summer-flowering deciduous shrubs do respond to being pruned back during early summer by producing new shoots lower down the pruned stem. The exact timing of the pruning will depend on the plant, the season and your local climate. All these shrubs flower on shoots produced during the previous season. So if you prune in spring you would lose the blooms for that year. Ideally, you should prune directly after the shrub has flowered. Your aim should not be to give an overall trim, but to make strategic cuts that will maintain the shrub's natural shape. After removing dead, diseased and damaged wood, thin overcrowded growth and then concentrate on wood that has produced flowers this year. As a rule, cut back each flowered stem by between a half and two-thirds, cutting just above a new shoot that will develop into next year's flowering stem.

Renovating old shrubs

Older shrubs may need more drastic pruning to reinvigorate them. For example, popular plants such as buddleias, kolkwitzia and flowering

SUMMER PRUNING SHRUBS

1 Philadelphus (illustrated) and some spring-flowering species, such as *Spiraea* 'Arguta' and *S. thunbergii*, become too dense and overcrowded if they are not pruned. Annual pruning keeps them compact and flowering well, and the best time to do this is immediately after flowering.

2 Reduce the shoots by one-third, cutting out the oldest and woodiest ones. Cut back the old stems to where a new shoot is growing lower down. Alternatively, if the shoot is very old and the bush is very congested, cut to just above the ground.

3 Brooms and genistas tend to become woody at the base as they age, with the flowers too high up the plants to look attractive. Keep them compact by regular pruning. Cut them back as soon as the flowers die and the seed pods are beginning to form.

The tender early-summer-flowering evergreen New Zealand tea tree (*Leptospermum scoparium* 'Lyndon') should be trimmed lightly after flowering to keep the shrub compact and tidy.

spiraeas can be pruned by removing one stem in three. Always choose the oldest and thickest stems to prune out so that the shrub will remain fresh, vigorous and free flowering.

Cultivars of lilac (*Syringa vulgaris*) often become tall and leggy, with the flowers borne very high up. You may be able to rejuvenate a neglected plant by sawing it down to a height of 30–90cm (1–3ft). This may sound drastic, and it will not flower for a year or two, but it should eventually shoot from the old wood and produce an attractive compact plant again.

4 Cut back each shoot to about halfway along the new green growth. Do not cut into old, woody growth because new shoots will be reluctant to sprout. Always cut back so that there are green shoots left on the plant to grow after pruning.

5 Lilacs benefit from careful deadheading. As soon as the flowering is over, cut the dead blooms back to the first pair of leaves below the flowerhead (no further, otherwise you might remove buds from which new flowering shoots will be produced).

No-prune shrubs

Abelia	Elaeagnus
Acer	Euonymus
palmatum	fortunei
Aucuba	Fatsia japonica
japonica	Genista lydia
Berberis	Hamamelis
thunbergii	Ilex
Choisya ternata	Magnolia
Cordyline	stellata
australis	Pieris japonica
Cotoneaster	Prunus
microphyllus	laurocerasus
Daphne	Sarcococca

Summer harvesting

By early summer many crops have reached maturity and are ready to harvest. It is important to pick each crop when it is in prime condition. Aim to harvest as quickly as possible but take care not to damage the vegetable in the process because this can encourage storage rots later. Pick vegetables that are young and tender for freezing but allow them to reach full maturity if they are destined for dry storage.

Asparagus

Established beds should be cropping from early summer for about six weeks. Stop harvesting during mid-summer. Do not start harvesting from new asparagus beds until they have been established for three years. Using a sharp knife, cut the spears 5cm (2in) below ground level when they reach about 10–15cm (4–6in) high. Use as fresh as possible after harvest or remove the lower scales and trim to length before blanching.

Beetroot (beets)

Pull roots for salads when young and tender – usually about golf-ball size. Lift maincrop beets before they become tough and inedible. Remove

Eat cabbages when they are fresh and crisp, when the heads are firm. Cut them off cleanly with a sharp knife. A second head sometimes grows from the stalk.

every other root from the row to leave the remainder to grow on and harvest in late summer. Once the leaves begin to wilt, twist off foliage from the root to stop them bleeding.

Broad (fava) beans Harvest early, as soon as the beans start to show, so they can be used immature, like snap peas, in early summer. Later, harvest maincrop before the beans are fully formed and the stem goes woody. Eat fresh or blanch and freeze.

Cabbages

Spring and summer cabbages should be cut when heads are firm and crisp and eaten fresh. It's sometimes possible to get a second crop by leaving a stalk about 10cm (4in) long in the ground and making an X-shaped cut in the top.

Carrots

Maincrop varieties should be available from early summer, 10 weeks after sowing. Pull selectively, aiming to remove them when the roots are

HARVESTING LEAFY CROPS

1 Harvest hearting lettuces when the "heart" feels firm. Use a sharp knife to cut through the stalk.

2 Spinach is a very easy crop to harvest. When you require some, simply cut away the young leaves with a pair of sharp scissors.

to remove them when the roots are 1–1.5cm (½–⅔ in) across. Thinnings of carrots can also be used in salads. On lighter soils pull carrots by hand, but on heavier ground you will need to ease them out with a fork. Refirm any that remain afterwards. Water the ground along the row the day before to make harvesting easier. Twist off the foliage immediately after harvest.

Early potatoes

Harvest when tubers are hen's egg size and the skin rubs off easily, which is usually when the flowers open on the plant. Excavate the soil alongside the row to make sure the tubers are large enough before you lift the whole plant. Eat fresh.

Globe artichokes

Established plants will be producing buds ready to be harvested by the end of early summer. Cut 5cm (2in) below the bud when the scales are still tightly closed. Once the terminal bud has been removed from each plant, new buds will be produced on sideshoots lower down for a late summer harvest. Eat fresh.

Peas

Harvest peas grown for their pods when the peas are just starting to form. Peas grown for their seeds should be harvested when pods swell and contain peas that are sweet and soft. Pick regularly to keep the plant producing new pods. Do not leave old pods on the plant, otherwise the peas will be dry and starchy and yields will drop off. Eat fresh or shell and blanch before freezing.

Perpetual spinach

Regularly pick over spinach, removing the leaves while they are small, to maintain a continuous

HARVESTING BEETROOT

Harvest beetroot (beets) by pulling it by hand from the ground. In heavier soils a fork may be needed to loosen the roots.

HARVESTING CARROTS

Short varieties of carrot can be pulled out by hand, but longer ones and those grown on heavier soils will need digging out with a fork.

crop. Larger leaves can also be harvested but discard the tough mid-rib before you cook them. Eat fresh or freeze.

Rhubarb

Start harvesting from established plants as soon as stems are large enough. Pull individual stems by holding them near to the base and

HARVESTING ASPARAGUS

Make an oblique cut 5cm (2in) below the ground. Asparagus plants should be left to build up for three years before cropping.

HARVESTING GLOBE ARTICHOKES

Harvest a globe artichoke when the scales are tightly closed by cutting the stem just below the head.

giving a sharp twist to break them away cleanly from the crown. Do not leave any broken stems on the plant because this can allow infections to take hold in the crown. Always leave three or four mature leaves on the plant to keep it growing vigorously and remove any flowering stems as soon as they are noticed. Eat fresh or freeze.

Pruning tree fruit

There are a number of advantages to be gained from pruning fruit trees in summer. Unlike winter pruning, which increases the vigour of a plant, pruning in summer tends to decrease the tree's response to being cut back. This means that this is a good time to prune if you want to keep a tree small. Pruning at this time of the year also helps to open up the canopy, so that those branches that remain will get more sunlight and the fruit they carry will be of a higher quality and will ripen earlier.

Why prune?

Neglected trees often produce their fruit out of reach, high up in the canopy, with few fruits set lower down. You can remedy this problem in summer by cutting back one or two of the main branches to a more horizontal side branch lower down. Any tree that has failed to set any fruit is more likely to put its energies into new growth, causing it to become overcrowded. If left unpruned, next year's crop is likely to consist of small, flavourless fruit that may be

Cherries are best pruned during the summer because they are less likely to be infected by the debilitating silver leaf disease.

PRUNING FAN-SHAPED APRICOTS

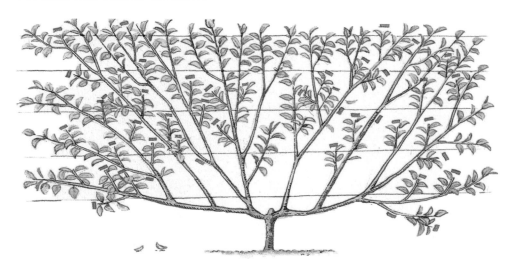

Once the fan has been established, the object of subsequent pruning is to maintain the shape. Cut out any shoots that are pointing in the wrong direction, especially those that point towards or away from the wall. Thin new shoots, leaving one every 15cm (6in). Prune the remaining shoots to five leaves in the spring and then again, after fruiting, back to three leaves.

so numerous that the tree fails to set any fruit the following year, starting the unsatisfactory cycle known as biennial bearing. The best way to deal with this sort of overcrowded growth is to remove all dead or damaged branches as well as any that are crossing or growing strongly vertically. Retain the most widely spaced and most horizontal-growing branches.

Summer pruning should only be carried out on well-established trees that have put on all their extension growth for the current year, otherwise pruning will encourage a thicket of sideshoots. If the base of the new shoot has started to turn brown and woody, the shoot will have stopped growing and is starting to mature. The growth should be stiff and not whippy when pulled downwards by the tip.

Plums and cherries

These trees, which are prone to a debilitating disease called silver leaf, are less likely to be infected when pruned in summer because there are fewer disease spores around then and the pruning cuts should heal more quickly when the tree is in vigorous

PRUNING FAN-SHAPED CHERRIES

To maintain the shape, remove any shoots that are pointing in the wrong direction. To ensure that there is a constant supply of new wood, cut back in summer all shoots that have fruited, as far back as the next new shoot. Tie these new shoots to the cane and wire framework.

PRUNING FAN-SHAPED PLUMS

Remove all new shoots that face towards or away from the wall. Then cut back all new shoots to about six leaves, leaving any that are needed to fill in gaps in the framework. In autumn, after cropping, further cut back the shoots to three leaves.

growth. Cherries are also prone to bacterial canker diseases which can be largely avoided by pruning in summer. It is not a good idea to prune heavily unless absolutely necessary. Once the initial shape is determined, most well-established trees do not need pruning apart from the removal of dead or damaged stems or branches. Simply prune to keep the canopy open and to maintain good health. Remove the dead or damaged branches first and thin the remaining ones as necessary.

However, it may be worth taking a risk with old, neglected cherries that fail to produce a decent crop by pruning heavily in summer. Prune back one in three of the oldest branches to a side branch lower down. New, vigorous and productive shoots may well grow in the years to come.

If suckers are growing around the base, remove these by pulling them off rather than cutting with secateurs (pruners) because pruning them will encourage new suckers to sprout.

Apricots

Most apricots are produced on the old wood, so little pruning is required other than to remove exhausted old wood every few years to maintain vigour and fruiting potential. Trees trained as fans should be pruned in summer by removing any laterals that are growing towards or away from the wall or fence and by cutting back the laterals that remain to 8cm (3 in). Any new laterals produced as the summer progresses should be removed during late summer.

Once the framework of a damson tree has been established, little pruning should be necessary apart from the removal of dead or damaged wood.

Codling moth traps

Apples and sometimes pears may be attacked by codling moths, which lay eggs on young fruitlets. The grubs feed on the flesh, causing the fruit to ripen and fall early. The flesh if tunnelled is full of excreta ('frass'). You can control codling moths to some extent by tying corrugated cardboard around the trunk in autumn to lure overwintering caterpillars. Destroy any that are found. You can also control the adults by using a pheromone trap that attracts the male moths, preventing them from mating with the females. One trap per five trees should be sufficient.

Pruning and propagating soft fruit

Summer is a good time to prune soft fruit, such as gooseberries and red and white currants, as well as raspberries, because you can combine harvesting with the pruning process. You need to prune trained forms of these bushes in summer to keep them in shape. Overcrowded and unproductive bushes can also be pruned now by removing one stem in three, taking out the oldest stems first. After three years all the old wood will have been replaced with new, vigorous and productive stems.

Pruning bushes

Gooseberries and red and white currants can be pruned in summer by cutting back all sideshoots to five leaves of this year's growth. The main leader of each bush is not normally pruned at this time of year unless it is diseased. For example, gooseberries, and sometimes currants, that have been attacked by gooseberry mildew can benefit from the tipping back of new growth. The disease starts as a white, powdery deposit on the shoot tips and youngest leaves but progresses to attack fruit, eventually distorting new growth. Opening up the bush and improving airflow, as well as

Check ripening strawberries every day and pick the fruits when they are red all over. Eat fresh straight away or keep them somewhere cool for a few days.

removing infected shoots, will help to control the disease. However, you will have to spray with a systemic fungicide as soon as symptoms are seen for effective control.

Pruning cordons

All the sideshoots on plants trained on a single main stem should be cut back to four leaves. If the cordon has grown beyond the top of its support, cut back the top shoot to a plump bud at the desired height. Alternatively, pinch out these shoots to the desired length when they have put on about 15cm (6in) of growth. Any suckers should be removed by pulling them out rather than trimming with secateurs (pruners).

Pruning after harvest

Blackcurrants, blackberries and raspberries can be pruned straight after harvesting is complete, or you can wait until autumn. The old, fruiting canes of blackberries and

raspberries should be cut down to ground level. Tie in new canes to their supports. Blackcurrant stems that have borne fruit should be cut out. Alternatively, combine the harvesting and pruning process to help save time and energy, by cutting out the fruit-laden branches of blackcurrants. These can then be

GROWING STRAWBERRIES

Place a layer of straw under the leaves of the strawberry plants in order to prevent the developing fruit from getting muddy or covered with dirt.

PRUNING BLACKCURRANTS

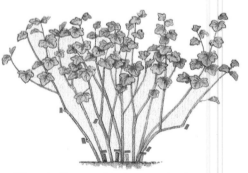

After planting, cut blackcurrant bushes back to a single bud above ground. The following winter, remove any weak or misplaced growth. Subsequent pruning should take place after fruiting and consists of cutting out up to a third of two-year-old or older wood in order to stimulate new growth.

LAYERING BLACKBERRIES

1 Choose a healthy shoot, then dig a hole near the tip and bend down the tip to bury it in the soil.

2 After a short period the tip will have produced roots. It can then be cut from the parent plant and replanted where required.

3 If you would like to have potted specimens, bury a flowerpot in the ground, fill it with compost (soil mix) and bury the tip in this.

taken to the kitchen where they can be stripped of fruit more easily and the spent stems discarded.

Propagate soft fruit

Strawberries produce their best crop during the second and third years after planting. Thereafter, the yields will drop off as the health of the crop deteriorates. For this reason it is a good idea to replace the whole crop every three or four years with

Once blackberry canes have fruited in autumn, cut them back to ground level and tie in new ones to replace those that have been cut out.

new plants. The cheapest way to do this is to raise your own plants by rooting runners from healthy, heavy cropping plants.

Strawberries can be propagated at this time of year by rooting runners. Simply sink a series of 9cm (3½in) pots full of fresh potting compost (soil mix) into the ground around the parent plant. Water the compost well, then select four or five strong, healthy runners and peg one plantlet down into each pot of compost using a piece of bent wire so that the base of the plantlet is in good contact with the moist compost. After a month or so, the plantlet will have rooted well and can be severed from the parent plant.

Blackberries and hybrid berries, such as tayberries, can be increased by layering. With these plants the tip of the shoot is pegged down in contact with the soil or compost in a pot. Dig a hole about 15cm (6in) deep and bury the shoot tip by replacing the soil. After the shoot tip has rooted, sever it from the parent plant, leaving 30cm (12in) of the original cane.

Raspberries naturally produce suckers alongside an established row and these can be removed once well

rooted by severing the stem from the main parent plant and replanting the rooting sucker as new stock if required. Red, white and blackcurrants are easy to propagate from hardwood cuttings in winter.

Cut back strawberries

Once the crop has been harvested, cut off all the old leaves back to the main crown and dispose of them or burn them. Do not compost them or leave them lying around the garden as they will help carry over pests and diseases to next year's crop. Runners should also be removed, unless you are using them to propagate new plants. If you used a straw mulch, you should remove this at the same time and destroy it.

Keeping crops growing well

Watering is a year-round task in the greenhouse, but the summer months are the most demanding. Plants growing in containers, such as pots and growing bags, are entirely dependent on you for their food and water, and this may mean watering more than once a day in summer. You can reduce the amount of time it takes by positioning your containers in one part of the greenhouse so they can be watered together.

When to water?

Different plants have different watering requirements, and it is essential that you check your plants regularly so that they are watered before they wilt and suffer stress. The simplest way to judge if a plant needs watering is to push your finger into the compost (soil mix) – if it is dry 2cm (¾in) below the surface the container needs watering. You can take a lot of the hard work out of watering by installing an automatic or semi-automatic system.

Automatic watering

Some watering systems allow plants in containers to draw just the right amount of water they need from a reservoir by capillary action. The pots are stood on a bed of damp sand or on a special fabric that draws the water from a reservoir. As the plant takes in moisture through its roots, water is drawn up from the bed of sand or capillary matting via capillary action to replenish it. You can make a capillary sand bed out of a sturdy box about 15cm (6in) deep that has been lined with thick black plastic sheeting. Place a 2.5cm (1in) layer of pea gravel inside to provide drainage and cover with a 10cm (4in) layer of horticultural sand. Firm, level and then stand the containers on top.

FEEDING AND WATERING IN THE GREENHOUSE

1 Plants should be watered before they show obvious signs of distress, such as wilting. With bushy plants it is not possible to judge simply by the visual appearance of the compost (soil mix), and touch is usually the best guide. Don't just feel the surface – push your finger down into the compost.

2 Moisture indicators, which show when the compost has dried out, for individual pots can be helpful for a beginner, who is uncertain when to water, or if there are just a few plants, but they are not a practical solution if you have a whole greenhouse or conservatory full of plants.

3 Capillary matting is an ideal way to water most pot-plants in summer. You can use a proprietary system fed by mains water or improvise with a system like the one illustrated. This uses a length of gutter for the water supply. You can keep it topped up by hand or plumb it into the mains.

4 If watering by hand, use the can without a rose unless you are watering seedlings. This will enable you to direct water more easily to the roots rather than sprinkling the leaves. Place a finger over the end of the spout to control the flow.

5 Use a liquid fertilizer applied with the water if you can remember to do it regularly. There are both soluble powders and liquids that can be diluted to the appropriate strength. Choose a high-potash feed for fruiting crops such as tomatoes.

6 Fertilizer sticks and tablets that you push into the potting soil are a convenient way to administer fertilizer if you don't want to apply liquid feeds regularly. Those releasing their nutrients over a period of several months need applying only once.

Watering and feeding are of critical importance throughout the lifetime of greenhouse crops. To achieve good yields from hungry crops, such as tomatoes, you may have to apply a liquid feed every week in addition to watering at least once a day.

Capillary matting is even easier. Lay the fabric on a thick sheet of black plastic placed on a level surface. Drape one end of the matting into a trough or short piece of guttering with the ends in place to act as the reservoir. Water the containers thoroughly from above to start the capillary action and keep the reservoir topped up as necessary.

Where a capillary watering system isn't practicable, such as with large containers and growing bags, you could opt for a drip watering system instead. You can buy bladder bags with a single drip nozzle that supplies water rather like a medical drip to individual plants or you could make your own out of an upturned plastic drinks bottle with the bottom removed. Drill a small hole in the lid and fit a loose galvanized screw into it, then stand the bottle vertically in the compost next to the plant. Any water poured into the bottle will leak out past the screw very slowly – providing water over many hours. Alternatively, you can set up an easy-to-install and reliable micro-bore irrigation system to water your entire greenhouse.

Feeding

Plants vary in the amount and type of nutrients they require. Fast-growing crops in containers will need feeding the most often – perhaps once a week. Plants that are grown for their fruits or flowers, such as tomatoes and chrysanthemums, should be given a high-potash liquid feed, while those grown for their foliage will do better with a feed that contains plenty of nitrogen. Permanent pot plants are best fed with a slow-release fertilizer when they are repotted; choose one that will provide nutrients for the whole season. Feed chrysanthemums until you can see colour in the breaking buds. Start feeding tomatoes in early summer once the first truss of flowers has set and stop feeding in late summer once the last truss has set. Start feeding cucumbers in midsummer when the first fruits start to swell. Always follow the manufacturer's instructions on the packet label for application rates.

Looking after greenhouse crops

A greenhouse provides the perfect environment for raising fast-growing tender crops such as tomatoes and cucumbers, but it is also a haven for the pests and diseases that attack them. There are a number of steps you can take to minimize the risks so that your plants grow strongly and crop well. Preventative measures will reduce the need for expensive chemical or biological controls.

Preventing problems

At the end of the growing season the greenhouse should be emptied and carefully cleaned so that pests and diseases cannot overwinter ready to attack the following year's crop. Even at this time of year you can practise good greenhouse hygiene by clearing out any dead or dying material before it becomes a source of infection. You can also make sure your crops are growing strongly so that they can shrug off attacks more easily. Avoid easy access for disease spores by making clean cuts with a sharp, clean blade when you are training your crops.

To get the most from your crops, you also need to be vigilant for problems and take action to control outbreaks quickly. Keep flying pests out of the greenhouse by covering vents and the door with insect-proof mesh and control those inside by hanging up sticky traps among the plants.

Biological controls

Many common greenhouse pests can be tackled by introducing their natural enemies into your greenhouse, a method known as biological control. The greenhouse or conservatory is an ideal place to practise biological control methods – the predators can be kept where they are needed and will thrive in the protected environment where they should multiply rapidly until control is achieved. For example, a parasitic wasp, *Encarsia formosa*, will control whitefly, while a predatory mite, called *Phytoseiulus*, can be used against spider mite attacks, and nematodes can be used to attack vine weevil larvae. Introduce the biological control as soon as you notice the first sign of the pest. You will need to remove any flying insect traps and stop spraying chemicals that might kill the biological control.

Care of greenhouse crops

Aubergines (eggplants) make bushier plants if the growing tip is pinched out when the plant is about 30cm (12in) high. Allow only one fruit to develop on each shoot. Pinch out the growing tips of these shoots three leaves beyond the developing fruit. Never let the plants dry out, and feed regularly. Mist to provide high humidity which is beneficial.

Melons Train the sideshoot of melons to horizontal wires, and pinch back the sideshoots to two leaves beyond each fruit that develops. Melons may require pollinating, in which case transfer the pollen from the male to female flowers with a small paintbrush. It may also be necessary to support developing fruits in nets strung from the ceiling.

USING BIOLOGICAL CONTROLS

1 Various forms of biological controls are available for a number of greenhouse pests including red spidermite, soft scale insects, mealybugs and thrips. *Encarsia formosa* is a tiny wasp that parasitizes whitefly larvae.

2 If vine weevil grubs destroy your plants by eating the roots, try controlling them in future with a parasitic eelworm. A suspension of the eelworms is simply watered into the compost (soil mix) in each pot in summer.

Pest and disease patrol

Spider mite Watch out for speckled, yellowing leaves on aubergines (eggplants), cucumbers, melons, begonias, fuchsias and pelargoniums. Examine the undersides of affected leaves as well as the plants' growing tips where the insects tend to congregate. If attacks are severe, webbing may also be present. This pest likes warm, dry conditions, so ventilate well and damp down surfaces. Try a biological control or spray a suitable systemic insecticide.

Whitefly Clouds of tiny white insects rise up when disturbed on crops such as aubergines, peppers and tomatoes. These sap-sucking insects congregate on the undersides of leaves and can be controlled using sticky traps, biological controls or a suitable contact insecticide.

Grey mould (botrytis) Felty patches appear on leaves, fruit and stems. Keep the greenhouse well-ventilated and clear away any infected material as well as yellowing leaves to reduce the chances of infection.

Sooty mould This black mould thrives on the sticky deposits left on the surface of leaves low down on the plant after being exuded by sap-sucking insects, such as whitefly and green- and blackfly, higher up. The mould weakens the plant by reducing its ability to photosynthesize. Wipe off with soapy water and control sap-sucking insects.

Aubergines (eggplants) are attacked by a range of common greenhouse pests including aphids, spider mites and whitefly.

SUMMER CARE FOR GREENHOUSE TOMATOES

1 If the plants are supported by strings, simply loop the string around the top of the shoot whenever necessary. It will form a spiral support that holds the stem upright.

2 If the tomato is supported by a vertical bamboo cane, use soft string wound twice around the stake and then loop it loosely around the stem before tying the knot.

3 Snap off sideshoots while they are still small. They will snap off cleanly if you pull them sideways. Do not remove sideshoots if you have a low-growing bush variety.

4 If fruits are failing to form, poor pollination may be the problem. Shake the plants each day, or spray the flowers with water, to spread the pollen from flower to flower. This is best carried out in the middle of the day.

5 Tomatoes respond well to feeding. Give them regular feeds with a proprietary tomato fertilizer that is high in potash to promote fruit production.

6 The lowest leaves often turn yellow as they age. Remove these, as they will not contribute to feeding the plant, and letting more light reach the fruits can help to ripen them. Snap them cleanly off the stem.

Midsummer

Midsummer is mainly a time to enjoy your garden, rather than do a lot of physical work in it. Most things are already sown or planted, and the emphasis is on weeding and watering as well as regular deadheading to keep the garden looking tidy and flowering well.

Use a hoe to control annual weeds on bare soil. Choose a warm, dry day so that the weeds wither and die quickly after being hoed off. If perennial weeds are a problem, they should be dug out by hand complete with roots to prevent them resprouting. Bindweed may be a problem at this time of year in established borders and can be tackled by strategically placing canes in the border for it to climb up. Slip out the cane once it is covered in twining stems and stuff this new growth into a plastic bag while still attached to the roots. This will allow you to spray it with a suitable weedkiller without affecting neighbouring ornamental plants.

Watering is another key job of the season. During prolonged periods of drought, you should aim to apply sufficient water to beds and borders to last for at least a week. The water should soak down to the roots where it can be used by the plants. Applying water little and often not only takes longer, but more water is lost through evaporation and it soaks only the top layer of the soil. This encourages plants to form shallow roots, making them less able to tap into reserves deep in the ground. Do not water indiscriminately; many plants can survive

longer dry periods than you might expect, and your main concern should be newly planted specimens. Although a lawn will turn brown in prolonged dry spells, it is not necessary to water, unless it is newly planted, because it will soon recover with the first rains of autumn.

To keep flowering displays looking their best, it is worth deadheading regularly. By removing the fading flowerheads you will not only improve the appearance of the plants, but extend the flowering period of many repeat-flowering favourites, such as roses, and get some perennials to put on a second display later in the summer. Although fresh herbs can be picked any time during the growing season, midsummer is the ideal time to harvest and dry them for winter use. Pick them in their prime, when their essential oils are at their most concentrated, producing the best aroma and flavour.

In the greenhouse, the perfect growing environment allows crops to grow strongly, but also provides ideal conditions for the pests and diseases that attack them. There are several steps you can take to reduce the problems, such as practising good greenhouse hygiene and tackling pest infestations early by using traps and introducing biological controls (the pest's natural enemies). Outside, problem pests of particular crops, such as pea moth and carrot fly, can be kept at bay by putting up insect-proof barriers or by altering your sowing times to avoid the pest altogether.

You can get bumper crops of your favourite fruit even in a small garden by growing them against walls and fences.

Summer bulbs, such as *Lilium martagon,* are an easy way to add a spectacular display of exotic blooms when you are enjoying your garden the most.

Griselinia   Weigela   heel, pulled from the parent plant
                                      with a little bark from the woody   pinks are often raised this way.

Propagating shrubs and climbers

Maintaining the pond

If it has been well sited, constructed and stocked, a pond will require a minimum of attention during the summer months apart from the occasional topping up after a hot spell to maintain water levels and help prevent water temperatures fluctuating too much. Small ponds and water features, such as gurgle ponds, that do not have a large reservoir of water may need topping up every day if they are operated during hot weather.

Protect fish

If you see the fish gulping for air at the surface during close, thundery weather it's worth playing a hosepipe on to the water surface to help increase oxygen levels. If the pond is fitted with a fountain or other moving water feature, turn this on to achieve the same result. The water temperature of shallow ponds that are stocked with fish may increase too much in prolonged hot spells, endangering the survival of the fish. If your fish look distressed, transfer them to a tank somewhere cool and shady until conditions improve.

Fish may also be at risk from predators outside the pond. If herons sometimes visit your garden, it is worth netting the pond in summer or putting up a low wire fence about 45cm (18in) high to

Introduce tender plants

Summer is the ideal time to add exotic-looking, tender aquatic plants, such as water hyacinths and water lettuce. Water chestnuts are the exception to this rule since although the plants are killed in winter, they produce 'nuts' that sink to the bottom of the pond in autumn and sprout the following spring to grow into new plants.

put them off preying on your fish.

Feed fish throughout the summer months as required, taking care not to overfeed them as surplus food will sink and rot in the water

CLEARING POND WEEDS

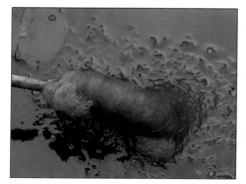

1 Left untreated, the filaments of blanketweed will quickly take over a pond. To clear the water, insert a cane into the water and twist it to wind the weed around it, rather like candyfloss.

2 Numerous tiny creatures live in blanketweed, and the removed weed should be left at the side of the pond for a while so that the creatures can escape and return to the water. Then put it on the compost heap.

3 Oxygenating and floating plants can soon take over small ponds. Lift out clumps and tear them apart, returning about a half to two-thirds to the water. Leave unwanted sections near the pond for a while.

4 Duckweed or other floaters can be useful initially in preventing green water, but they soon spread and need constant thinning, otherwise they can prevent more desirable plants from growing well.

5 Remove duckweed using a fine-mesh net before it has a chance to spread. You will need to check for it on a regular basis because even a small colony can quickly spread in the right conditions.

6 Even a pond that is clear of pond weeds can become infested by small amounts being introduced on new plants. Always check new plants carefully, looking on the undersides of leaves to check they are clean.

Clear water

Hot summer weather can also upset the ecological balance of a pond so that the water turns green with algae. This can be controlled quickly and easily using a pond algicide, but make sure you follow the instructions carefully so that you don't affect other aquatic residents. If you do not want to use chemicals you can clear the surface by scooping out blanket weed by hand. Simply use a stick or bamboo cane to twist up the filamentous blanketweed algae into a green blob wrapped around the cane so that it can be removed from the pond. Leave the weed at the side of the pond overnight to allow any aquatic creatures to escape back into the pond before putting it on the compost heap. For a long-term solution, consider installing a filter, which will remove the algae before it has time to bloom. You can also prevent algae forming in the first place by placing a special barley-straw pad into the pond. It is thought that the bacteria found on it feed on the algae, keeping the water clear — even during hot spells.

If duckweed is a problem, use a fine-mesh net (the sort sold for

Thin overcrowded lily pads before they cover the entire surface of the pond.

WATER LEVEL

Top up the level of water in the pool in summer when evaporation levels are high. This is especially important if you have a watercourse running continuously.

rockpool fishing at the seaside) to scoop up the tiny floating plants. Leave the plants on the side of the pond for 24 hours so that any trapped creatures can escape.

Tidy plants

It's not too late to add new plants to your pond in midsummer, although you'll get maximum benefit if you plant up your pond earlier in the year. Existing repeat-flowering marginal plants will benefit from regular deadheading to tidy the displays and

encourage further flushes of blooms. Remove rampant plants and thin them to prevent them from swamping their neighbours. Overcrowded waterlilies should also be thinned out so they do not cover the entire surface of the pond.

Use a garden hose to dislodge and drown pests, such as blackfly and thrips, which can form colonies on waterlily pads. Lush marginal plants such as marsh marigolds can suffer from mildew. Cut off affected leaves to encourage new, disease-free growth.

Growing and training vegetables

To keep vegetables growing well, they need to be given room to grow and not allowed to run short of water or nutrients. Most garden soils contain sufficient nutrients to grow most vegetables as long as you apply plenty of well-rotted organic matter when the ground is cultivated. Regular maintenance throughout the summer will ensure optimum cropping.

Feeding vegetables

On poor soils a few hungry crops, such as Brussels sprouts, cabbages, cauliflowers and maincrop potatoes, will need to be given extra feed to do well. This is usually given as a base dressing before the crop is planted as well as a side dressing during the life of the crop. Most soils contain plenty of phosphate and potash, so for leafy crops choose a high-nitrogen fertilizer to boost yields. Potatoes and root crops, on the other hand, will produce a lot of topgrowth at the expense of roots and tubers with this feeding regime, and should be given a fertilizer that's high in phosphate instead. Fruiting crops, such as tomatoes and courgettes (zucchini), do best with a fertilizer that provides a high proportion of

EARTHING UP LEEKS

As the leeks grow, earth (hill) them up by pulling the soil up around the stems to blanch them. This will give the leeks a better flavour.

potash. With such conflicting demands, often the best option is to use a balanced, all-purpose feed, which provides these three major nutrients in equal amounts.

Pest patrol

The best way of keeping pests under control is to ensure your crops are growing well and be vigilant so that you can catch outbreaks early and take appropriate action.

Aphids Blackfly on broad (fava) beans are a common sight and will move to other crops, such as French and runner beans. Other types of

PROTECTING CAULIFLOWERS

Cauliflowers are sometimes scorched by the hot sun. Protect from discoloration by covering them with the inner leaves.

aphids also attack brassicas, courgettes and lettuce. If you garden organically, you may wish to wait for natural predators to bring outbreaks under control, but plants will be weakened and yields lost. Aphids can also spread debilitating viruses, which could destroy the whole crop. However, you can give natural predators a hand by rubbing off early colonies of insects and removing the tips of broad beans on which blackfly congregate. As a last resort, apply a suitable insecticide.

Carrot fly Inconspicuous shiny black flies lay their eggs near the stems of

TRAINING OUTDOOR TOMATOES

1 If you are growing a cordon variety (one that is growing as a single main stem, supported by a cane), keep removing sideshoots as they develop in the leaf axil – that is, where the leaf joins the stem.

2 Regular tying in to the support is even more important outdoors than in the greenhouse, because strong winds can break an unsupported stem and shorten the productive life of the plant.

3 As soon as the plant has set the number of trusses (sprays) of fruit likely to be ripened in your area, pinch out the top of the plant. In many areas you can only reasonably expect to ripen four trusses.

BLANCHING CELERY

1 Blanching celery stems makes them taste sweeter. When the stems are 30cm (12in) long, tie them loosely together just below the leaves.

2 Fasten a collar of cardboard around the stems. They will eventually blanch – that is, become white – because of the lack of light.

3 Although soil can also be pulled up around the stems to blanch them, a collar will stop soil from getting into the crown.

carrots and related plants. Grubs hatch and burrow into the roots, ruining the crop. You can prevent this pest by using physical barriers or by sprinkling a suitable soil insecticide into the seed drill before sowing. Late crops sown in early summer will not be affected.

Onion fly This tiny insect lays its eggs next to onions and related crops. The grubs hatch and burrow into the developing bulbs, killing seedlings and ruining larger bulbs. Following a strict crop rotation will help prevent this pest, but you can also apply a suitable soil insecticide to the seedbed before sowing.

Pea moth Adult moths are active in early and midsummer, laying eggs next to the flowers on pea plants. The grubs burrow into the developing pods and eat a young pea. Crops sown in early or late spring are less affected than those sown in mid-spring because they flower before or after the time when the adult moths are on the wing. However, you can still usually use the undamaged peas by sorting through the crop at harvest time. The alternative is to apply a preventative spray at flowering time.

Outdoor tomatoes

Tomatoes that have been grown outside need less attention than greenhouse varieties, especially if you grow the kinds on which you leave on the sideshoots. Feeding and watering are necessary if you want a good crop of quality fruits. Regular watering not only ensures a heavy crop but also reduces the risk of splitting through uneven watering, which sometimes happens if dry weather produces hard skins that can't cope with a sudden spurt of growth following a wet period. Add a liquid fertilizer to the water, at the rate and frequency recommended by the manufacturer. How well your crop does depends on a combination of variety, care and climate. In cold areas, outdoor tomatoes can be a disappointing crop, but in warm areas you will almost certainly have more fruit than you can eat.

Outdoor tomatoes require less attention than those grown indoors and can be trained using attractive supports in a prominent position.

Harvesting and storing herbs

Herbs can be picked for culinary use at any time during the growing season, and a few, such as thyme, can be harvested in small amounts during the autumn and winter too. If you want to harvest herbs for drying and storing, the best time will depend on the part of the plant you want to collect: leaves, flowers, roots or seeds.

Harvesting

All herbs should be picked when they are in their prime. Avoid old, diseased

HARVESTING HERBS

Harvest herbs when they are at their peak, usually before they flower. Cut them on a dry day, avoiding times when they are wilting in the heat. Harvest the best leaves, not the older leaves lower down the plant.

or discoloured parts, and try to pick in the morning after the dew has evaporated but before the sun has dissipated the essential oils that give herbs their distinctive taste and aroma. Don't be tempted to pick wet herbs for drying and storing because these are more likely to go mouldy. Cut the material cleanly from the parent plant using a sharp pair of scissors or secateurs (pruners). Avoid collecting large batches of herbs all at once, because there will inevitably be a delay before some are prepared for storage. Heaps of unprepared herbs are likely to heat up and deteriorate.

Leafy herbs should be picked before the plants come into flower. This is the stage when their essential oils are at their most concentrated and producing the best aroma and flavour. Small-leaved herbs, such as thyme and rosemary, should be picked on the stem, while the leaves of large-leaved herbs, such as bay, can be picked individually off the parent plant. Flowers are best harvested as they start to open – pick single blooms or whole flowerheads as appropriate. Seeds are best picked as soon as they are ripe

Collect herbs, like this marjoram, when they are at their best. Small-leaved herbs should be picked attached to the stem, while larger-leaved herbs can be picked as individual leaves.

(when the pod has turned from green to brown), and roots are usually removed while the plant is dormant during the winter months.

Drying

Leafy herbs dry best in a well-ventilated place that's dark and warm – an airing cupboard is ideal. Aim for a temperature of 35°C (95°F), although anything above 20°C (68°F) would do. Hang the herbs up

HARVESTING MARJORAM FOR DRYING

1 Small-leaved herbs, such as marjoram, are easily air-dried. Cut bunches of healthy material at mid-morning on a dry, warm day.

2 Strip off the lower leaves, which would otherwise become crushed and damaged when the stems are bunched.

3 Twist a rubber band around a few stems to hold them tightly together. Gather as many bunches as you need.

DRYING HERB SEEDS

1 Pick seedheads just as they are ripening. At this stage the seeds should readily come away from the stalks. Place them on a tray and leave the seeds for a few days in a warm, dry place until they have completely dried.

2 Make sure that the seeds are completely dry and then sieve them to remove any debris and bits of seed husks before putting them into a glass jar with an airtight lid. Label clearly and store in a cool, dry, dark place.

FREEZING HERBS

The best method of storing soft-leaved herbs, such as parsley and mint, is to freeze them. Chop up the leaves and place them in ice-cube trays. Top up with water and freeze. This helps maintain the herb's colour.

in bunches or lay them in open racks so that they dry quickly and thoroughly. Within a week the herbs should be so dry that they rustle. Strip the leaves from their stems and store each herb in individual airtight containers. Seedpods are best dried in paper bags to catch the seed.

Storing

The best way to store dry herbs is in clearly labelled, airtight opaque containers so that they are protected from direct light. Better still, keep

them in a dark cupboard. Herbs can also be preserved in herb oils and vinegars, which have many culinary uses. You can create single flavours or mixed herbs to taste. This is a good way to store herbs such as basil that do not dry well. Other soft-leaved herbs, such as parsley and mint, can be stored frozen in ice cubes, which helps preserve their flavour and colour. The ice cube can then be added to summer drinks or added to stews and casseroles as required. Whole sprigs of other

herbs can also be frozen for winter use. Either wrap them in foil or lay them on trays to freeze.

Herb mixtures

Different herbs can be combined in a number of distinctive mixtures. *Bouquet garni,* for example, is a combination of several herbs, such as bay, parsley, marjoram and thyme. Sprigs of the herbs are tied together or placed in a muslin (cheesecloth) bag, which is cooked with the dish and removed before serving.

Herbs to dry

Bay	Lemon verbena
Caraway	Mint
Clary	Rosemary
Coriander	Sage
Dill	Savory
Fennel	Tarragon
Lemon balm	Thyme

Herbs to freeze

Basil	Lovage
Borage	Marjoram
Coriander	Mint
Dill	Parsley
Lemon balm	Rosemary

DRYING HERBS

Bunches of herbs can be dried by hanging them in a dry, well-ventilated place where they are out of direct sunlight.

HERB MIXTURES

Grow herbs in individual pots, which can be kept in a larger container and replaced when the plants are past their best.

Summer pruning trained fruit trees

Shaped and trained apple trees are normally pruned twice a year – once in summer and again in winter. Summer pruning controls the amount of growth produced each year and maintains the basic shape; winter pruning consists of thinning overcrowded fruiting spurs on old plants. In late spring the new growth at the ends of the main shoots is cut back to its point of origin, but summer pruning is the most crucial in terms of maintaining the trained shape.

Pruning apples and pears

On trained forms of apples and pears, all mature new shoots that originate directly from the main trunk and are over 23cm (9in) long should be cut back to three leaves once extension growth is complete.

SUMMER PRUNING ESPALIER APPLES

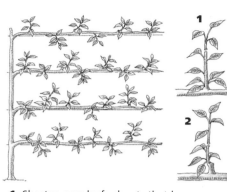

1 Shorten new leafy shoots that have grown directly from the main branches back to three leaves above the basal cluster of leaves. This should be done only once the shoots have dark green leaves and the bark has started to turn brown and is woody at the base. In cold areas it may be early autumn before the shoots are mature enough.

2 If the shoot is growing from a stub left by previous pruning – and not directly from one of the main stems – cut back to just one leaf above the basal cluster of leaves.

SUMMER PRUNING CORDON APPLES

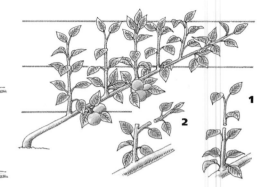

1 A cordon is pruned in exactly the same way as an espalier, although, of course, the basic shape of the plant is different. Just cut back shoots growing directly from the main branch to three leaves above the basal cluster of leaves.

2 Cut back shoots growing from stubs left by earlier pruning to one leaf above the basal cluster. Well-established trees may become congested with fruiting clusters, so these may need thinning periodically.

Pears grown as cordons are a space-efficient way of growing fruit in a small garden. If correctly pruned, heavy crops can be produced from a single row of trees.

This does not include the clusters of leaves found at the base of such shoots. All mature shoots that originate from the sideshoots (laterals) on the main trunk should be cut back to one leaf beyond the cluster of leaves at their base. If the new shoots have not turned brown at the base and are easily bent when pulled downwards from the tip they are not sufficiently mature and should be left until late summer or early autumn before they are pruned. Always use a sharp pair of secateurs or a pruning knife so that any cuts made are able to heal quickly, reducing the risk of disease attack.

Summer pruning other fruits

Grapes Outside, prune sideshoots (laterals) carrying bunches of developing grapes back to two leaves from the supporting wire. Subsequent new shoots (sub-laterals) should be cut back to one leaf. Allow one truss to develop per lateral during the early years, increasing to two or three per lateral once well established. All unwanted growth should be removed back to the main framework of stems. Alternatively, train using the traditional guyot system described below. In the greenhouse, pinch out non-fruiting laterals after they have developed six leaves and sub-laterals to just one leaf.

Figs Figs grown as free-standing bushes should have the tip of each new shoot pinched out after five leaves to encourage new fruit-bearing shoots to form lower down the stems. Trained forms of figs should have half of their new sideshoots (laterals) cut back in this way. These will bear fruit next year. If grown in an unheated greenhouse, prune the sideshoots back to just above the fourth leaf and in a heated greenhouse prune back to two leaves.

Peaches On trained forms prune out any laterals that are pointing in the wrong direction, such as towards the wall support, to maintain the overall shape. Also, after harvest, cut back fruited laterals to a replacement lateral lower down. Tie in new shoots to the supporting framework.

Trained forms of apples and pears make attractive and productive garden dividers that dont take up too much space.

SUMMER PRUNING GRAPES

Train new shoots vertically, removing any sideshoots that develop on them to one leaf. Allow vertical fruiting shoots to grow on the horizontal branches, removing any sideshoots. Cut back above the top wire to three leaves.

SUMMER PRUNING FIGS

Pinch out the growing tips of about half of the young shoots that are carried on the main framework branches. You should do this towards the end of midsummer. As the shoots develop, tie them to the wires.

SUMMER PRUNING COBNUTS

Late summer Established trees should be pruned in late summer. Strong lateral growths are broken off by hand to about six to eight leaves from the base and left to hang.

Renovating permanent plants

Overgrown permanent container plants can be renovated at this time of the year if they are looking straggly or going bare at the base, or if they have grown unmanageably large. Now is also a good time to propagate many indoor plants.

Air-layering

Some plants that produce stiff, upright growth, but have grown too tall or have become bare at the base, and that do not root readily from cuttings, can be propagated using this method. It is usually safer than taking cuttings, because the new plant is not cut from the parent until it has formed roots.

Aglaonema, cabbage palm, leopard lily, finger aralia, dragon tree, fatsia, rubber plant, Swiss cheese plant, schefflera, philodendron, and orange and lemon trees can be propagated in this way. Plants can be air-layered at almost any time, but early-midsummer is ideal because they are growing vigorously at this time.

Division

Plants with a fibrous root system, like calatheas and most ferns, are more likely to divide successfully. It's also a useful technique for rejuvenating plants that produce bulbs and rhizomes, such as baby's tears, aspidistras, asparagus and haworthia.

Once a plant has filled its pot, if it is not practical to move it to a larger one, division may revive it and will give you a number of extra plants. It's worth noting that a few flowering plants bloom better if kept slightly pot-bound. House- and greenhouse plants can be divided throughout the year, but late spring and early summer are particularly good times. Turn the pot upside down and knock out the rootball. Tease apart or slice up the roots with a sharp knife so that each division has plenty of roots and shoots. Repot each new division into fresh compost (soil mix).

Layering

This is used to propagate many climbers and trailers that have outgrown their allotted space. Kangaroo vine, grape ivy, creeping fig, trailing fig, ivy, wax plant and sweetheart vine can all be regenerated in this way. Simply select a healthy, low-growing shoot and remove several leaves from just behind the tip. Then peg the shoot down into a pot of moist compost. Keep well watered and the layer will root in a couple of months and can then be severed from its parent. Spider plants produce plantlets naturally that are easy to root in moist compost.

AIR-LAYERING

1 Layer the plant above the bare area, just below the leaves. If you are using the technique on a multi-stemmed plant just to increase stock, remove a few leaves from the point where you want to make the layer.

2 Carefully make an upward slit about 2.5cm (1in) long, below an old leaf joint. Take care that you do not cut more than halfway through the stem, otherwise the shoot may break.

3 Make a sleeve out of plastic sheet. It does not have to form a tube as you can wrap it round the stem then make a seal. Fix the bottom of the sleeve a short distance below the cut, using a twist-tie or adhesive tape.

4 Brush a small amount of rooting hormone (powder or gel) into the wound, to speed rooting. Then pack a little sphagnum moss into the wound to keep it open. Pack more damp sphagnum moss around the stem.

5 Once the sleeve is full of moss, secure at the top with another twist-tie or tape. Make sure that the moss is kept moist, and carefully check for roots after a month or so. When well rooted, sever from the parent to pot up.

TAKING LEAF PETIOLE CUTTINGS

1 The kind of cuttings taken from African violets are known as leaf petiole cuttings and include a length of stalk. Select a young but fully grown, healthy leaf, and cut it off cleanly near the base.

2 Trim the stalk about 2.5cm (1in) below the leaf blade and insert it so that the leaf blade sits just in contact with the cutting compost (soil mix). Insert individual cuttings in small pots, or several together in larger ones.

3 Keep the compost moist but not wet, and the air humid. If you do not have a propagator, enclose the pot in a plastic bag, held with a rubber band, but make sure that it does not touch the leaves.

Leaf cuttings

Some plants, including African violets and streptocarpus, root readily from leaf cuttings. Two different methods are shown here: leaf petiole cuttings, for which the whole leaf and stalk are used; and leaf sections, for which just a part of a leaf is needed. Although you can root them at almost any time of the year, spring and early-midsummer are best because the young plants will grow quickly.

Stem tip cuttings

Other plants, including begonia, crassula, orchid cactus, fittonia, hibiscus, impatiens, kalanchoe, maranta, pelargonium and Christmas cactus, can be propagated from cuttings taken from a healthy shoot tip with leaves. In this case, cut just above a leaf joint 5–10cm (2–4in) below the shoot tip. Remove the leaves from the bottom two-thirds of the cutting and then insert it into a pot of fresh compost. Within a month or so, the cutting should have rooted. With crassula and christmas cactus, you can also break off a single leaf and insert that in a pot of free-draining compost.

TAKING LEAF SECTION CUTTINGS

1 Streptocarpus and sansevieria are among the houseplants that can be propagated from leaf sections. Choose a healthy, mature leaf that is not very old, and with a sharp knife cut it into evenly sized slices 5–8cm (2–3in) wide.

2 Insert the bottom third of each section in the compost (soil mix), making sure the side originally nearest the leaf stalk forms the base. Keep the cuttings in a warm, light place, out of direct sun.

Crassula ovata is an attractive houseplant that likes a sunny position, so is ideal for adding interest to the greenhouse or conservatory. It is easy to propagate from cuttings. Starry white or pink flowers are produced in autumn.

Planting and maintaining the flower garden

Spring-flowering bulbs are now becoming widely available, but exactly when you plant them will depend largely on whether the ground has been cleared of summer plants. If you are planting in beds, it is best to let the summer bedding continue to flower for as long as possible, and you may prefer not to disturb the last of the summer colour in herbaceous borders just yet, but it is best to plant as soon as possible in vacant ground and in containers. It is also worth spending time on late flowering chrysanthemums and dahlias to get the best displays possible.

Planting bulbs

If you have a lot of bulbs to plant over a wide area, individual planting holes may be more appropriate than excavating several large holes to take a group of bulbs. There are special long-handled planting tools that are useful for individual bulbs, but an ordinary long-handled trowel is just as good. You can use a normal trowel with a handle of conventional length, but it makes planting more tedious if the area is large. Check from time to time to make sure that the holes are being made to the correct depth. After checking a few it will be easy to judge by eye. Make a hole large

enough to take the bulb easily (it must not become wedged in the hole, because the roots will then be exposed to dry air and will not grow). Return the excavated soil. If you are planting a large area, you can shuffle it back in with your feet, then rake the surface level.

Planting depth

The depth and spacing of the bulbs should depend on the type of bulb you are planting. As a rule of thumb, a bulb should be covered with soil equivalent to twice its own depth. This means that a 5cm (2in) high bulb should be planted in a 15cm

PLANTING BULBS FOR SPRING

1 Fork over the ground before planting, and if the plants are to be left undisturbed for some years, add some well-rotted organic material. If your soil is heavy, most bulbs will also benefit from the addition of some sharp sand or grit.

2 Rake a slow-acting fertilizer, such as bonemeal, which contains mainly phosphate, into the surface, or apply it to the planting holes. Alternatively, apply a controlled-release fertilizer that provides nutrients according to the soil temperature in spring.

3 If you are planting a permanent display in a bed or border and have space, dig out a hole about three times the depth of the bulbs and wide enough to take the number of bulbs you wish to plant. Make the hole irregular for a more natural, informal effect.

4 Space the bulbs so that they look like a natural clump. Wide spacing will allow for future growth and natural increase, but if you intend to lift the bulbs after flowering much closer spacing will create a bolder display.

5 Set the bulbs on their base. Draw the soil back over the bulbs, being careful not to dislodge them in the process. Firm the soil with the back of the rake rather than treading it, which may damage the bulbs.

6 If you are likely to cultivate the area before the shoots come through, mark where bulbs have been planted and label. Alternatively, make a record in a notebook of where the bulbs have been planted for future reference.

CARING FOR DAHLIAS AND CHRYSANTHEMUMS

1 To produce larger flowers, pinch out the side buds behind the crown (central) flower bud of dahlias, while they are still small. Many chrysanthemums are also disbudded, but how and when you do it depends on the cultivar, so be guided by a specialist catalogue.

2 The best way to control pests and diseases is to spray at the first signs. Often it may be possible to prevent spread simply by pinching off and destroying the first few affected leaves. The discoloured chrysanthemum leaves show signs of leaf miner damage.

3 Chrysanthemums and dahlias benefit from regular feeding. Even if you used a slow-release fertilizer to see them through most of the summer, they will probably respond to a boost now. Apply a quick-acting general fertilizer or a high-potash formulation.

(6in) hole. Larger bulbs should be spaced 8–10cm (3–4in) apart, and smaller bulbs 2.5–5cm (1–2in) apart. If you are trying to create an instant natural-looking effect, plant the bulbs more densely than this. But if you are prepared to wait, plant at the standard distance and the bulbs will spread naturally. Some bulbs, such as daffodils, spread mainly by offshoots from the bulb so they form larger and larger clumps. Others, such as crocus, seed themselves more widely.

Most bulbs have an easily identifiable top and bottom, but some, and many corms and tubers, can cause confusion because they lack an obvious growing point. If in doubt, just plant them on their side – the shoot will grow upwards and the roots down. A few bulbs that do have an obvious top are planted on their side because the crown tends to rot in wet soil, though these are rare exceptions. *Fritillaria imperialis* is sometimes planted this way. It is also worth planting vulnerable bulbs on a bed of grit or coarse sand to allow good drainage around the base.

Dahlias and chrysanthemums

At the end of summer and into autumn, dahlias and chrysanthemums come into their true glory, just as most flowers have passed their best. Some types are simply left to produce masses of blooms with no intervention, but those grown for large flowers are usually selectively disbudded (see above). This produces fewer but larger blooms. Both types of plant need plenty of feeding and a careful watch has to be kept to prevent pests and diseases spoiling them. Alternatively you can promote a mass of smaller flowers later by removing the terminal bud only.

Disbud dahlias to get larger blooms on single stems that are suitable for the show bench and for use in arrangements.

Maintaining shrubs and hedges

Permanent feature plants, such as hedges and groundcover, need to be attended to at this time of the year. A hedge that has been allowed to grow out of control or one that has bare patches can be an eyesore. This is the time to carry out the essential maintenance that will prepare such features for winter and keep them looking good next year.

Trimming a hedge

Hedges need regular trimming to promote dense bushy growth from the base to the top. Most formal hedges are best trimmed in late summer with a pair of shears or a powered hedgetrimmer. Large-leaved hedges should be cut with secateurs (pruners) so that you avoid cutting through individual leaves, which could look unsightly. Slow-growing hedging plants, such as yew, holly and beech, need trimming only once a year, but faster-growing hedges, such as privet and box-leaved honeysuckle (*Lonicera nitida*), will require trimming regularly from late spring. Informal hedges also need pruning to keep them in shape. If it is a flowering hedge or one that bears a crop of decorative berries you will need to prune at the right time. For example, berberis, escallonia and *Ribes sanguineum* should be trimmed immediately after flowering, if necessary.

It is important to shape an established hedge so that it grows well and remains healthy. The easiest shape for most formal hedges is to create a square-sided profile with a domed or slightly sloping top. Use a coloured line held taut between canes at either end of the hedge as a guide. If you live in an area that regularly gets heavy snowfalls in winter, it is important to create a smoothly domed top so that the snow is shed naturally and doesn't accumulate on the top and push the hedge out of shape. You can either shape the top by eye or cut a template out of wood

KEEPING HEDGES IN TRIM

1 Cutting a hedge also includes clearing up the trimmings afterwards. One way of making this task a little less onerous is to lay down a cloth or plastic sheet under the area you are clipping and to move it along as you go.

2 When you are using shears, try to keep the blades flat against the plane of the hedge because this will give an even cut. If you jab the shears forward with a stabbing motion, the result is likely to be uneven.

3 A formal hedge looks best if the top is kept accurately level. This can be done by inserting poles at the ends or spaced at intervals along the hedge, with strings stretched between them to use as a guide.

4 Keep the blades flat when you cut the top of a hedge. If it is a tall hedge, you will need to use steps or a platform rather than reaching up at an angle. Make sure any support is held very stable.

5 Power trimmers are much faster than hand shears and, in consequence, things can go wrong faster as well, so concentrate on what you are doing and have a rest if your arms feel tired. Wear adequate protective gear.

6 Some conifers are relatively slow growing and produce only a few stray stems that can be cut off with secateurs (pruners) to neaten them. Secateurs should also be used for large-leaved shrubs, such as laurel.

TRIMMING GROUNDCOVER

1 Groundcover is often neglected and tends to collect all kinds of litter and rubbish. Take time to regularly remove any litter that is lurking between the leaves.

2 Most groundcover will look better if it is trimmed back at least once a year. Here, a lesser periwinkle (*Vinca minor*) is given a much-needed trim.

3 Regular trimming will encourage groundcover plants to grow more densely, with fewer straggly stems. They will look tidier and healthier.

to use as a guide. Hedges with very dense growth, such as yew and most other conifers, should not be cut with vertical sides, but trimmed in a tapering wedge shape that is wider at the base than at the top. This shape allows the base of the hedge to get plenty of light so that it will be more likely to remain densely clothed in foliage. Before you cut, you can spread plastic sheeting along the hedge to make it easier to clear up the clippings afterwards.

REVERSION IN SHRUBS

Green-leaved shoots have appeared in this *Spiraea japonica* 'Goldflame'. If left, they will take over the whole plant because they are more vigorous. The remedy is simple. Cut the offending shoots back to that part of the stem or shoot where the reversion begins.

When to trim hedges?

Evergreen hedges	Growth rate	When to trim
Buxus sempervirens	Slow	Midsummer
Chamaecyparis lawsoniana	Fast	Early summer and late summer
x *Cupressocyparis leylandii*	Very fast	Early summer
Euonymus japonicus	Slow	Late summer
Griselinia littoralis	Medium	Late summer
Ilex aquifolium	Slow	Late summer
Ligustrum ovalifolium	Fast	Late spring to late summer
Lonicera nitida	Fast	Late spring to late summer
Prunus lusitanica	Slow	Late summer
Taxus baccata	Slow	Late summer
Thuja plicata	Medium	Late summer

Deciduous hedges		
Carpinus betulus	Medium	Late summer
Fagus sylvatica	Slow	Late summer
Prunus cerasifera	Medium	Late summer

Flowering hedges		
Berberis darwinii	Medium	After flowering
Berberis x *stenophylla*	Medium	After flowering
Berberis thunbergii	Medium	After flowering
Crataegus monogyna	Medium	Late winter
Escallonia cultivars	Medium	After flowering
Fuchsia magellanica	Fast	Mid-spring
Garrya elliptica	Medium	After flowering
Ribes sanguineum	Medium	After flowering
Rosa	Medium	Early spring

Harvesting and storing vegetables

The harvest season is now in full swing on the vegetable patch, and you will be kept busy picking and digging up a wide range of crops, probably every day. Some of them you will want to use immediately, while you will be storing others to enjoy through the colder months. You can use the following as a guide to make the most of your labours.

Aubergine (eggplant)

Cut the fruit from the plant using a sharp knife when it's ripe and fully coloured – the flavour quickly deteriorates if they are allowed to become overripe. Store fruits for up to two months or cut each fruit in half, or peel and dice, before blanching and then freezing.

Broccoli and calabrese

Harvest broccoli on a 10cm (4in) stalk when the heads have formed but the flowers are still in tight bud. Calabrese can be cut with a 2.5cm (1in) stalk when the main central head is still firm with tight buds. Leave plants to grow on and produce sideshoots to be harvested later. Regular harvesting encourages better yields. Eat fresh or blanch and freeze.

Courgettes (zucchini)

Remove young fruits from the plant when they are 10–15cm (4–6in) long. Do not allow them to get any larger, otherwise the plant will stop producing new fruit. They should be eaten fresh, but will remain in good

A simple way of "stringing" garlic is to thread a stiff wire through the dry necks of the bulbs. The bulbs can also be tied on string.

condition in a refrigerator for about a week after harvest. Alternatively, slice and freeze for later use.

French beans

Harvest when young and crisp just as they start to swell, but before they become stringy – usually about 10cm (4in) long. Do not leave old beans on the plant, or subsequent yields will be reduced. You should pick over the plants regularly. Hold the stem of the plant as you pick to prevent it being ripped out of the ground. Eat fresh or trim, blanch and freeze.

Onions

When leaves topple in late summer, the crop is reaching maturity. Do not bend the leaves over, but let the crop dry out and go dormant naturally. Once the foliage is dry and brown, lift the crop and move on to drying racks for at least a week. Outdoors is best if the weather is dry and sunny, but if it rains they should be moved to a well-ventilated place under cover. In wet years, it may be necessary to cover the row with cloches to help them dry out before moving them indoors.

RIPENING AND HARVESTING ONIONS

1 The traditional practice of bending the leaves of onions over is no longer recommended as it encourages diseases in storage. Let the foliage die down naturally.

2 As soon as the foliage has turned a straw colour and is brittle, lift the onions with a fork and leave them on the surface with their roots facing the sun for a few days to dry off.

3 To complete the ripening process place the bulbs on wire mesh supported above the ground so that air can circulate freely.

4 If the weather is damp, cover the bulbs with cloches until you can store them. Use damaged bulbs first.

HARVESTING SQUASH

Harvest a courgette, marrow (zucchini) or other squash by cutting it off right at the base with a sharp knife.

HARVESTING RUNNER BEANS

Harvest runner beans when they are large enough and still fresh and pliable; discard the older, tougher beans.

HARVESTING TOMATOES

Harvest tomatoes when they are fully ripe, which will usually be when they turn red. Leave the stalks on.

Potatoes

Wait until the topgrowth has started to die down on maincrop potatoes before lifting. Cut off the remaining foliage and leave the crop for two weeks so that the tubers mature. Before you harvest, excavate at the side of the row to make sure the tubers are sufficiently mature and that their skins do not rub off. Harvest when the weather and soil are dry and store dry in paper sacks.

Shallots

If planted early, these can be lifted in midsummer. If you planted late it may be late summer before they are ready to harvest. Lift the bulbs in dry weather when the leaves die back. Wait for a week for the bulbs to ripen and the remaining foliage to dry. Store only perfect bulbs in nets or trays, or strung up together.

Runner beans

Pick beans while they are small and tender. Harvest regularly so that you do not leave old beans on the plant, which will slow the production of new flowers and pods and reduce subsequent yields. Eat fresh or blanch and freeze.

Sweet corn

Check that the cobs are ripe when the silky tassels start to turn brown. Press a thumbnail into individual grains on the cob until the juice is released. If it is clear and watery leave to ripen further, if creamy it is ready to harvest. Pick each cob individually by holding the main plant firmly and twisting the cob free. Eat fresh or blanch and freeze.

Tomatoes

The first fruits ripen two to three months after planting. Harvest fruit when it is fully ripened and starting to soften, by gently lifting the fruit and breaking it from the truss at its "knuckle joint". Eat fresh or freeze.

Turnip and swede (rutabaga)

Leave in the ground until needed. Then lift individual roots carefully.

It is essential that onions and shallots are completely dry before they are stored. Place them in trays or nets in a cool but frost-free place.

Harvesting and storing fruit

Harvest fruit when it is in prime condition, taking care not to damage it because this will encourage storage rots later on. Fruit for storing dry should be picked slightly under-ripe, while crops for bottling or freezing are best fully ripe, but not over-ripe. As soon as the fruit is harvested, transfer it to somewhere cool and complete the storing process as quickly after harvest as possible.

Storage methods

The easiest way to store fruit is to freeze it. To help retain flavour, it is best to freeze in layers of dry sugar or in syrup. However, soft fruit can be frozen dry on open trays before being bagged or boxed. Making surplus fruit into sweet preserves is another option. The pectin in the fruit gels with the sugar and acid to thicken the preserve and bacteria cannot survive in the sugary environment.

Apples and pears Harvest when slightly under-ripe but when the fruit comes away from the branch with its stalk intact when you gently lift and twist. Trees will need picking over several times to harvest the fruit

Storing apples and pears

Apples	Harvest time	Store until
'Cox's Orange Pippin'	early autumn	late winter
'Discovery'	late summer	eat fresh
'Egremont Russet'	early autumn	midwinter
'Greensleeves'	early autumn	late winter
'Grenadier'	late summer	early autumn
'Idared'	mid-autumn	early spring
'James Grieve'	early autumn	eat fresh
'Jupiter'	early autumn	late winter
'Katja'	late summer	late autumn
'Laxton's Superb'	late autumn	midspring
'Sunset'	early autumn	midwinter
'Worcester Pearmain'	early autumn	early winter
Pears		
'Conference'	mid-autumn	late winter
'Doyenné du Comice'	early autumn	early winter

in the right state for storage. Fruit exposed to direct sun will ripen first and shaded fruit last. Choose perfect, average-sized fruits to store. Large fruits tend to rot more easily in storage and small fruits tend to shrivel. Different varieties store for different periods, so keep them separate in the store. Keep in a cool, frost-free place so that the fruits are not touching — special moulded paper trays in ventilated cardboard

boxes are ideal. Inspect fruits regularly and remove any that are showing signs of deterioration. Apples and pears can also be bottled, frozen or puréed.

Blackberries Pick slightly under-ripe for freezing and fully ripe for eating fresh or turning into jam.

Blackcurrants Pick the fruit complete with stalk when the berries are fully coloured. Eat fresh or turn into jam.

STORING APPLES

Apples can be stored in trays in a cool, dry place. It is best if they are laid in individual screws of paper or moulded paper trays so that the individual fruits do not touch. The length of storage time depends on the variety.

STORING SOFT FRUIT

Soft fruit such as raspberries and hybrid berries is best placed in small individual containers as it is picked to prevent it being squashed and spoiling. Store in a refrigerator or other cool place.

STORING PEARS

Pears can last many months depending upon the variety. Lay them in a box so that the fruits do not touch and air can circulate around them. The best varieties for storage are 'Conference' and 'Doyenné du Comice'.

Cherries Easier to harvest in the early morning when fully ripe, with the stalk intact to prevent the fruit bleeding. Eat fresh or remove stones (pits) before bottling or freezing.

Gooseberries Pick while still under-ripe and green for bottling and freezing, but wait until fully ripe and softening slightly for eating fresh.

Grapes Harvest grapes when they are ripe by removing the whole bunch from the vine along with a little of the woody vine on each side of the bunch using a pair or scissors or secateurs (pruners). Eat fresh.

Peaches and nectarines Gently twist the fruit as it rests in the palm of your hand to see if it is ready to pick. Ripe fruit will be well coloured and softening slightly near the stalk. Eat fresh, freeze or bottle.

Plums Harvest when fully ripe if eating fresh, slightly under-ripe for cooking and preserving. Pick with the stalk intact. Halve and stone before bottling or making into jam.

Raspberries Pick when fully coloured but still firm to the touch when each fruit is easily detached from its "plug". For larger hybrid berries, harvest with scissors to remove the fruits complete with their stalks. Eat fresh, freeze or turn into jam.

Red and white currants Pick when ripe by removing the whole strings of fruit. Remove stalks before eating fresh, freezing or turning into jam.

Strawberries Harvest when the fruit is fully coloured but still firm. Pick by holding the fruit in the palm of your hand while pinching the stalk off between finger and thumb. Eat fresh or turn into jam.

Apricots When fully ripened, the fruit can be picked cleanly from its stalk. Eat fresh, dry or freeze.

Apples and pears are removed from the tree with a twist of the wrist. The stalks should remain attached to the fruit.

Blueberries Pick when ripe and fully coloured. Eat fresh or freeze.

Nuts Filberts and cobnuts should be picked when the husk starts to turn yellow. Eat them fresh or dry and store.

Harvesting soft fruit and plums for storage

	Harvest time
Blackberries	
'Bedford Giant'	midsummer
'Oregon Thornless'	late summer
Blackcurrants	
'Ben Lomond'	midsummer
'Malling Jet'	late summer
Gooseberries	
'Careless'	early summer
'Leveller'	early summer
Plums	
'Czar'	midsummer
'Early Rivers'	midsummer
'Oullin's Golden Gage'	late summer
'Victoria'	late summer
Raspberries	
'Glen Clova'	early summer
'Malling Admiral'	midsummer
'Malling Delight'	early summer
'Malling Jewel'	early summer
'Malling Leo'	midsummer

Apples should be picked over several times during late summer and early autumn to make sure that each one is harvested at exactly the right stage of maturity.

Propagating and planting in the greenhouse

Pelargoniums (popularly known as bedding geraniums) and tender fuchsias can be potted up and overwintered in a frost-free place to provide cuttings next spring. Many gardeners prefer to take cuttings now, however, and to overwinter the young plants in a light, frost-free place. These will make good plants for next summer, or you can use them to provide more cuttings next spring. Indoor bulbs that are specially prepared for early flowering should also be planted as soon as they become available.

Propagating fuchsias

Softwood cuttings can be taken for as long as new growth is being produced, but at this time of year semi-ripe (semi-mature) cuttings root easily and are simple to take. Pull off sideshoots about 10cm (4in) long, with a 'heel' of old main stem attached. Trim off the lowest leaves and trim the end of the heel to make a clean cut. If you have taken cuttings without a heel, trim the stem straight across beneath a leaf joint. Cuttings will usually root without aid, but a hormone rooting powder can speed the process. Insert several cuttings around the edge of

You can have hyacinths flowering by midwinter if you plant specially-prepared bulbs now. These will flower earlier than they would naturally. As nutrients are stored in the bulbs, they can survive for a season without soil, and they can look decorative in gravel or a special glass container. The water level should never touch the bulb, only the roots.

an 8–10cm (3–4in) pot filled with a cuttings compost (soil mix). Label the cuttings, water and place them in a coldframe, greenhouse or on a light windowsill. Keep the compost damp, and pot up individually when well rooted. Protect from frost. Check the rooted cutting occasionally and remove yellowing leaves.

Propagating pelargoniums

Take cuttings from non-flowering shoots (if you have to use shoots with flowers, cut off the blooms). A good guide to length is to cut the shoot off just above the third joint below the growing tip. Remove the lowest pair of leaves with a sharp knife, and remove any flowers or

SOWING SPRING-FLOWERING POT-PLANTS

1 Sprinkle the seeds as thinly and evenly as possible over the surface. Large seeds, such as cyclamen, can be spaced individually. Cover with a sprinkling of the sowing mixture if needed (follow the advice on the packet).

2 Stand the pot in a container of water. Letting the moisture seep up into the compost from below like this avoids the risk of seeds being washed away or into clumps were you to water the pot from above.

3 Most seeds will germinate successfully if covered with a sheet of glass or placed in a plastic bag to reduce water loss. Seeds that germinate slowly or erratically benefit from being in a heated propagator.

buds. Trim straight across the base of each cutting, just below the lowest leaf joint. You can dip the ends in a rooting hormone; they usually root readily without, but the fungicide in some powders is useful. Insert about five cuttings around the edge of a 13cm (5in) pot containing a cuttings compost and firm gently. Make sure the leaves do not touch. Keep in a light, warm position but out of direct sun.

Other tender perennials

Many summer bedding plants that are less than hardy are perennial and can be overwintered successfully. Popular types such as artemisia, ballota, cosmos, diascia, dicentra and helichrysum can be lifted and potted up to be overwintered as plants. Alternatively, rooted cuttings can be taken now. Another option is to overwinter the plants, force them into growth during early spring and take cuttings then.

Sow flowering pot plants

Provided you can keep your greenhouse frost-free during the winter, it is worth sowing a few flowering plants to bloom next spring. Some suggestions are given in the box below, and those that are hardy, such as *Calendula* and *Limnanthes*, can even be grown in an unheated greenhouse provided you do not live in a very cold area.

Planting hyacinth bulbs

For early flowering indoors or in the greenhouse, you must choose bulbs that have been 'prepared' or 'treated'. The term may vary, but it means that before you receive the bulb it has been stored under specially controlled conditions that make it think that more of its resting period has elapsed. It looks no different, but it believes that winter is more advanced than it really is and that it needs to grow and bloom quickly.

Ordinary, untreated hyacinths can also be planted now, but they will flower later in the season. It is a good idea to pot up bulbs of both kinds, separately, to spread the flowering period. If you buy potted bulbs in spring, wait until they are showing colour to be sure they are the ones you want.

PLANTING HYACINTHS FOR WINTER OR SPRING FLOWERING

1 If you are using a bowl without drainage, use a special bulb compost (soil mix) based on peat with charcoal added to keep it sweet. If you use a container with drainage holes, any ordinary compost can be used. Place drainage material in the bottom of the container.

2 Place a thin layer of compost in the container, then space the bulbs close together but make sure they are not touching. An odd number will look better than an even number (three or five bulbs are usually planted in a single bowl).

3 Pack more compost around the bulbs, but leave their 'noses' exposed. Water, without wetting the tops of the bulbs. If there are no drainage holes, be very careful not to overwater them.

4 Stand the containers in a cool, shady position and cover them with grit, peat or coarse sand. If the containers have no drainage holes, protect them from rain to prevent waterlogging, which will cause the bulbs to rot.

Seeds to sow now

Browallia
Calendula (choose a very dwarf variety)*
Cineraria
Cyclamen (for home and greenhouse)**
Exacum affine
*Limnanthes douglasii**
*Linaria maroccana**
Primula acaulis (cultivated primroses)*
Primula malacoides
Schizanthus

* These are tough plants that will tolerate some frost and are suitable for an unheated greenhouse in mild areas
** Cyclamen should flower in midwinter the following year (i.e. after about 16 months)

Autumn

Autumn can be an Indian summer or the first taste of winter, so you will need to keep a close eye on weather forecasts. Normally the shortening days and lower sun will mean temperatures slowly decrease as the season progresses. Misty mornings and dewy evenings become commonplace, creating an eerie atmosphere in the lower light levels. Be watchful and vigilant as the nights become colder. In some areas quite severe frosts are common in early autumn, and in others light frosts may not occur until mid-or late autumn, if at all. Listen to the weather forecasts and take in or protect vulnerable plants if frost is expected. Think seriously about winter protection for plants on the borderline of hardiness, and be prepared to give early winter shelter, perhaps in the form of a windbreak, for newly planted evergreens. A little protection can ensure that many plants survive instead of succumbing to winter winds and cold.

Japanese maples are one of the best small trees for autumn colour, with leaves turning brilliant shades of yellow, red and orange.

Early Autumn

The weather in early autumn is still warm enough to make outdoor gardening a comfortable experience, and although the vibrant flowers of summer may be gone, there are plenty of delights to be enjoyed in the form of bright berries and flaming foliage, not to mention late-flowering gems such as chrysanthemums and asters. Apart from bulb planting, and protecting frost-tender plants, there are few really pressing jobs at this time of year.

Once the grass has stopped growing, the lawn may be given its final cut – the timing will vary depending on the weather and where you live. It is therefore an ideal time to clean and service your lawnmower. Early autumn is also the perfect time to complete lawn maintenance tasks such as raking out thatch, eradicating moss, feeding and aerating, to improve the quality of your lawn. You can also start a new lawn from scratch using turf or sowing seed. After a long summer of heavy use lawns are often showing signs of wear with brown patches under play equipment and around access points, humps and hollows, and broken edges. Fortunately, they are all relatively easy to repair at this time of the year.

Make the most of autumn leaves by collecting them up promptly and composting them. It is a good idea to clear leaves from your lawn and other low-growing plants regularly to prevent them being smothered and suffering stress before the onset of winter. Rock-garden plants are particularly vulnerable because they are liable to rot under a blanket of fallen leaves, especially if the weather is wet. Although you can add them to a compost heap, if there are a lot of leaves you would be better off using them to make leafmould. Once decomposed, this fibrous material can be used as a general soil improver, a planting mixture or a mulch.

There's still time to plant most spring-flowering bulbs in the garden or containers. Daffodils, crocuses and other popular bulbs should be planted as soon as possible, otherwise flowering may be delayed the following spring. Tulips are the exception: they should be planted in late autumn or early winter for the best results.

In the greenhouse, you can extend the season by removing any shading materials and cleaning the outside of the greenhouse to enhance light levels as much as possible. There's still time to sow a few annuals and perennials destined for the garden and you can keep the greenhouse productive by sowing winter lettuce. Outside you can extend the harvest period by covering with cloches outdoor crops such as lettuce so that they continue to grow and tomatoes so that they have time to ripen before the first serious frost. Most tender crops will be harvested over this period and any surpluses carefully stored for winter use. If you grow a lot of vegetables from seed, you can also save money at this time of year by saving your own seed from selected plants that have been allowed to flower and set seed.

Trees and shrubs that take on autumnal lives, such as this cut-leaf maple, provide much-needed colour at this time of year.

Early autumn is the perfect time to carry out maintenance tasks, as well as essential lawn repairs.

Planting spring and summer flowers

If frosts have not put an abrupt end to your summer bedding display, the plants will undoubtedly be looking sad and dejected by now. Even if you do not plan to replant with spring bedding, the garden will look tidier if the old plants are cleared away and the ground dug over. If they are not diseased, most can go straight on the compost heap, but this is a good time to harvest some ripe seed for sowing next year, or straight away if the plants are hardy enough.

Gladioli can be left in the ground only in mild areas where the soil is well drained. If your soil does not remain wet, and if frosts are always light and do not penetrate far into the soil, they should survive. In cold areas, however, gladioli will be killed if they remain in the soil, so lift them before there are penetrating frosts. Gladioli flower reliably from year to year, so they are almost always worth saving. The offsets or cormlets (small corms) that form around the base will reach flowering size within two or three years if they are potted up and kept in frost-free conditions until spring. Cormlets may not come true to type, however.

The sweetly scented ice plant (*Sedum spectabile*) brightens the garden in late summer and early autumn, and is a magnet for bees and butterflies.

Plant spring displays

Fork over the ground after clearing it of summer bedding plants. Fertilizer is not normally needed, but bonemeal, which is very slow-acting, or another slow-release product, is worth adding if the soil is impoverished. Bulbs should be planted as soon after purchase as possible. If you have raised spring bedding plants yourself, water them well about an hour before lifting them with as much soil around the roots as possible. Plants, such as forget-me-nots and double daisies, bought from garden centres are usually sold in trays or strips. Don't be afraid to break them if this allows you to release the rootball with as little root disturbance as possible. Space the plants out on the surface, allowing for the bulbs, before planting. Space the bulbs out, then begin planting from the back or one end.

CLEARING SUMMER BEDDING

1 Plants like this will do more good on the compost heap than they will left on show. Bare soil can look neat and tidy as long as you remove weeds and other debris.

2 Bedding plants generally have shallow roots and are easy to pull up by hand. If some have deep roots, simply loosen the roots with a hand fork before you start.

3 Old bedding plants, as long as they are not diseased, are ideal for the compost heap. You can collect them all together before filling your compost bin.

Plant lilies for summer

Lilies are often planted in spring, but you can also plant them now except in very cold areas. The bulbs are less likely to dry out, which can result in failures. Most lilies prefer a slightly acid soil (pH 6–6.5), but some, including *Lilium candidum*, will do well in alkaline soils. Lilies demand a well-prepared site, so dig the soil deeply and work in as much well-rotted manure or garden compost as you can spare. Add plenty of grit to improve drainage if the soil tends to be wet. Lilies look best in groups rather than as isolated specimens, so excavate an area of soil to a depth of about 20cm (8in), large enough to take at least four or five bulbs. Add coarse grit or sand unless the soil is very well drained. Add a sprinkling of bonemeal or a slow-release fertilizer, because initial feeding is more important than with bedding bulbs used for a single season. Space the bulbs about 15cm (6in) apart and make sure that they are deep enough to be covered with about twice their own depth of soil. Sprinkle more grit or coarse sand around the bulbs to deter slugs and reduce the risk of waterlogging. Place small canes or sticks around the

LIFTING AND STORING GLADIOLI

1 Loosen the soil with a spade or fork before attempting to lift the plants.

2 Trim off most of the foliage, leaving just a stub to dry off. Shake off most of the soil.

3 Leave the lifted plants in a dry, well-ventilated place for a few days to dry off. When the remains of the old stems have shrivelled, trim them off and remove the cormlets that have grown around the base.

4 Dust with fungicide by shaking in a bag containing a little fungicide. Then store the corms in paper bags in a dry and cool but frost-free place. Label clearly. Pot up the cormlets and keep frost-free.

planting area before you return the soil to remind you to avoid damaging the emerging shoots when you hoe in spring. Remember to label.

4 Dig over the ground and remove any perennial weeds. If there are a lot of annual weeds, you can bury them by turning the soil with a spade, otherwise use a fork.

5 Whether or not you are replanting with spring bedding, rake the ground so that it is neat and tidy. On heavy soils, leave clods on the surface to be broken down by frost.

Storing garden canes

Bamboo canes deteriorate after a season or two in use, especially if they have been left in the ground for a long period. Extend their life by cleaning and preserving them. Store them in a dry place rather than leaving them exposed in the garden. Knock off most of the soil, then scrub the canes with a stiff brush and garden or household disinfectant. Stand the ends that have been in the soil in a bucket or container partly filled with a wood preservative and leave overnight to allow the preservative to penetrate. Bind the cracked ends of canes with tape. Bundle the canes to keep them tidy and store in a dry place until needed next year.

Preparing the lawn for winter

The time consuming task of mowing will now be coming to an end, but there are other tasks that can usefully be done now to keep your lawn in good condition. Clearing fallen leaves is essential, otherwise the grass will turn yellow, and if moss is a problem, you can take steps to eradicate it now. Moss-killing chemicals are only a temporary solution, however — to discourage moss, improve drainage by aerating the lawn, and feed as necessary to keep the grass growing strongly.

Removing thatch and moss

If moss is a problem in your lawn, treat with a moss-killer and allow it to turn brown before raking or scarifying (otherwise you'll just spread the moss around the lawn). Raking out thatch and moss from your lawn by hand is tiring. If you have a large lawn, you may wish to invest in a powered lawn rake. This will do the job rapidly and efficiently.

Spiking

If part of your lawn is used as a short cut or has been compacted through constant use, from summer games for example, you can improve

COLLECTING AND COMPOSTING LEAVES

1 Don't let leaves lie on your lawn. The grass beneath will turn yellow and be prone to disease and the leaves will harbour pests. On a small lawn, rake them up with a lawn rake.

2 Leaves on paths and drives are best brushed up with a broom or besom. Alternatively, buy or hire a garden vacuum that will clear leaves from all parts of the garden.

3 You can buy special tools to lift the leaves without too much bending, but two pieces of wood are also an effective way to lift them once they have been brushed into a heap.

4 Leaves can be added to the compost heap or bin, but some rot down slowly, so it is best to compost a large amount on their own. Leaf mould is a valuable soil improver.

it now by aerating it. Spike small areas with a garden fork pushed at least 10–15cm (4–6in) into the ground, spacing the holes a few

centimetres/inches apart. Wiggle the fork backwards and forwards each time to open up the holes. Take the drudgery out of aerating large areas

MAINTAINING THE LAWN

1 Over the years, grass clippings, dead grass and other debris form a thatch on the surface of your lawn. This affects growth of the grass and should be removed with a lawn rake. Raking also removes moss.

2 If grass growth is poor, aerate the lawn. You can do this by pushing the prongs of a garden fork into the ground to a depth of at least 15cm (6in), covering the entire area with holes that are no more than 10cm (4in) apart.

3 Brush a soil improver into the holes. Use lawn sand or a mixture of fine soil and sand if the ground is poorly drained. Alternatively, use peat, a peat substitute or sifted, well-rotted compost if the ground is already sandy.

by using a hollow-tined aerator that removes a core of soil efficiently. Then brush a 50:50 mixture of sifted garden soil and sharp sand (or just sharp sand on poorly drained lawns) into the holes. This will improve the drainage and aeration in the surface layer of the lawn.

Feeding

Most lawns don't require feeding in autumn, but if yours has seen excessive wear and tear during the summer months you might want to give it a boost now. Don't be tempted to use a spring lawn feed because this contains too much nitrogen. Nitrogen encourages lush, leafy growth that will be easily damaged by frost and is prone to diseases. Instead, choose a proprietary autumn lawn feed that will promote good root growth and tough topgrowth.

Weeding

Single weeds can be removed with an old kitchen knife or a spot weedkiller. Make sure you remove the tap root as well as the top growth when you remove each weed. If the weeds are more widespread, a combined weed and autumn feed product should be applied.

Routinely clear fallen leaves from around deciduous trees, like this cut-leaf maple, each autumn to prevent them from smothering low-growing plants and grass.

Collecting leaves

Never waste the leaves shed by deciduous trees and shrubs. They will make excellent leafmould if you rot them down, but if left on the ground, they can damage areas of grass and smother small plants. For small quantities, fill punctured black plastic sacks with moist leaves and tie the top to seal them in. Tuck the bags out of the way and the leaves will rot down. For crumbly leafmould suitable for use as a soil improver or planting mixture for next spring, mix a few handfuls of grass clippings in with each sack. For large quantities, make a special cage by driving four strong posts into the ground and wrapping chicken wire around them. Fill with leaves. If the leaves are dry, sprinkle them with water and cover the top with a piece of carpet to weigh them down and encourage decomposition.

4 If your lawn is in poor condition and needs reviving, apply an autumn lawn feed. It is essential that you use one that is specially formulated for autumn use, as spring and summer feeds will contain too much nitrogen.

5 If the grass contains a lot of moss, apply a moss-killer recommended for autumn use. The mixture known as lawn sand, sometimes used to kill moss, contains too much nitrogen and will encourage sappy growth.

Wildflower meadows

Autumn is the ideal time to tidy up wildflower meadows that contain summer-flowering plants. Once the wildflowers have set seed, use a scythe to cut the meadow back. For larger areas, hire a powered mechanical version.

Leave the cut material to dry so that any seed has time to ripen and scatter before the trimmings are gathered up and placed in a compost bin for recycling

Repairing lawns

Threadbare lawns are a common sight at this time of the year after a summer's wear and tear. The stresses caused by drought are compounded by constant use and abuse during the summer months. Fortunately, early autumn is an ideal time to deal with many lawn problems. Any repairs made now will have time to bed in over winter while the grass is not being cut to ensure a fresh green lawn next spring. Now is also the perfect time to make a new lawn, by sowing seed or laying turf.

Humps and hollows

Uneven patches can appear on any lawn at any time, and are usually first detected when pale and dark green patches are seen after the lawn has been cut. Where there are humps, the grass is cut short and often scalped by the passing lawnmower blades, while grass in the dips remains long.

If the problem is widespread, then the best solution for dealing with hollows is to spike the lawn with a garden fork after it has been cut, then add a topdressing of finely

REPAIRING A BROKEN EDGE

1 Use a half-moon edging tool or a spade to cut a rectangle around the affected area, making sure that you cut back to firm soil.

2 Push a spade under the rectangle, starting from the broken edge. Keep the thickness of the slice of grass as even as possible.

3 Reverse the turf so that the undamaged part of the turf is against the edge of the bed and the broken edge is within the lawn. Fill the hole created by the damaged area with sifted soil and firm it down well.

4 Sow grass seed in the patched area, matching the type of grass if possible. Brush soil into the joints to help the grass knit together quickly and water well. Protect the newly-sown area from birds.

Alternatives to lawns

Although lawns are the traditional first choice for most people, there are other options, especially in situations where lawns are difficult to grow or maintain, such as in heavily shaded areas where even shade-tolerant grass struggles to grow, at the bottom of steps where the lawn remains permanently threadbare or on steep banks, which are difficult and dangerous to mow.

Low-growing, easy-care evergreen groundcover plants can provide a low-maintenance alternative to a lawn. You can also use groundcover plants in conjunction with attractive hard landscaping materials.

sieved topsoil, which should be spread out evenly. Make sure you do not add more than a 1cm (½in) layer at any one time because this will suffocate the grass. If the hollows are deeper than this you will have to make several topdressings, spaced out over the course of a growing season so that the grass has time to grow up through the topdressing between applications. Alternatively, spread out applications over several seasons to achieve a perfectly level surface to your lawn.

Humps need to be tackled individually. Using a sharp spade or half-moon edging iron, make an H-shaped cut into the lawn with the

cross-bar of the H cutting through the hump you are trying to correct. Then, carefully undercut the turf from this cut and peel back the grass on either side to leave an oblong area of soil exposed. Take away soil as necessary to correct the hump before firming and replacing the peeled-back turves. Firm again with the back of your spade and check that the area is now even using a straight-edged piece of timber as a guide. Finally, fill any cracks with a 50:50 mixture of sieved garden soil and sharp sand, before watering well. This method can also be used to deal with hollows, adding sieved topsoil to raise the level rather than taking soil away.

Early autumn is the ideal time for essential lawn maintenance after a summer's hard wear and tear. Sharp edges against beds and borders will greatly improve the lawn's appearance.

Bare patches

Whether they are caused by heavy use or excessive shade from overhanging shrubs the solution to bare patches is basically the same. If they are caused by heavy wear you will need to relieve any compaction first by spiking. If shade is the problem you will need to cut back or thin out the overhanging foliage and use a shade-tolerant seed mixture when you resow. Following this preparation, prick over the bare patch with a garden fork and apply a well-balanced, all-purpose fertilizer, gently working it into the surface layer. Level and scatter grass seed at the rate of 20–35g per square metre

(1–1½oz per square yard), then cover the seed with a light scattering of sieved garden soil. Water well and cover with bird-proof netting. Keep well watered until the grass seedlings are well established.

Broken and uneven edges

Although broken or uneven edges can occur on any lawn, they are a particular problem in gardens with a light sandy soil, where the entire lawn edge may need to be recut every year. You can install a mowing strip along the edges (see page 46). Isolated broken edges are easy to repair by turning around a section of turf.

DEALING WITH UNEVEN EDGES

You can tidy an uneven edge at any time, but doing it in autumn will relieve the pressure at busier times of year. Hold a half-moon edger against a board held in position with your feet. This is not usually an annual job.

Planting container bulbs

Spring-flowering bulbs are an excellent choice for containers because they provide eye-catching colour early in the year and can be cleared out after flowering so that the pots and tubs can be used for summer bedding displays. You can also combine bulbs in permanent displays with trees, shrubs and perennials. Choose just one or two varieties in complementary or contrasting colours rather than a haphazard mixture.

Getting started

Almost any container will do provided it has drainage holes so that it doesn't get waterlogged, but for larger bulbs it will need to be at least 20cm (8in) deep. Most bulbs can be potted up using an all-purpose potting compost (soil mix), but for permanent displays use a loam-based compost, such as John Innes No. 2, which will keep its structure for longer. Plant bulbs at the normal recommended planting depth for permanent displays, but you can get away with shallower planting for temporary displays as long as each bulb is planted at least one bulb's depth below the surface. For large-flowered bulbs, make sure the container is stable with a wide base, so that it will not topple over in strong winds.

Take care that the compost does not dry out, and this may mean watering in winter. Add a mulch to conserve moisture and also to keep down weeds.

Bulbs and spring bedding

Some of the best container displays for spring combine bulbs with spring-flowering bedding plants, such as forget-me-nots (*Myosotis*), double daisies (*Bellis*) and polyanthus (*Primula*). This is often more effective than filling the container with bulbs alone, and it means that the container looks less bleak after planting, while the period of flowering is greatly extended. Put the plants in first, then the bulbs between them. If you plant the bulbs first, it can be difficult to remember their positions, and they are likely to be disturbed when you insert the plants.

Bulbs for impact

Displays of spring bulbs are less predictable than those of summer flowers, and it can be especially disappointing when different bulbs planted in the same container flower at different times. The consolation is that this does at least extend the period of interest. A good alternative is to plant single-subject displays

PLANTING BULBS FOR A SPRING WINDOW BOX

1 Cover the drainage holes with a layer of material to prevent the compost (soil mix) from falling out when you water and to aid drainage, such as broken pots or pieces of chipped bark (sold for mulching).

2 Add a 2.5cm (1in) layer of compost. Unless the planting is to be permanent, you can mix in some old compost previously used for summer bedding, since bulbs do not need a lot of nutrients.

3 You can pack in more bulbs by planting in layers. Place large bulbs, such as daffodils or tulips, at the lower level. Space them slightly apart so you can trickle compost in between the bulbs. Add more compost.

4 Position the smaller bulbs, such as crocuses and scillas, so that they lie between the larger bulbs. Small crocuses will be swamped by tall daffodils, so choose miniature or dwarf daffodils to keep a suitable balance.

5 Top up with more compost, but leave 2.5cm (1in) of space at the top for watering and perhaps a decorative mulch. Because the windowbox will look bare for some months, add winter-flowering pansies for interest.

PLANTING A PERMANENT CONTAINER

1 For a container with year-round interest, you can base the display on permanent evergreens such as dwarf conifers and ivies. The gaps can then be filled with colourful bulbs, followed by bedding plants, if you like.

2 Position the bulbs on the surface so that they are evenly spaced around the edge. Dwarf bulbs that multiply freely, such as scillas, chionodoxas, and *Anemone blanda*, will usually improve year after year.

3 Plant the bulbs with a trowel and water well. If adding bulbs to a container with established plants, try not to disturb the roots; the same applies if you add bedding plants later.

that, although often brief, are frequently bolder. By planting *en masse* and cramming in lots more bulbs you can enhance the overall display, especially if you are using small bulbs, such as crocus, grape hyacinths, scilla and chionodoxa, which can be planted almost touching. Larger bulbs, such as daffodils, hyacinths and tulips, are better spaced slightly, leaving at least half a bulb's width between bulbs.

Longer-lasting displays

Tubs, large pots and urns allow you to be more creative with your plant combinations. You can plant bulbs around permanent deciduous or evergreen shrubs or in multiple layers that flower at different times so that you get a continuity of flowers over a longer period. In a single container you could combine an early-spring-flowering crocus with a mid-spring-flowering dwarf daffodil and late-spring-flowering tulip to give a display through the entire season. Choose bulbs that should be planted at different depths. In this example, the tulips would be planted 15cm (6in) below the surface, the daffodils 10cm (4in), and the crocuses 5cm (2in).

PLANTING A LATE SPRING CONTAINER

1 Choose a large pot, and cover the drainage holes with broken crocks. Add a layer of grit for extra drainage. Tulips like a very well-drained compost (soil mix), so it is a good idea to mix some grit into the compost too. Part-fill the container, allowing room for the tulips to be planted under twice their own depth of compost.

2 Tulips are usually planted in late autumn or early winter, to reduce the risk of disease, but in a container the risks are minimal and they can safely be planted now. Choose a late-flowering variety, and arrange them on the compost, nose upwards. Cover with more compost, bringing the level to within 2.5cm (1in) of the rim of the pot.

3 Wallflowers should flower about the same time as late-flowering tulips. Choose a complementary colour, preferably scented. If bought in a bunch, separate them carefully before planting, and choose those with the best root systems if you have too many.

4 Plant the wallflowers above the tulips, firming the compost gently around the roots. Water the container well, and allow to drain. It should be kept just moist, but not too wet, throughout the winter, and watered more frequently when growth begins.

Extend your harvests

If you have cloches that you normally use to protect your crops in spring, make the most of them by extending the end of the season as well as the beginning. They can be used to get late sowings off to a flying start as well as help extend the productive life of tender crops by protecting them from early frosts.

Practical matters

Late sowings of quick-growing crops, such as lettuce 'Little Gem', can be grown on quickly under cloches for a late autumn harvest, while hardy crops, such as early carrots, summer cauliflowers and peas, can be started now under cloches and overwintered to be ready to harvest well before their spring-sown counterparts. This is the traditional way of filling the gap between the last of this year's crops and the first of those sown next spring. Other crops to try include broad (fava) beans, early calabrese and leaf beet. Some hardy crops, such as spinach and endive, also benefit from protection if an early frost threatens. Again, use spare cloches or cover with a double layer of garden fleece to insulate against the cold.

Save large barn cloches for large crops such as tomatoes, and use tent and plastic tunnel cloches for low-growing crops such as lettuce.

CUTTING DOWN ASPARAGUS HAULMS

In the autumn, as the asparagus fronds are turning brown, cut them down to about 2.5cm (1in) above ground level. Apply a mulch of well-rotted compost along the trench to replenish the soil for the next season.

Cordon tomatoes can be untied from the supports and laid horizontally on a bed of straw so that they too can be covered with cloches for the last few weeks. Green tomatoes can be ripened indoors if they have reached a reasonable stage of maturity. If left on the plant, harvest as soon as a severe frost is forecast.

Saving your own seed

If you grow a lot of vegetables each year, it might be worth leaving a few plants of each crop to mature and set seed so that they can be collected and stored ready for next year. On fruiting crops, such as tomatoes, you need only save one or two fruit to ripen fully, while with peas it's a matter of leaving a few pods on the plant at harvest time. Bear in mind that with beans, which need to be picked regularly to ensure a continuous crop, leaving pods to mature on a plant will slow the rate of new pod development and so reduce overall yields. So wait until the end of the season to leave a few pods to mature and choose the most productive plant. Collect the fruits when they are fully ripe and starting

PROTECTING OUTDOOR TOMATOES

1 Frost will kill tomatoes, but you can often extend their season and ripen a few more fruits on the plant with protection. Low-growing bush plants can be insulated with a bed of straw and covered with a large cloche.

2 Cordon-trained tomatoes must be lowered before they can be protected. Remove the growing tip, any ripe fruit and yellowing leaves, then untie the plant from its support and remove the stake.

3 Lay a bed of straw on the ground and lower the plants onto this. If you lay all the stems in the same direction, you will have a neat row of tomatoes that can be easily covered with cloches. Remove ripe fruit every day.

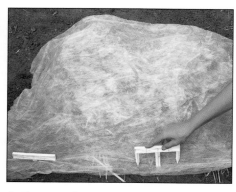

4 Fleece can be used to offer wind protection and enough shelter to keep off a degree or two of frost, though it does not warm the air during the day in the same way that glass or other rigid materials will do.

PUTTING CLOCHES IN PLACE

1 Winter and mooli radishes are frost-hardy, but to encourage further growth before bad weather sets in, cover with cloches. If not already sown, start them off under cloches in a mild area, provided the soil is still warm.

2 Try sowing lamb's lettuce and winter purslane as a cold weather crop. They don't need cloche protection except in cold areas, but the cover will ensure a better supply of more succulent leaves.

3 Put the cloches in position over the rows before the cold weather has had time to check growth. With only a little protection like this the plants will crop more freely and over a much longer period.

to soften (tomatoes and marrows) or have dried out and become hard (peas and beans).

With crops that are normally picked before they flower, such as lettuce, root crops and brassicas, you'll have to leave at least two plants of the same variety to mature and flower. Two are normally required because their flowers need to cross-pollinate to set seed. You may have to wait until the following year before this happens with brassicas and crops in the onion family.

Planting garlic

You can plant garlic from the supermarket, if it looks healthy, but varieties sold for gardeners are more likely to succeed, especially in cooler climates. Garlic needs a cool period before it sprouts in spring so it can be planted any time during autumn and winter. Prepare the ground by thoroughly digging and removing weeds, and on poor soils rake in a base dressing of general fertilizer, about two weeks before planting. Any time after the weather conditions

turn cold in your area you can plant garlic cloves; this is usually in early autumn in the coldest areas, and in late autumn in milder gardens. Plant on ridges to aid drainage if your soil is heavy. Use a dibber or small trowel to plant each clove 10–15cm (4–6in) apart, using a garden line as a guide. Plant vertically with the pointed tip facing upwards in holes twice the depth of the clove.

PLANTING GARLIC

1 Use a dibber to make holes in the ground for each clove, at 10–15cm (4–6in) intervals. A line of string held on two pegs will help you to keep the row straight.

2 Plant the cloves just below the surface of the ground so that the bulbs are upright, firming them in so that they are covered to their own height with soil.

Harvesting will be peaking by early autumn, but you can extend the cropping period of many outdoor vegetables by taking action to protect them now.

Storing vegetables

One of the biggest challenges when growing vegetables is making sure that harvested crops can be kept in tip-top condition until they are needed in the kitchen. Fortunately, many vegetables are easy to store either in the ground where they are growing or in a frost-free shed or garage. Most of those that don't store well can be blanched and frozen, or preserved in other ways.

Storing outside

Most root crops, including carrots, swedes (rutabagas) and turnips, as well as hardy vegetables such as leeks and Brussels sprouts, can be left in the ground until they are needed. If you have light soil, root crops can be left in position all winter without deteriorating. Mark the rows with canes or labels so that you know where to dig after the topgrowth has died down. If you live in an area that is prone to hard frosts, you will need to protect the vegetables with an insulating layer of straw held in place with netting, so that you can harvest the crops successfully even when the soil is frozen solid. The main disadvantages of leaving the crop in the ground are that they may have to be harvested when the soil is very wet or frozen, and you'll inevitably suffer winter losses from pest and disease attacks.

Storing inside in sand

On heavy soil in cold areas, digging up vegetables may be difficult or impossible for much of the winter. In this case, it is best to lift the root crops in autumn when the soil and weather conditions are favourable and keep them in trays or boxes of moist sand in a frost-free shed or garage. Less hardy crops, such as beetroot (beets), will need to be

TRADITIONAL POTATO STORAGE

1 Lift the tubers with a fork once the foliage has died down. Leave the potatoes on the surface for a couple of hours so that the skins dry off and harden. Do not leave them overnight or slugs will damage the tubers.

2 Sort the potatoes before storing them. It is sufficient to grade them into four sizes: very small, small, medium and large. Use the smallest ones immediately and only store the medium and largest sizes.

3 Place the largest potatoes in sacks to store in a cool but frost-proof place. If you can't get paper sacks, use black plastic sacks. Make slits in these for ventilation, but keep away from light.

4 If you have a large crop, make a traditional clamp in the garden. Line a shallow depression with a layer of straw at least 10cm (4in) thick.

5 Pile on the potatoes carefully, then heap a thick layer of straw over the top. It must be thick enough to provide good insulation.

6 Mound earth over the straw, but leave a few tufts of straw sticking out of the top. These will allow a little ventilation.

One of the problems of a productive vegetable plot is how to avoid wasteful gluts. Be prepared for the harvest season so that all the vegetables are picked and stored in the peak of condition.

stored in this way. Choose only the best roots to store and make sure they are not damaged because this will encourage storage rots to develop. Remove the leaves before storage, twisting off beetroot foliage rather than cutting it to reduce bleeding. Lay the roots horizontally in layers of damp sand so that they do not dry out. Use up the smallest roots first.

Storing inside in sacks

Potatoes, on the other hand, should be stored in dry, dark and frost-free conditions. It is essential to keep them in the dark, otherwise they will go green and become inedible. The best option is to place them in special double-skinned paper sacks, which can be tied at the top to exclude light. Then make sure the temperature in your store never falls below freezing. You can help prevent damage from cold by insulating the sacks with sheets of polystyrene (styrofoam) and by laying them on old wooden pallets to improve air circulation. If storage space is limited, you could try using the traditional clamping method. It looks primitive but works well except where winters are very severe.

Storing inside in jars

Crops such as beans and peas can be kept dry in airtight containers such as old jam jars. Make sure the crop is fully ripe and the pods are brittle before removing the dry seeds and storing them in labelled containers.

Storing inside in nets

A few crops, such as onions, marrows and cabbages, are better stored in nets. They will need to be kept in a cool, well-ventilated area that is frost-free and dry during the winter months. Netting bags and old tights (pantyhose) are both suitable, or you could try your hand at braiding members of the onion family into ropes. These crops can also be stored successfully in open trays, provided they are kept well ventilated.

Extending the greenhouse season

The greenhouse can still be a busy place in early autumn, with many crops still growing strongly. You might be harvesting this year's crops as well as planning ahead for next year and sowing seed for early flowers and vegetables. Now is also a good time to plant bulbs in pots for blooms early next year.

Practical matters

Plants will need as much light as they can get at this time of the year, so remove the shading and clean the glass in the roof and sides of the greenhouse. Check that the heater is in good working order well before you need to use it. Tip back

Clear away any greenhouse shading to maximize light levels for growing crops in the greenhouse and make final preparations for winter.

BRINGING IN POT PLANTS FROM THE GARDEN

1 Clear away and put on the compost heap the mulching material if the pot has been plunged into the ground and mulched to reduce the need for regular watering.

2 If the pot does not come up easily, insert a garden fork a little distance away and loosen the surrounding soil so that you can lever it out without damaging the pot or plant.

3 Remove leaves and debris from the surface of the compost (soil mix), which will almost certainly have become contaminated. Wipe the pot clean with a damp cloth, and be especially careful to clean the bottom of the pot so that it does not make a mess indoors.

4 Always check for pests and diseases before bringing it in. If the plant has thick or glossy leaves, wipe them over with a proprietary leaf shine to improve their appearance. Plants left outdoors almost always become splashed with mud and dirt.

tomatoes that have reached the top of their supports and remove lower leaves as they start to yellow to encourage the remaining fruit to swell and ripen as quickly as possible. Also space out potted plants on the staging to increase air circulation around them and reduce the incidence of disease. Watch out for any outbreaks of grey mould (*Botrytis*) in particular from now on, because this disease thrives in damp, stagnant air, which can be found in a closed greenhouse in autumn. Reduce watering, too, as plant growth slows, and pack away capillary watering systems to reduce the overall humidity in the greenhouse. Remove any yellowing foliage or other debris from around your plants to keep them healthy.

Late sowing

You can still sow a few annuals and perennials in early autumn for planting out in the garden. Autumn-sown plants will make sturdier specimens and flower more quickly than those sown during early spring. Overwintering lettuce can also be sown now in pots or seed trays for planting out into the greenhouse border after the summer crops have been removed. Try varieties such as 'Cynthia', 'Kwiek' and 'Novita', sown in succession for cropping in late winter and early spring when there is little else around. Cauliflowers can be sown now for overwintering in pots and planting out in their final position during the spring for crops in mid- to late spring – well before the spring-sown crops.

Winter colour

A greenhouse that's kept frost-free is ideal for forcing hardy spring bulbs. Pot up bulbs of narcissi, early tulips and hyacinths so that their tips can be seen just poking through the surface of the compost (soil mix). Stand in a cool, dark place, such as a deep sand bed or box full of peat, where the root system can be allowed to develop. Check them periodically to see if the shoots have started to break and that the root system is developing well. In late autumn take the containers out of the plunge bed and clean them up before standing them in a well-shaded spot, such as under the staging, so that they can get used to being in the light. Gradually increase the light levels until they can be put in full sun.

Greenhouse shading

To maximize light levels, remove greenhouse shading when the weather cools down. If you applied a shading wash earlier in the year, clean it off now. Most can be rubbed off with a duster when the glass is dry. Internal or external shading material such as blinds or nets can also be removed now. You may be able to use the same internal fixings to secure winter insulation.

USING UP SPARE BULBS

1 If you have some bulbs left over from border planting outside you can use them to boost indoor displays by planting now. Do not worry if the bulbs have already developed some shoots, but take care that they are not damaged as you plant them up.

3 Water the container well and allow to drain. If you wish, mulch with moss to retain the moisture as well as to add an attractive finish.

Keep cool and well-ventilated until they start to show colour in the bud, when they can be moved to their flowering position.

Pots from the garden

Many winter- and spring-flowering houseplants, such as Christmas cactus and some orchids, and solanums, grown for their winter berries, can spend the summer outdoors as they look uninteresting at this stage. Bring them in before

2 Fill the container with moistened bulb fibre. If you are using ordinary potting compost, place a layer of grit in the bottom of the container to aid drainage. Plant the bulbs so that they are close but not touching, with the top half left exposed.

4 You may need to support the leaves and stems with twigs. Only do so if you notice that the stems are beginning to flop, but then act immediately. Beech twigs are ideal, as they branch well all the way up the stem.

the first frost threatens (see opposite).

Lift the pots and clean with a moist cloth. Remove any loose debris and compost from the surface of the pot and top up with fresh. Check the plant for signs of pests and disease, especially around the crown and the undersides of leaves where pests like snails might hide.

Not so hardy plants grown in containers on the patio, such as sweet bay and citrus, should also be moved to a well-lit frost-free place.

Naturalizing bulbs

Growing bulbs in a natural setting where they can be left undisturbed to spread and multiply is not only one of the most effective ways of growing them but is undoubtedly the easiest. The bulbs will flower year after year with the minimum of maintenance, adding interest to otherwise dull areas. You can naturalize bulbs in lawns, in borders and under the canopy of trees.

Naturalizing in grass

Choose bulbs that are adapted to the use you wish to put them to. Most bulb catalogues provide useful advice and there are often special deals on cultivars that have been bought in bulk for naturalizing.

You will need an area of grass that you don't mind leaving unmown until early summer to allow bulb foliage to die back naturally. In a small garden, the best bulbs to choose are those that flower in late winter or early spring, such as snowdrops and crocuses. These should have died down almost completely by the time you are ready to give the lawn its first cut of the season. Alternatively, if you like to start mowing early, grow them towards the edge of the lawn where they can be appreciated and yet allowed to die down naturally after flowering. In these areas you'll be able to include bulbs such as daffodils, fritillaries and grape hyacinths.

Naturalizing in beds and borders

Areas that are regularly cultivated for planting seasonal bedding, for example, are not really suitable for naturalizing bulbs because you are likely to dig up the dormant bulbs by mistake unless they are clearly marked. But areas that are left

NATURALIZING BULBS INDIVIDUALLY IN GRASS

1 Scatter the bulbs on to the turf in a random fashion and plant them where they fall, but try to allow a distance of about 8–20cm (3–8in) between each one.

2 Dig a deep, square hole of about a spade's width and about 25cm (10in) deep, depending on the size of the bulb. You may need to go deeper than one spade's depth.

3 Put a layer of grit or sand in the bottom of the hole, then plant the bulb, base down. Cover the bulb with loose soil and replace the top divot. Firm down gently.

4 A special bulb-planting tool, which takes out a core of soil, will save time if you want to plant a lot of bulbs individually. Scatter the bulbs randomly as before.

5 Push the bulb planter into the soil, twisting it a little if the ground is hard, then pull it out with the core of soil. Release the core of soil and place the bulb at the bottom of the hole.

6 Pull off a little soil from the base of the core (to allow for the depth of the bulb), then replace the core in the hole. Firm gently. Fill any gaps with sieved garden soil.

relatively undisturbed, such as between shrubs and trees, can be effectively planted with naturalized bulbs. They will do particularly well between late-leafing deciduous specimens, where they can get plenty of light during early spring. Naturalized bulbs also combine well with late emerging perennials and hardy ferns, because these plants will help disguise the yellowing bulb foliage as they grow. Choose bulbs such as winter aconites, anemones, bluebells, grape hyacinths, crocuses, daffodils, fritillaries, snowdrops and chionodoxas.

Saving tender bulbs

Do not discard your dahlias – lift the tubers before frosts penetrate the ground and store them for next year. Even seed-raised plants will have formed tubers that you can store. Lift the dahlia tubers once the first frosts have blackened the foliage. Use a fork to lift the tubers, to minimize the risk of damaging them. Cut the old stem off to leave a stump about 5cm (2in) long. Stand the tubers upside-down so that moisture drains easily from the hollow stems. Using a mesh support is a convenient way to allow them to dry off. Keep in a dry, frost-free place. After a few days the tubers should be dry enough to store. Remove surplus soil, trim off loose bits of old roots and shorten the stem to leave a stump. Label each plant and dust with fungicide. Pack the tubers in a well-insulated box with peat, vermiculite, wood shavings, or crumpled newspaper placed between them.

A spare bedroom or cool but frost-free garage are suitable places for storage. Keep bulbs, corms and tubers where you can easily check them about once a month to make sure they are all still sound. If you notice any signs of rot, remove and destroy the affected tubers.

NATURALIZING BULBS IN SMALL AREAS OF GRASS

1 If you have a lot of small bulbs, such as crocuses and winter aconites (*Eranthis*), to plant in a limited area use a spade or half-moon edger to make an H-shaped cut.

2 Slice beneath the grass with a spade until you can fold back the turf for planting. Do this with care to get an even turf that can be folded back without cracking.

3 Loosen the ground before planting, as it may be very compacted. If you want to apply a slow-acting fertilizer, such as bonemeal, work it into the soil at the same time.

4 Avoid planting in rows or regimented patterns. You want the bulbs to look natural and informal, so scatter them and plant more or less where they fall.

5 For larger bulbs, make deeper holes with a trowel. Plant them so that they are covered with about twice their own depth of soil. Use a spade to dig out a hole for a group of bulbs.

6 Firm the soil, then return the grass. Firm again if necessary to make sure it is flat, and water if the weather is dry to make sure that the grass grows again quickly.

Planting new shrubs and hedges

Autumn is the best time to plant most shrubs and hedges, since they will need less watering than those planted in spring. The main exception are evergreens, which should be planted in mid- to late spring so that they are not exposed to cold, drying winds before they become established. Now is also a good time to prune rambling roses, which can quickly become very large if not kept under control.

Adding new plants

In autumn the existing garden displays are still fresh in your mind, so you will be in a better position to decide what new additions you need.

Do not prune rambling roses in the first year, but thereafter prune in autumn after flowering by removing any dead or diseased shoots and reducing sideshoots by about two-thirds.

PRUNING A RAMBLING ROSE

1 Prune a rambling rose after flowering but while the new shoots are still fairly pliable. Older, congested plants can be more off-putting than younger ones, but all ramblers are fairly straightforward to prune.

2 First, cut out any dead or damaged shoots or those that are very weak and spindly. Do not remove very vigorous, young shoots. Work methodically, cutting shoots back in sections.

3 Cut out old stems that have flowered, but only where there are new shoots to replace them. Shorten the sideshoots on old stems that have been retained (those that have flowered) by about two-thirds.

4 Tie in the flexible shoots to the support. Wherever possible, tie loosely to horizontal wires or a trellis. This will prevent the whippy shoots from being caught by the wind and getting damaged or harming others.

And because it is not a busy time of year in most gardens, it means you have plenty of time to consider all the options and are less likely to make mistakes.

One of the most common pitfalls when adding new shrubs to a bed or border is to plant them too close together. This means that you will either have to move one or more shrubs when they get overcrowded in a few years, or spend a lot of time pruning them to keep them within bounds. But don't be tempted to buy large specimens to fill the borders and create an instant effect. Not only is this expensive, but older plants will not establish as quickly and will soon be overtaken by the faster-growing smaller plants.

If you are planting a completely new bed of shrubs, fill the gaps between with fast-growing plants, such as buddleia and mock orange, which will quickly grow and provide a colourful display while the slower-growing permanent shrubs are getting established and filling out. The filler plants can then be removed as necessary over the following

PLANTING A HEDGE

1 Prepare the ground thoroughly, as a hedge will be there for a long time and this is your only opportunity to improve the soil. Clear it of all weeds and their roots and dig deeply.

2 Take out a trench about 25cm (10in) deep. Set up a line of garden twine to make sure that the row is straight. Place the excavated soil to one side of the trench.

3 Add as much well-rotted garden compost or manure as you can spare, then fork it into the base of the trench to improve the soil and encourage deep rooting.

4 Return the soil to the trench, adding more organic material as you do so. Then apply bonemeal and rake it in. Don't apply fast-acting fertilizers at this time of year.

5 Bare-root hedging comes bundled together, with the roots in a bag of peat or soil. If you cannot plant immediately, simply dig the hedging into a spare piece of ground.

6 Dig large holes at the appropriate spacing. A typical spacing is 38–45cm (15–18in), but it may be different for some plants, so always check the recommended spacing first.

7 Check that the plants are set at the correct depth and firm them in well, treading around them to remove any large air pockets, which could cause the roots to dry out.

8 Water thoroughly, and be prepared to water regularly in dry spells for the first year. Protect new hedging with a windbreak in exposed gardens.

seasons. The second option is to smother the ground between the shrubs with complementary groundcover plants underplanted with colourful bulbs. Or you could plug the gaps with a sowing of hardy annuals in spring. These will grow and flower in their first year before dying in autumn. Most will readily self-seed so you won't need to sow afresh each spring. They will also die out naturally as the permanent shrubs take over the bed, using up the available light, moisture and nutrients.

Container-grown or bare-root?
Most garden plants are sold in containers, which are convenient because they needn't be planted

immediately. Some trees and shrubs (particularly hedges and roses) ordered by mail order from specialist nurseries may arrive bare-root, however, with their roots wrapped in moss and a protective sleeve. These

are plants that have been lifted from the field; they are often cheaper than container-grown and can be just as good if planted promptly. Bare-root plants are also sometimes available at garden centres and other outlets.

Autumn pond care

Although ponds need little routine maintenance, there are a few end-of-season tasks that are essential if you want to keep your plants and fish (if any) in good condition. Clear out any dead or dying plant material, which will rot and foul the water over the winter. Overgrown plants can be trimmed back, but leave removed material on the side of the pond overnight so that any trapped pond creatures have a chance to make their way back to the water.

Fallen leaves

Stop autumn leaves getting into the pond by covering it with a fine-mesh net held taut above the water. If leaves congregate on the netting, clear them away to prevent the net from sagging into the water. Large ponds that are too big to net can be protected by erecting a low, fine-mesh fence around the perimeter to catch any wind-blown leaves. Clear these up regularly and turn them into leafmould.

Tender aquatics

Some aquatic plants, such as the water lettuce (*Pistia stratiotes*) and *Salvinia auriculata*, will be killed by frost, even though they can multiply rapidly outdoors in summer. Fairy moss (*Azolla filiculoides*) sometimes survives a mild winter in favourable areas, but as an insurance policy overwinter a few plants in a frost-free place. Net a few plants that are still in good condition. They may already be deteriorating in the cooler weather, so don't save any that appear to be rotting or badly damaged. Put a handful of the plants into a plastic container – such as lunch box or ice cream container – full of water. Don't cram them in so that they are overcrowded. Use extra containers rather than have all the plants touching. Some gardeners put a little soil in the bottom to provide nutrients. Keep the plants in a warm, light place, such as a heated greenhouse. You might also be able to keep them on a well-lit windowsill. Top up or change the water occasionally to prevent it from becoming stagnant.

Miniature waterlilies

With the exception of tropical waterlilies, which are usually only

An established, well-balanced pond needs little additional work in autumn, but carrying out a few seasonal tasks now will keep it in good order and help prepare it for the winter months ahead.

AVOIDING ROTTING LEAVES IN THE POND

1 Protect the pond from the worst of the leaf fall with a fine-mesh net. Anchor it just above the surface of the pond. Remove the leaves regularly, and eventually remove the netting.

2 If you are not able to cover your pond with a net or don't like the appearance of one, use a fish net or rake to remove leaves regularly to prevent them rotting and fouling the water.

3 Trim back dead or dying plants from around the edge of the pond, especially where the vegetation is likely to fall into the water, where it will decompose.

grown by enthusiasts with heated pools, waterlilies are very hardy and are usually planted deep enough not to come to any harm in cold weather. Miniature waterlilies are sometimes used for raised miniature pools, in a half-barrel or shrub tub for example, and these are vulnerable. Because the container is raised above the ground, in very severe weather the water can freeze solid throughout. Try wrapping your pool in several layers of bubble insulation material, or move it into a cool greenhouse for the winter.

Protect pond pumps

If you leave a pump in your pond over winter, ice may damage it. Remove submersible pumps from the water before penetrating frosts cause the water to freeze deeply. Don't just take the pump out of the pond and leave it where moisture can enter — it should be stored in a dry place. Clean the pump before you put it away. It will probably be covered with algae which can be scrubbed off. Remove the filter and either replace it or clean it. Follow the

manufacturer's instructions. Make sure all the water is drained from the pump. If your pump is an external one, check that the system is drained. Read the manufacturer's instructions, and carry out any other servicing necessary before storing the pump in a dry place over winter. It may be necessary to send it away for a service, in which case do it now instead of waiting until spring. Replace the pond pump with a pond heater during the winter to prevent the surface of the pond freezing over.

OVERWINTERING TENDER AQUATICS

1 Net a few plants in good condition. They may already be deteriorating in the cooler weather, so don't save any that appear to be rotting or badly damaged

2 Put a handful of the plants in a plastic container of pond water. Don't overcrowd them — use extra containers rather than allow them to touch. Some gardeners put a little soil in the bottom to provide nutrients.

3 Keep the plants in a light, frost-free place, such as a greenhouse. You might be able to keep them on a cool windowsill. Top up or change the water occasionally so that it does not become stagnant.

Creating winter interest

Filling containers with winter-flowering plants is one of the quickest and easiest ways of brightening up your garden. Whether positioned on the patio or placed next to a well-used path or doorway, they'll give months of pleasure when little else in the garden is providing interest. It's also worth having a few winter containers where you can see them from the house. For example, you could plant up a winter hanging basket and even a window box outside the kitchen window to add a little sparkle to the view.

Recycling plants

You don't need to spend lots of money on new plants each autumn because many garden plants can be given a temporary home in a garden container for the winter months. Self-seeded hellebores and rooted runners and sideshoots from groundcover plants, such as ajugas and bergenias, as well as unwanted divisions from overgrown evergreen perennials that have been divided earlier in the year, can all be used.

Some plants can be saved and recycled from summer displays, too. For example, the small-leaved ivies used in hanging baskets and as trailers around the edge of summer containers can be reused in almost any winter arrangement. Similarly, the hardy grey-leaved senecio (*Senecio cineraria*), which is often included in bedding displays, can be used to add interest to winter containers, too.

Winter containers are of particular value because there is little else to catch the eye. Here, pansies and variegated ivy have been combined for a long-lasting display.

PLANTING A WINTER HANGING BASKET

1 Line the hanging basket with a suitable organic material. Conifer branches, as shown here, are an ideal material.

2 Fill the lined basket with a suitable potting compost (soil mix) to about one-third of its depth, spreading it evenly over the base.

3 Position the plants first to see how they will look. Fill in the spaces between the plants with more potting compost.

4 Any gaps between the plants can be filled with small bulbs or bedding plants to provide a riot of spring colour.

Adding seasonal fillers

Many evergreen shrubs and perennials are worth buying for winter containers. These days garden centres sell them as very small plants so they will not take up too much space. Shrubs with colourful foliage, such as cultivars of *Euonymus fortunei*, or small-leaved hebes will provide colour and structure to the arrangement. A few berrying plants are worth adding, such as the superb *Skimmia japonica* subsp. *reevesiana* with its compact clusters of bright red fruit that last all winter, or pink-berried pernettyas, which look a treat when accompanied by pink and white winter-flowering dwarf heathers. In a larger container you could try winter-flowering jasmine, small upright and prostrate conifers, or *Viburnum tinus*, which flowers for a long period from late winter. Whatever the weather, make sure you water the container or basket from time to time, as needed throughout the winter months, so that the plants do not run short of moisture.

PLANTING A WINTER WINDOWBOX

1 Assemble all the necessary materials. These include the window box, crocks, a good potting compost (soil mix) and the plants. If the box is light, assemble it on the ground. If not, then assemble it in position.

2 Holes in the bottom are essential to allow good drainage. Stop the compost from being washed out by placing crocks over these. If very good drainage is needed, then a layer of gravel can also be added.

3 Partially fill the box with compost, gently tapping the sides to make sure that no air gaps remain. Never over-firm soil-less potting mixes, which can become waterlogged and airless, and the plants will suffer.

4 Place the plants on the compost to work out the arrangement and check their positions before finally planting. Make sure that they are planted in the compost at the same depth that they were in their pots or trays. Plant them fairly close for an instant effect.

5 A selection of small bulbs will make a useful additional display for the window box. The bulbs can be planted in among the main plants and are best planted in groups of three so that they give a fuller display. Water the basket thoroughly once it is planted.

6 Topup the windowbox with compost so that the surface is about 2.5cm (1in) below the rim to allow for easy watering. Add a layer of gravel to prevent soil from splashing against the leaves. Water well and keep watering as necessary throughout the winter months.

Giving a colour boost

Winter-flowering bedding plants and the earliest of the spring bulbs can be combined to create an ever-changing and colourful display right through the winter months. Winter bedding plants are sometimes disappointing as some varieties tend to flower only in mild spells. For the best performance in cold weather, choose the many colours of the Universal Series of winter-flowering pansy and Crescendo Series polyanthus. They can be bought in mixed or single colours so you can create complementary or colour-coordinated schemes. Choose stocky plants that are just coming into flower so that you can be sure of the colour.

Ornamental cabbages are another good source of winter colour, with rosettes of leaves variegated in pink, cream, white and green.

Late winter-flowering bulbs are well worth adding at planting time to extend the display into spring. Crocus, scilla, snowdrops, dwarf daffodils and tulips are worth including. You can also drop in some ready flowering potted bulbs which are available from garden centres in early spring, to give winter containers a fillip.

Keep winter-flowering pansies in a sheltered position if you want continuous colour through the winter months.

Overwintering herbs

Gathering fresh herbs from the garden allows you to enjoy them at their best, and if you plan ahead you can ensure a regular supply all winter long. A few shrubby herbs, such as rosemary and bay, can be cropped all year without special protection. However, because they are borderline hardy it would be best to grow them in containers in colder areas so that they can be moved inside in winter. Alternatively, cover them with garden fleece during cold spells.

Keeping herbs going

Perennial herbs, such as chives, mint and oregano, which would naturally die down in autumn, can be kept growing much longer by covering selected plants with cloches. In milder areas you might be able to keep them growing all winter using this technique. Evergreen herbs, such as thyme and sage, can also be encouraged if they are protected to continue growing to provide useful material for the kitchen throughout the winter months.

In colder areas it is worth potting up a few herbs if you can keep them somewhere frost-free throughout the winter. An insulated coldframe, greenhouse, conservatory or porch would be ideal, but you could also keep a pot or two growing on a cool bedroom windowsill. Lift the plants complete with roots and soil and transfer to a large pot. If you lift sufficient to fill several pots of each herb you will be able to use them in succession, so that the first has a chance to put on more growth before you revisit it. Vigorous growers, such as mint, can be grown from a few fleshy roots planted into a pot or seed tray. Cover the roots with compost and keep moist until shoots appear, then place in a well-lit spot.

A few herbs, including parsley and chervil, can be sown late under protection to provide late winter pickings. Sow in containers of fresh compost (soil mix) and keep them

POTTING UP HERBS FOR WINTER USE

1 Mint is an easy plant to force indoors, or in a coldframe or greenhouse, because it is naturally vigorous. Lift an established clump to provide a supply of roots to pot up.

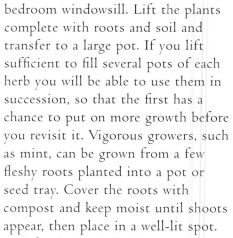

2 Be careful to select only pieces with healthy leaves (diseased leaves are common by the end of the season). You can pull pieces off by hand or cut through them with a knife.

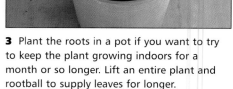

3 Plant the roots in a pot if you want to try to keep the plant growing indoors for a month or so longer. Lift an entire plant and rootball to supply leaves for longer.

4 If you want a supply of tender fresh leaves early next spring, cut off the tops and put the roots in seed trays or deeper boxes, then cover them with soil. Keep them in a greenhouse or even a protected coldframe.

5 Chives also respond favourably to lifting for an extended season. Lift a small clump complete with rootball and soil to pot up. If it's too large, you should be able to pull it apart into smaller pieces.

6 Place the clump in a pot of ordinary soil or potting compost (soil mix), firm well, and water. It should continue to provide leaves after those outdoors have died back, and will produce new ones earlier next spring.

PROTECTING SWISS CHARD

In cold areas, Swiss chard needs some form of winter protection. Any form of cloche or portable coldframe can be used.

CUTTING BACK GLOBE ARTICHOKES

Cut down all stems to ground level when the plant dies back in the autumn. Replace plants after three or, at most, four years.

HARVESTING LEEKS

Harvest the leeks by digging under them with a garden fork. As you do this, pull them from the ground with the other hand.

outside until temperatures start to drop at night. Pot up the seedlings when they are large enough to handle and place them in a coldframe or greenhouse or on the kitchen windowsill to keep them growing throughout the autumn and winter. They will then provide useful harvests from midwinter onwards.

Some herbs, including borage, fennel and tarragon, cannot be overwintered using these methods and so will need to be frozen or dried if you want to use them during the winter months.

Straw protection

Vegetables such as celery and beetroot (beets) also benefit from protection in cold areas. Pack straw among and between the plants in the blocks or rows. It does not matter if the tops of the leaves are exposed – you are only protecting the edible part. Mature celery will usually survive some frost, but the straw protection is useful if it turns very cold before you are ready to lift it. In mild areas beetroot can be left unprotected, but the straw does help to keep plants in better condition for longer in cold areas.

Protect Swiss chard with cloches or garden fleece during the autumn for the best quality growth, especially in gardens that experience penetrating frosts.

Making compost

Making garden compost allows you to mimic the natural recycling of organic matter that occurs in the soil. It is also a convenient way of getting rid of a lot of bulky waste, and saves you money because you do not have to buy in so much organic matter to boost the fertility of your plot. Making your own compost is, therefore, good for the wider environment, your soil and the plants you are trying to grow.

What you need
You do not need any special equipment to compost successfully. Just pile the material up in a heap and it will eventually break down at the centre. However, to get the compost to break down evenly in the shortest possible time, you would be better off buying or making a compost bin. Aim for the largest size that you have room for: the greater the volume, the more quickly the compost will break down. A bin holding 1 cubic metre (35 cubic feet) is ideal, but smaller sizes can also work well. If you have a large garden that produces a lot of waste, build three bins side by side, so that one can be filled while the second is rotting down and the third is being emptied of well-rotted compost.

Traditionally, compost bins are made from scrap wood, but this rots with the heap and so needs replacing every few years. Making a bin from wood, however, does allow you to build it to fit the space you have available. You can buy manufactured bins that have been pressure-treated against rot so that they last a lot longer. Most ready-made bins, however, are made from plastic. Make sure your ready-made bin is large enough for your needs and has some ventilation (you may need to drill some holes), and that it is easy to access the compost once it is ready for use.

What you can compost
You can recycle virtually any organic waste from the garden or kitchen in a compost bin, but for the composting process to be completed as quickly as possible you will need to mix the different types of material in the bin. You can do this either by mixing the dry and moist ingredients before they are added to the compost heap, or by adding them unmixed in alternate layers not more than 15cm (6in) thick. Dry ingredients include old newspaper and straw and moist ingredients

MAKING COMPOST

1 A simple compost bin, which should be about 1m (3ft) square and deep, can be made using cheap, pressure-treated fencing timber, or by nailing four flat pallets together.

2 Pile the waste into the bin, taking care that there are no thick layers of one material. Grass clippings will not rot down if the layer is too thick because air cannot penetrate.

3 It is important to keep the compost bin covered with an old mat or a sheet of plastic. This will help to keep in the heat generated by the composting process, prevent it from cooling down too much in winter and also stop the compost from getting too wet in bad weather, which slows down the process.

4 After about a month, turn the contents of the compost bin with a fork to let in air and to move the outside material, which is slow to rot, into the centre to speed up the composting process. If you have several bins, it is easier to turn the compost by transferring it from one bin into another.

5 When the bin is full, you may want to cover the surface with a layer of soil and use it to grow marrows (large zucchini), pumpkins or cucumbers. If you want to use the contents as soon as possible remove one of the sides for access. Otherwise, keep the compost covered with plastic or an old piece of carpet.

HOW TO ADD ORGANIC MATERIAL

1 Organic material such as well-rotted garden compost or farmyard manure is high in nutrients. Fork in when the soil is dug. For heavy soils, this is best done in the autumn.

2 If the soil has already been dug, the organic material can be lightly forked in or left on the surface. The worms will complete the task of working it into the soil.

3 In autumn, and again in spring, top-dress established plants with a layer of well-rotted organic material. This will also help to suppress weeds and conserve soil moisture.

include grass clippings and annual weeds. Any woody materials, such as prunings, should be chopped up with secateurs (pruners) or processed through a garden shredder before being added. Don't include any diseased plant material, and never add meat, fish, fat or other cooked foods, which will attract vermin.

Perennial weed roots and annual weeds that are setting seed might survive the composting process and be spread around your garden when the compost is used. You can use them in the compost if you first leave them to rot in a bucket of water; otherwise, throw them away or bury them deeply in a specially prepared trench.

Composting efficiently

Even when you have the right sized bin and the right mixture of ingredients, there is a lot you can do to help it compost more efficiently. The first trick is to give the heap a kick-start by adding a proprietary compost activator or a spadeful of well-rotted compost from a previous bin each time you add a new layer of material to the bin. This will introduce the right microbes as well

as providing them with the perfect environment to work efficiently. Do not allow the heap to dry out or get too wet (which will slow down the composting process) and cover it with a lid in winter to help retain heat within the heap. To ensure the heap composts evenly it will need to be turned after a month. It should

produce sweet-smelling, crumbly, fibrous compost in just a few months in summer and around six months in winter.

If the compost does get too wet, empty the bin completely and then return the compost while mixing in a dry material, such as shredded newspaper, as you go.

Woody material can be added to the compost heap but it needs to be chopped up finely beforehand so that it rots down quickly.

Heating the greenhouse

You only need to heat your greenhouse over the winter months if you intend to use it to grow tender crops year round or want to overwinter tender plants. If you want to overwinter just a few plants, consider investing in a high-top, thermostatically controlled electric propagator instead, which can be placed on the staging and will cost a lot less to run than heating the entire greenhouse. If you do decide to heat your greenhouse over winter, insulation will reduce the cost. You could also just heat a part of the greenhouse, dividing the area off with insulation material.

Heating the greenhouse

You can choose among electric, gas and paraffin powered heaters. Choose a thermostatically controlled electric fan heater if you have an electricity supply to your greenhouse. This will control the temperature automatically, switching on and off as required. Using an electric heater means you don't have to worry about topping up the fuel tank or replacing the gas bottle, and you don't have to ventilate the greenhouse to get rid of fumes. If you choose a low-tariff night-rate electricity supply for your greenhouse heater it will be even cheaper. The size of the heater should depend on the volume of air you want to heat. The minimum size for a well-insulated 1.8 × 2.4m (6 × 8ft) greenhouse will be a 2kW heater in milder areas and a 2.5kW heater in colder areas. In a larger greenhouse it is worth partitioning off an area to be heated with thermal screens. A larger heater doesn't necessarily cost more to run, because if it is thermostatically controlled, it will turn on and off when needed. The advantage of a larger heater is that it is better able to provide the heat required when temperatures drop quickly.

Insulating the greenhouse

Insulation will help to cut down heating costs, but even if you don't heat your greenhouse during the winter, insulation will provide some extra protection for any not-quite-hardy overwintered plants.

Proper double-glazing is not very practicable or cost-effective for most amateur greenhouses where high temperatures are not normally maintained. Clear plastic sheeting is the most practical choice as it can be taken down at the end of the cold season and used again if stored carefully for the summer. Single thickness, heavy-duty plastic lets through plenty of light, and is cheap to buy, but it is not the most effective material for conserving heat. Bubble plastic is more efficient because air trapped in the bubbles cuts down heat loss. If possible, choose bubble plastic that is thick, with large pockets of air. It lets through less light, but is more efficient at reducing heat loss.

In colder areas this may not be sufficient insulation. One option is to cover the floor and sides, up to the level of the bench, with polystyrene (styrofoam) blocks.

A large, high-roofed greenhouse is perfect for letting in the sun, but expensive to heat in winter – heated propagators could be the answer.

Thermal screens made of clear plastic or special translucent fabrics are widely used commercially to conserve heat. Fixed horizontally over the plants, they are usually pulled across at night and drawn back during the day. Stretch supporting wires along each side of the greenhouse, over which the fabric can be draped or pulled. If you have a large greenhouse, it may be more economical to heat just part of it. Use a vertical screen to partition off the end to reduce the total volume that is to be heated. Try to seal the edges to minimize draughts.

INSULATING THE GREENHOUSE WITH BUBBLE PLASTIC

1 There are many proprietary fasteners for securing plastic sheeting to the inside of a metal greenhouse. Details may vary, but they slot into the groove in the metal moulding and can be secured with a twisting motion.

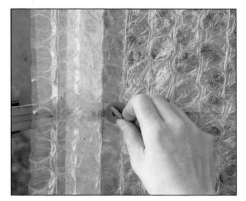

2 With the main part of the clip in place, the top is pushed or twisted into position, clamping the plastic liner. If you use thick bubble plastic, you may need to buy clips designed for the extra thickness.

3 You may find it easier to line the sides and roof separately. If you decide to do this, make sure that the sheets of plastic overlap in order to provide a seal or use transparent tape to seal the joins.

4 You can fix the insulation to a timber-framed greenhouse with drawing pins (thumbtacks) or special pins sold for the purpose. Use plenty of pins to keep the sheets of insulation in position.

5 If you don't want to fix the insulation directly to the wooden frame, suction fixers can be attached to the glass. These can also be used for metal-framed greenhouses. Moisten the plastic before pressing into place.

6 Secure the liner to the cup with the special pin provided, or use a drawing pin. This is a useful way of attaching insulation to the inside of doors and vents, which need to be opened and closed independently.

7 Whichever method of fixing you choose, you should always insulate the ventilators separately. Although you need to conserve heat as much as possible, some ventilation is essential on warm days, otherwise the greenhouse will get too hot.

8 To avoid too much warmth being lost between the sheets where they join, seal the joins with transparent adhesive tape. Do not use parcel tape because this will cut down the amount of light that can enter the greenhouse.

Overwintering tender plants

Many tender perennials, such as marguerites and osteospermums, which are widely used in summer containers and bedding schemes, can be successfully overwintered and used as the basis for displays next year. This could save you a great deal of money and will give you the chance to keep unusual plants from year to year. There are several ways you can overwinter tender perennials, but the method you choose will depend on the species you are trying to overwinter.

In the border
Some plants, including *Senecio cineraria*, chocolate cosmos, daturas, fuchsias and penstemons, are almost hardy and can be given sufficient protection outside in the garden in most areas. Once the foliage has died back, cover the ground with a deep mulch of dry leaves or chipped bark to provide insulation. In an exposed garden net the pile or surround it with pieces of wood to keep it in place. On lighter soils, you can even bury plants such as fuchsias and pelargoniums in shallow trenches to provide the insulation cover. Dig a trench about 30cm (12in) deep, line it with straw, then lay the plants on this. Cover the plants with more straw and return the soil. Dig them up in spring, pot them up and keep in warmth and good light to start into growth again. If the winters are not too harsh, many of the plants should survive.

In a coldframe
The protection offered by a coldframe will allow you to overwinter a larger range of plants, including *Calceolaria integrifolia*, diascias, glechomas, helichrysums and verbenas. Insulate the sides and top of the coldframe with layers of bubble plastic or blocks of polystyrene (styrofoam). The plants can be planted or packed in boxes. Check them periodically and remove any dying foliage. Water if necessary during mild spells in late winter and early spring.

In the shed
Frost-free sheds and garages are suitable for overwintering all the above plants, as well as tuberous begonias, cannas and impatiens.

OVERWINTERING PELARGONIUMS

1 Lift the plants before the first frost if possible, though they will often survive a light frost if you take them in promptly afterwards.

2 Shake as much of the soil off the roots as possible, to minimize the amount of space the plants will take up in storage.

3 Trim the longest roots back to about 5–8cm (2–3in) long, to make potting up easier. Also remove any damaged foliage.

4 Shorten the shoots to about 10cm (4in), and trim off any remaining leaves. Although this looks drastic, new shoots will grow in spring, and you will be able to use these for cuttings if you want more plants.

5 The most effective way to store pelargoniums for the winter is in large trays at least 15cm (6in) deep. Half-fill with potting compost (soil mix), position the plants and add more compost to cover the roots.

6 If you want to overwinter your pelargoniums on a windowsill indoors, you may find it more convenient to use large pots instead of trays. Water well initially, then only when the compost becomes almost dry.

OVERWINTERING TENDER FUCHSIAS

1 If your fuchsias have been grown in pots during the summer, take them into the greenhouse. If planted in the ground, lift with a fork and remove excess soil.

2 Pot up the plants individually, or in large boxes if you have a lot of plants, then put them in a frost-free place, such as in the greenhouse or on a light windowsill indoors.

3 Tidy up the plants by removing old leaves and pinching out any soft green tips. You must keep the plants cool but frost-free. Water sparingly when the soil is almost dry.

Trim the plants back and pack them in wooden boxes or trays filled with a mixture of equal parts potting compost (soil mix) and sharp sand. To prevent the roots drying out, line the box with perforated plastic sheeting beforehand. Check occasionally to make sure the compost doesn't dry out completely.

In the greenhouse

All tender perennials can be overwintered if you have a greenhouse. If it is unheated, you can overwinter all the plants listed so far plus

euryops, felicias, gazanias and lobelias. Place the plants in an insulated box after trimming them back.

In the house

Indoors you can overwinter the most valuable and unusual tender perennials. Pot them up into containers that are large enough to accommodate their rootballs. Keep them somewhere light but out of direct sun in a cool room that is free of frost – an unheated bedroom, porch or conservatory is ideal. This is the best way of overwintering precious plants and other prized specimens.

Cuttings

Fuchsias and pelargoniums can be rooted from cuttings taken in spring or autumn. If you are overwintering old plants, you can use them to provide plenty of cuttings in spring. If you took cuttings in late summer or the autumn, however, your young plants will still be growing actively. Make sure that you keep these plants in good light and reasonably warm – they will then probably retain their foliage. If conditions are favourable, pelargoniums may even flower during the winter months.

Tender fuchsias that are being grown outside can be overwintered in a frost-free place indoors and will provide early cutting material for new plants in spring.

Late autumn

A last-minute spurt of action is often needed at this time of year, to get the garden ready for winter and ensure protection for plants that need it. In cold areas winter will already have taken its grip, but in warmer climates there are still many mild days to be enjoyed. Take advantage of them before colder temperatures and strong winds drive you indoors.

It is also important to keep on top of other routine tasks if the weather is mild. There will be plenty of weeding to be done, especially in mild spells, since weeds seem to keep growing more vigorously than other plants – they may begin colonizing spaces where garden plants have died down. You should also carry on clearing fallen leaves from around the garden. If left, the leaves will provide a haven for slugs and other pests. Any remaining vegetable crops should be harvested and stored, unless they are hardy enough to be left outside. Even hardy root crops may be best lifted now if your soil is heavy.

A mild spell in late autumn is an ideal time to clean the greenhouse. It is likely to be less full than in spring, and it is important to start the season of cold, dull days with clean glass to allow in all available light, and an environment as free as possible of pests and diseases. The aim is to prevent pests and diseases overwintering on bits of old plant material or in cracks and crevices. This may not prevent your plants being attacked next year, but it will delay any outbreaks.

Any outdoor plants that are likely to be damaged by winter weater can be protected now. Evergreens such as conifers may need protection from strong winds, especially when newly planted. Alpines and some other plants are more susceptible to damage from rain, though the low temperatures will not harm them – these can be sheltered by a glass 'roof'.

Late autumn is an ideal time to plant deciduous trees. The secret to success when planting is to prepare the ground well and plant firmly so that the roots cannot move. Staking is essential for larger trees to prevent them being rocked by the wind. After planting make sure the tree does not run short of water until well established, which could mean watering during dry spells for the first few years. Many trees and shrubs can also be propagated from cuttings taken in late autumn – useful for producing large quantities for a hedge, for example. No special facilities or equipment is needed since the hardwood cuttings are rooted in a trench in the garden.

In the fruit garden, take this opportunity to plan areas. Choosing the right crop for each position and planting them in carefully prepared soil will mean they need less attention thereafter. You can also carry out many pruning tasks on an established plot. For example, neglected apples and pears can be brought back into shape and cropping by pruning at this time of the year, while bush fruit and canes can be given their annual prune.

Late autumn is an ideal time to prune fruit trees. Start by removing any dead or weak growth as well as any crossing branches.

A heated greenhouse can be full of colour right through the winter but it is very expensive maintaining high temperatures throughout the coldest months.

Planting trees

It is essential to plant a new tree well if it is to establish quickly. Making sure the roots are secure in the soil and never run short of moisture are the two key components to successful planting. Most trees are sold in containers these days and can be planted at any time of the year but will establish more quickly if planted in autumn when the soil is moist and still warm. Bare-root trees are best planted in autumn.

Spacing

Like shrubs, trees need to be spaced at the correct distance if they are not to cause trouble later on. You will need to find out the approximate mature height of adjacent trees (by looking on the plant labels or consulting a good plant encyclopedia) and using the following simple calculation: add the heights together and then divide by two for the correct planting distance. For example, if you are planting a tree that will reach 15m (45ft) alongside a tree that will reach 11m (33ft), they should be planted 13m (39ft) apart (11m + 15m = 26m, 26m ÷ 2 = 13m; 45ft + 33ft = 78ft, 78ft ÷ 2 = 39ft).

Trees should always be planted well away from your house and other buildings, otherwise their roots may interfere with underground drains and the foundations and, in extreme cases, cause subsidence. As a rule, don't plant most trees nearer than their mature height. Some types of trees, such as poplars and willows, have more questing roots than others, so plant these even further away.

Planting

After preparing the ground by digging thoroughly and removing perennial weeds and other debris, excavate a planting hole about twice as wide and a little deeper than the rootball of the tree you are planting. On heavy soils, prick the sides of the hole to break up any clay so that the roots are not prevented from growing out into the surrounding soil. Then add well-rotted organic matter or proprietary planting mixture and lightly fork it into the soil at the bottom of the hole. After watering the rootball thoroughly, position it in the hole and check the depth using a cane – the tree should be at the same depth as it was in the pot or ground (look for a change in bark colour on bare-rooted trees). Trim damaged roots from bare-root trees and uncoil any circling roots at the base of container-grown specimens. Reposition the rootball in the hole, then add about 15cm (6in) of excavated soil while keeping the trunk upright. Shake bare-rooted trees to make sure that soil trickles

National tree planting week occurs in late autumn each year, and this is an ideal time to plant deciduous specimens, while the soil is still warm and moist.

PLANTING A TREE

1 Place a strong stake of rot-resistant wood or one treated with preservative in the hole, knocking it in so that it cannot move.

2 Place the tree in the hole, pushing the rootball up against the stake, so that the stem and stake are 8–10cm (3–4in) apart.

3 Backfill with soil and firm it down around the tree with the heel of your shoe. Top up with soil if necessary.

4 Although it is possible to use string, proper adjustable rose or tree ties with a spacer provide the best type of support. Fix the lower one 15cm (6in) above the soil level.

5 Fix the second tie near the top of the stake, slightly below the head of the tree. Do not make the tie so tight around the stem that it will constrict expansion as sap flows in spring.

6 Water the ground around the tree thoroughly and mulch the surface of the soil with chipped bark, well-rotted organic matter or a proprietory plant mulching mat.

between the roots, thus avoiding air pockets. Firm, and then add the next layer of soil. Repeat the process until the hole is filled. Water thoroughly and mulch with a thick layer of well-rotted organic matter.

Staking

If the tree is over 1.5m (5ft) tall it should be staked to prevent it being blown about in the wind. Drive a sturdy 1.5m (5ft) stake into the hole before planting, to leave about 60cm (24in) above the surface after planting. Position the stake slightly off-centre and on the windward side of the tree. After planting, attach the stake to the tree using adjustable tree ties, one at the top and one close to the ground. Container-grown trees may be better staked after planting by driving the stake in at an angle to avoid damaging the rootball.

Recommended trees

Acer griseum
Amelanchier lamarckii
Betula pendula 'Youngii'
Crataegus laevigata 'Paul's Scarlet'
Fagus sylvatica 'Purpurea Pendula'
Malus 'John Downie'
Prunus cerasifera 'Nigra'
Pyrus salicifolia 'Pendula'
Rhus typhina
Sorbus 'Joseph Rock'

Propagating plants

Late autumn is an ideal time for taking cuttings of many plants, particularly if you are short of time. Hardwood cuttings root more slowly than most softwood or semi-ripe cuttings, which you can take in spring and summer, but they need less attention. Most don't need heat, and because you plant them in the open ground (or in a coldframe), watering won't be onerous. Many plants experience a surge of root growth at this time of year, so cuttings taken now have a good chance of success.

Take hardwood cuttings

This is the best time to take hardwood cuttings of many popular trees and shrubs. Some will root in a prepared patch of ground, but most will root more quickly if covered by a coldframe. You could also try rooting a few of the more difficult subjects in a heated propagator.

Traditionally, hardwood cuttings 15–23cm (6–9in) long are taken in late autumn or early winter, depending on the type of growth the plant makes. Trim each cutting with a straight cut just below a leaf joint at

Deciduous ceanothus can be propagated from basal cuttings put in a coldframe.

the bottom and remove any soft growth towards the tip by cutting at an angle just above a bud. Prepare a slit or V-shaped trench and half-fill it with sharp sand or grit. Insert the cuttings 15cm (6in) apart so that the bottom two-thirds of each is buried. Firm the soil back around the cuttings and water well. In cold areas you can cover the cuttings with an open-ended cloche or coldframe. Keep well watered. Plant out rooted cuttings the following autumn.

Using a propagator

In a heated propagator, make the cuttings 10–15cm (4–6in) long and prepare in the same way. Evergreen shrubs, which are difficult to root outside, should have all but the top pair of leaves removed. Wounding the base of the cutting by scratching a little bark, about 1cm (½in), away from the base to one side, and dipping the base in hormone rooting powder can help to encourage rooting. Insert in pots full of cuttings compost (soil mix) and water well. Set the temperature for 15°C (59°F), reducing to 10°C (50°F) after a couple of weeks. Rooting should be complete by the time the propagator is needed in early spring.

Shrubs from cuttings

Hardwood cuttings are usually successful with *Buddleja* (butterfly bush), *Cornus alba* (dogwood), *Cornus stolonifera* (dogwood), *Deutzia*, *Forsythia*, *Ligustrum ovalifolium* (privet), *Philadelphus* (mock orange), *Ribes sanguineum* (flowering currant), roses (species and hybrids), *Salix* (willow), *Spiraea*, *Tamarix* (tamarisk), *Viburnum* (deciduous) and *Weigela*, among many others. *Aucuba japonica*, *Ceanothus* (deciduous) and *Hypericum* can be propagated from heel or basal

Buddleias are easy to root from hardwood cuttings taken during late autumn.

cuttings now. You should be prepared to experiment or consult a specialist book.

Trees from hardwood cuttings

Some trees can also be propagated from hardwood cuttings, and *Platanus* (plane), *Populus* (poplar) and *Salix* (willow) are particularly easy. If propagating trees, decide whether you want a multi-stemmed tree or one with a single main stem. If the latter, set the cuttings deeper in the trench so that the top bud is just below the surface of the soil.

Plant out layers and rooted cuttings

Rooted layers prepared in spring and hardwood cuttings inserted last year will be ready for planting out in their final positions if they have rooted well. They can be severed from their parent and then transplanted with as much soil around the roots as possible. Rooted cuttings can either be potted up to grow on or planted out in the garden. Poorly rooted layers can be left for another year.

TAKING HARDWOOD CUTTINGS

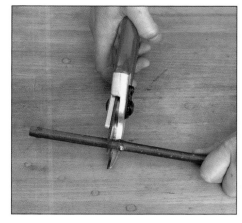

1 Choose stems that are firm and pencil thickness. The length of the cutting will depend on the plant, but about 15cm (6in) is appropriate for most. Make a cut straight across the stem, just below a node.

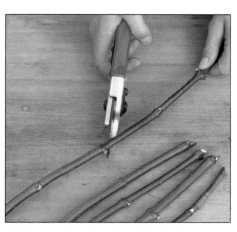

2 Using a pair of secateurs (pruners), make the second cut about 15cm (6in) above the first. Make the cut above a node, but this time at an angle so that you will know which is the top and which the bottom of the cutting.

3 Although a rooting hormone is not essential, it can increase the success rate, especially with plants that are difficult to root. Moisten the bases of the cuttings in water before dipping in the powder.

4 In addition to the usual powder, you can also use liquid and gel rooting hormones, in which case you do not need to dip the end in water first. Treat only the base end of each cutting. Shake off any excess.

5 Make a slit trench with a spade, a little shallower than the length of the cuttings. Choose an unobtrusive and fairly sheltered spot in the garden to leave the cuttings undisturbed for a year.

6 Sprinkle some grit or coarse sand in the base of the slit if the ground is poorly drained. This will help to prevent waterlogging around the cuttings. Firm lightly to make sure there are no air pockets.

7 Insert the cuttings 8–10cm (3–4in) apart, upright against the back of the slit, leaving about 2.5–5cm (1–2in) above the ground.

8 Firm the soil around the cuttings, to eliminate the pockets of air that would cause the cutting to dry out.

9 Water the cuttings and label. Continue to water them in dry weather, especially during the spring and summer months.

Pruning apples and pears

Late autumn is the ideal time to plant new trees and to prune existing ones. If you are growing more than one tree you will have to take into account both the rootstock and the pollination time. By choosing apples or pear varieties that blossom at the same time you can ensure a better set. Trees on dwarfing rootstocks can be planted 1.5m (5ft) apart, while trees on vigorous rootstocks should be spaced up to 7m (25ft) apart. Fruit trees are planted in the same way as ornamental trees.

Pruning fruit trees

Despite a popular belief that apple and pear trees are difficult and time-consuming to keep in shape, if you buy trees that have been well trained, they will require the minimum of care. Apples and pears can be divided into two groups: some apple varieties produce fruit at the tips of their branches (known as tip bearers); while others and most pear varieties bear fruit on spurs produced on older wood. Most pruning involves the removal of dead or diseased wood, maintaining the overall shape and the thinning of fruiting spurs (see below).

Renovating neglected trees

If you leave a tree unpruned for a number of years it may well keep producing a good crop of fruit but they are likely to be variable in size and to be carried high up on the tree. Often, neglected trees will crop well in alternate years, producing a large crop of undersized fruit one year followed by a relatively lean year the next. If your tree answers this description, then late autumn is an ideal time to prune to put things right. Always start by cutting out any dead, diseased or dying branches.

Quick growth

Good vigour but little fruit is more often a problem with well-established young trees than old ones. Upright shoots are growing well and producing lots of leaf but few fruits. You could try summer pruning to

SPUR PRUNING AN APPLE BUSH TREE

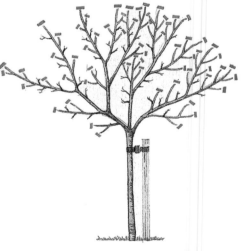

After planting, cut back the leader to about 75cm (30in) above the ground. Leave any sideshoots that appear just below this cut but remove any others lower down. The following year, reduce all new growth by about half. This will form the basic framework. Subsequent pruning is restricted to reducing the length of new growth by about a third and removing overcrowded growth.

When pruning pears, remove any dead, dying or weak growth, then remove crossing or very upright shoots, to leave a healthy tree of well-spaced branches.

help reduce the size and vigour, or you can use a technique called festooning, which requires no pruning at all. Simply tie all the whippy upright shoots down by their tips to hold them as near horizontal as possible – anchoring the end of each string to a sturdy stake. The sap in the stems will then be slowed and less upright growth and more blossom (and subsequently fruit) will be encouraged.

An older tree that makes a lot of growth often develops a thicket of crossing branches in the centre that prevent light getting in and encourage disease problems. Few fruits will be borne on these branches and any that are produced will be small and very late ripening. Thin out any crossing branches, removing the weakest and least well positioned. Then remove any vertical shoots from the centre of the crown to open it up to light and air. Finally, step back from the tree and see if

PRUNING A DWARF PYRAMID PEAR

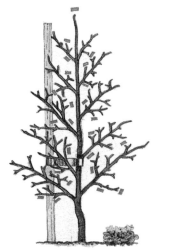

After planting, cut back the leader by about a third. Cut back the sideshoots to about 15cm (6in). In the first summer, cut back the new growth on the main side of the shoots to about five leaves and on the secondary shoots to three leaves. Thereafter, cut back new growth on the main stems to five leaves and reduce other new growth to one leaf. During the winter, thin out any congested spurs.

A poorly pruned fruit tree will become less and less productive as the seasons pass and may not produce a crop at all.

there are any other branches that can be pruned back to help balance the shape of the canopy.

Neglected trees will often put all their vigour into the most vertical and highest branches. This means that the best fruit is often carried well out of reach at the top of the canopy. This can be a serious problem in a heavy cropping year, because these vertical branches tend to be weak and liable to break under a heavy load. All these problems can be overcome by shortening the main upright limbs back to a well-placed side branch lower down growing out

at as near the horizontal as possible. Again, the aim is to end up with a lower canopy of well-spaced branches with an open centre.

Slow growth

Poor vigour and no fruit is usually associated with old, neglected trees that have practically stopped growing. You can increase the vigour and fruit production by pruning selected branches back by about a half to stimulate growth while maintaining the tree's overall shape. It may take several years before the tree is completely reinvigorated.

Pruning soft fruit

Soft fruit is generally simple to prune, mainly because all parts of the plant are within easy reach and the job can usually be done with secateurs (pruners). The aim, however, is the same as with tree fruit – to produce vigorous, healthy bushes and canes that bear good quality fruits year after year. As a matter of routine, always start by cutting out any dead, diseased or damaged stems.

Blackberries and hybrid berries

These fruit on one-year-old shoots, so after harvest, cut out all the fruited stems back to ground level. This will leave all the new shoots produced this year to fruit next year. If there are too many new shoots, thin out the weakest. Tie the remaining shoots to their support. If the plants have been allowed to get overgrown, you will have to wear thick, thornproof gloves and use a pair of long-handled pruners to cut out all but the new stems produced this year.

Blackcurrants

The best fruit is borne on one-year-old branches, so when pruning an established bush the aim is to remove the oldest shoots and encourage new ones. Prune while the plant is dormant. The easiest pruning method is to treat them the same way as many popular shrubs, using the one-in-three pruning method. Simply cut out one-third of the stems, starting with the oldest. This is the best method of rejuvenating an old, neglected plant because after three years' pruning all

Red currants fruit on old wood and can be trained as bushes or cordons, which are usually trained vertically.

PRUNING RASPBERRIES

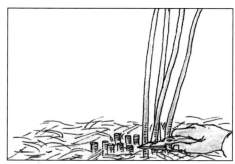

1 Provided you are sure the variety is autumn-fruiting, simply cut all the canes down to ground level while they are dormant using a pair of secateurs (pruners).

2 On summer-fruiting raspberries, cut the old canes (dark stems) that fruited this summer to just above the ground. Tie in the remaining shoots to support wires if necessary.

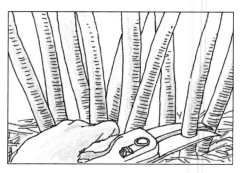

3 If the raspberries have been growing undisturbed for several years, the clumps may have become congested. Thin out surplus canes to be spaced about 8cm (3in) apart.

PRUNING BLACKCURRANTS

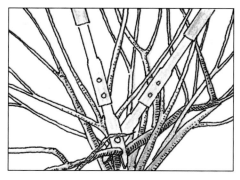

1 Cut back to their point of origin any diseased, damaged or badly placed shoots, leaving the strong, vigorous stems.

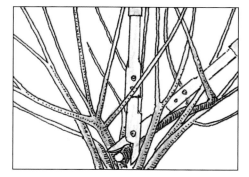

2 Start pruning only once the plants are old enough to fruit reliably. Cut back one-third of the oldest shoots close to the base.

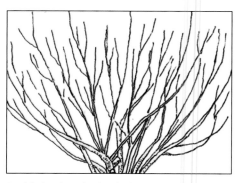

3 This is what the bush should look like after pruning, with plenty of well-spaced young shoots that will fruit next year.

PRUNING GOOSEBERRIES

1 If the job was not done after harvesting, cut back any low branches near the soil to an upward-pointing bud, and remove any badly placed and crossing branches. Try to ensure that the centre of the bush is left open.

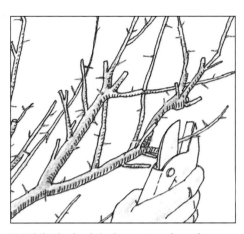

2 While the bush is dormant, reduce the length of new summer growth at the tips of the main shoots by about half. Then go along each main branch and prune back the sideshoots to two buds from the old wood.

3 If the plant is old, cut out one or two of the oldest shoots, until you find a younger one to take over. You will need a pruning saw or loppers for the old wood. Thin the remainder for an open, well-balanced shape.

the stems will be young and vigorous. If you are short of time, pruning can be carried out at harvest time.

Gooseberries

These fruit on shoots that are a year or more old, and continue to fruit quite well even if you neglect pruning. But the spines on the stems make the fruit difficult to harvest unless the bush is pruned annually. The aim is to develop a well-balanced open shape – rather like a wine goblet, with well-spaced branches and an open centre. This also helps prevent gooseberry mildew, which can be a serious problem on congested bushes. You can bring an old, neglected bush back into shape by removing all the crossing shoots that congest the centre of the bush. Thin the remainder to produce an open, well-balanced shape. This regime can also be carried out at harvest time.

Raspberries

Summer-fruiting raspberries fruit on shoots that are one year old. As soon as fruiting is over, loosen the canes from their support and cut all the

fruited stems back down to ground level using a pair of secateurs. Tie in the most vigorous new canes to the support so that they are spaced 8.5cm (3in) apart, cutting out any surplus canes back to ground level. Make sure that all tall canes are securely fastened to the wires to prevent wind damage. This pruning can be carried out any time after fruiting.

Autumn-fruiting raspberries bear fruit on canes grown during the current year, so pruning is even easier. In this case, simply prune all the canes back to ground level after they have produced their fruit in the autumn.

Red and white currants

Unlike blackcurrants, these fruit on shoots that are at least two years old. The fruit-bearing shoots develop when the sideshoots are pruned. The bushes are usually grown on a short length of clear stem (known as a 'leg'), but can also be grown as bushes or trained as cordons. If pruning was not carried out in the summer, start by removing any crossing or overcrowded shoots, to allow plenty of light into the centre of the bush. Then shorten last summer's growth at the tip of

each main shoot by half. Finally, cut back the sideshoots to within one or two buds of the main stem. This will encourage fruiting. On an old bush it may be necessary to cut out some of the older shoots that no longer fruit well, but try to leave a vigorous young sideshoot to replace each one.

Gooseberries can be grown as bushes, cordons or standards. When pruning, aim to keep the centre of the plant as open as possible to encourage good air circulation when in leaf.

Cleaning up the greenhouse

Annual cleaning is essential to maintain the efficiency of the greenhouse: even a little dirt on the glass can make a significant difference to the amount of light that reaches the plants, and pests and diseases that are allowed to overwinter are more likely to become unmanageable the following year. If you can, it's always best to take advantage of the less busy season for the chore of cleaning, rather than waiting until you need to start sowing in spring. And any permanent plants in the greenhouse will benefit from the extra light during the dark days of winter.

Getting started

Choose a mild spell so that all the permanent plants can be stood outside without risk for a couple of days. Clear out any of the remaining crops and any debris as well as all temporary staging and shelving to leave the greenhouse as clear as possible. Take down all temporary shading material, and clear out any piles of empty pots, seed trays and unused bags of compost (soil mix). Deconstruct and disinfect watering systems, such as capillary matting, that are still in use. Turn off the electricity supply at the mains, and remove all electrical equipment.

Greenhouse structure

Using a suitable diluted disinfectant and a hard-bristle brush, scrub down all the internal surfaces in the greenhouse, including the floor, permanent benches and staging. Make sure you clean right into the corners, scrubbing the greenhouse base right up to the frame. Use a toothbrush to clean the mouldings of aluminium glazing bars and clean other areas with wire wool. Wash down the inside of the glass with

During a mild spell in autumn, take the plants that live year round in the greenhouse to a sheltered spot in the garden so that you can clean the greenhouse thoroughly.

disinfectant solution. Make sure the overlaps between panes of glass are cleared of algae, which reduce light transmission during the winter months. Use a plastic plant label or similar to scrape out stubborn moss and algae. Finally, rinse down the whole of the inside of the greenhouse with clean water from a hosepipe.

Clean any remaining shading wash from the outside of the greenhouse glass and use a floor mop or broom to wash down the outside of the roof with a household detergent. There is no need to sterilize the outside of the greenhouse. Wash the sides and ends and carry out any essential maintenance, such as replacing cracked panes of glass and clearing out the gutters.

Pots and seed trays

Clean all empty pots and seed trays that have been used during the course of the season using the same

diluted disinfectant (check that the product you are using is suitable for use on plastic, however). Scrub the insides to remove any remaining compost and rinse in clean water. Don't keep open bags of unused compost for next year's sowings because it will no longer be sterile. It is far better to buy fresh next year and use any waste compost as a soil improver when planting in the garden.

Greenhouse plants

Permanent plants that couldn't be removed from the greenhouse will need to be protected from the cleaning process under a sheet of plastic. Once the greenhouse is clean, remove the covering and inspect the plants to check for pests and diseases — removing any infected material. Wipe the pots of the plants placed outside during cleaning with a moist cloth. Check for signs of pests and disease before returning them inside.

GREENHOUSE CLEAN-UP

1 If you have not already removed the remains of summer shading, do it as soon as possible. Shading washes like this are easy to wipe off with a duster if dry. If left, they will reduce light levels inside the greenhouse.

2 Whether or not summer shading has been used, clean the glass. The easiest way to clean the outside is with a brush or cleaning head on a long handle. Scrub to remove debris. Rinse with clean water.

3 The inside of the glass should be washed with a suitable diluted disinfectant. Using a spray mister is a convenient way to apply the solution. make sure all traces of algae, dirt and grime are removed.

4 Algae often grow where the panes of glass overlap, an area that also traps dirt. Try squirting a jet of water between the panes, then dislodge the dirt with a thin strip of rigid plastic (a plastic plant label is ideal).

5 Squirt a jet of water between the joints where panes overlap to move the loosened dirt and algae. You may need to repeat the process to dislodge stubborn pieces of dirt. Rinse thoroughly to remove traces of disinfectant.

6 Dirt and soil also accumulate where the glass joins the base, and this can be a breeding ground for pests and diseases. Use a label or a small tool to lift the soil out of the crevice, then douse with a garden disinfectant.

7 Fumigation is a good way to control a number of pests and diseases that may be lurking in nooks and crannies around the greenhouse. Check the manufacturer's instructions to make sure it is suitable for your type and size of greenhouse.

8 It is worth disinfecting the frame and staging, whether or not you fumigate the greenhouse. Use a proprietary garden disinfectant diluted in water and scrub all surfaces thoroughly. Rinse with clean water afterwards.

9 Diseases are easily carried over from one plant to another on old pots and seed trays. When you have time between now and spring, wash them all using a garden disinfectant, scrubbing them thoroughly. Rinse with clean water afterwards.

Winter

A well-planned garden will not be devoid of colour or interest during the winter months, and working outdoors can be a real pleasure. Even when the garden is stripped bare there is much to appreciate in the variety of textures, colours and unexpected scent. The lingering brilliance of autumn fruit and dramatic presence of architectural seedheads are joined by the beautiful bark of many trees and shrubs as well as the bonus of winter flowers. Dramatic skeletal frameworks of fading foliage and seedheads combine with contorted twigs to add charm to the winter garden. Try bold rudbeckias with the thistle-like sea hollies and teasel alongside the skeletal form of hydrangeas for a seasonal highlight after a hoar frost. Nearby, add a few tried and trusted winter bloomers, such as winter jasmine, with its cheerful yellow flowers, and snowdrops, which come in so many different varieties that with careful planning you can have some in flower throughout the winter.

Evergreens are the backbone of the winter garden. Coloured forms, such as this variegated holly, will help light up beds and borders whatever the weather.

Moving trees and shrubs

Autumn and early winter are the best times to move established deciduous trees and shrubs. Wait until mid-spring before you transplant evergreens, including conifers. If your soil is very heavy and poorly drained you might be better off delaying the move of deciduous trees and shrubs until spring, but you will have to keep them well watered throughout the summer. By transplanting now you can be sure that the soil is moist and still warm enough to encourage quick rooting.

Preparing the plants

Always thoroughly soak the plants you are intending to move 24 hours before you want to move them to help prevent the rootball cracking and falling away from the roots. Ideally, move the plants during dull weather or when rain is forecast.

Preparing the new hole

Prepare the planting hole before you start digging up the shrub or tree. Clear the ground of perennial weeds and other debris and improve the water-holding capacity of the soil by incorporating plenty of well-rotted manure or other organic matter.

If shrubs or trees outgrow their allotted space they can be moved while they are dormant during autumn or winter. Get help with large specimens, because the rootball will be very heavy.

MOVING A SHRUB

1 Before you begin to dig up the shrub, make sure that the planting site has been prepared and the hole properly excavated. Water the plant well the day before moving it.

2 Dig a trench around the plant, leaving a large rootball (the size depends on the size of the plant). Sever cleanly any roots that you encounter to release the rootball.

3 Dig under the shrub, cutting through any vertical taproots that hold it in place. Take care that you do not break up the rootball when you are severing thick roots.

Cutting the rootball

The size of the rootball should depend on the size of the tree or shrub you are transplanting. As a rough guide, aim to make the rootball about the same diameter as the spread of a shrub and about one-third the height of a tree. The depth of the rootball will also depend on the soil type: deepest on light, sandy soils; and shallower on heavy clay soils. Small trees and most shrubs are easy to move, especially if they are relatively young. First of all clear the loose soil from around the stem and then cut a vertical slit trench around the shrub to mark the diameter of the rootball and sever any roots that are close to the surface. Make a second slit trench about 30cm (12in) further out and then excavate the soil between the slits to create a flat-bottomed trench as deep as the intended rootball. Undercut the rootball using your spade, severing all the roots you come across until the rootball is completely freed.

With large shrubs and trees you would be better off pruning the roots the year before you want to transplant, by digging the trench around the rootball to sever all the roots near the surface. This will encourage new feeder roots to develop in the soil near to the plant, which will form part of the rootball.

Moving the rootball

Rock the freed rootball over to one side and slide a sheet of strong fabric or plastic underneath. Then rock the plant the other way so that half the fabric can be pulled through. With small rootballs, you can simply tie the fabric around the main stem to hold the soil in place. With large rootballs, you will need to reinforce this with strong string or even rope. Carefully lift or drag the trussed-up rootball to the new planting hole and settle it into place at the same depth it was at previously.

If the rootball is large or you are tackling it on your own, use a short, smooth plank as a slide to help you pull the rootball out of the hole. Then lay the rootball on a piece of thick plastic and drag this to the prepared planting hole. The plastic will slide easily over the soil, grass or paving causing the minimum of damage. To move the rootball up steps use a short plank as a slide.

Check bulbs in store

Don't wait until it is time to plant your tender overwintering bulbs before checking them for rot.

1 Check bulbs, corms and tubers being overwintered in a frost-free place once a month. By eliminating diseased or soft bulbs or corms, you will prevent the rot spreading.

2 If you discover any soft or diseased bulbs in store, discard them and dust the others with a fungicide if you have not already done so.

4 Rock the plant to one side and insert some sacking or plastic as far under the plant as you can. Rock the shrub in the opposite direction and pull the sacking through.

5 Tie the sacking around the main stem. If the combined weight of the plant and rootball is very heavy, get help to move it. Tie a length of wood or metal to the sacking and lift it out.

6 Lower the shrub into the prepared planting hole. Remove the sacking and make sure that the plant is in the right position and at the correct depth. Refill the hole and water well.

Knowing your soil

The type of soil you have in your garden will have a great influence on the way you garden and what you can grow. It is useful, therefore, to get to know what your soil is like from the outset. That way, you are likely to make fewer mistakes. You can, of course, learn quite a lot by looking at what is already growing well in your own garden and in your neighbours' plots.

Soil structure

Seeing whether drought-loving Mediterranean plants or hungry plants such as roses are happy in your garden will be a good guide to the type of soil you have, and you can also learn a lot by feeling the texture. Simply wet a small lump of soil and rub it between finger and thumb. If it feels slippery and slimy the soil probably contains a lot of clay particles, if it is gritty then sand is predominant. If it is neither, it is probably a balanced mixture of sand, silt and clay, known as a loamy soil.

Clay soils The tiny particles in clay soils will compact together, especially when walked on, so that water cannot drain away and air cannot penetrate. In spring clay soils tend to be cold and wet and are difficult to work. In summer they can dry out to form solid lumps. However, the water retention means clay soils are generally fertile.

Sandy soils The particles in sandy soil are mainly much larger and of an irregular shape, so do not pack down, resulting in lots of air pockets that allow water to drain freely through the soil. This means that nutrients are easily washed out (known as leaching). In spring sandy soils are easy to work and tend to warm up quickly, but in summer they often dry out.

Silty soils With particle sizes between those of clay and sand, silty soils are generally free-draining but hold on to moisture better than sandy soils. However, unlike sandy soils they are easily compacted if walked on when wet.

TAKING A PH TEST

1 Place the soil in the test tube until it reaches the mark on the side

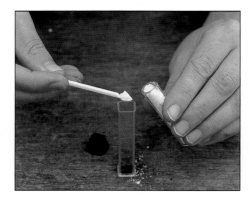

2 Put a layer of barium sulphate powder into the tube level with the mark. This compound helps the solution to clear rapidly and makes the pH reading clearer.

3 Pour in a little of the indicator solution up to the mark shown on the tube. Be careful not to put in too much because this can make the solution dark and difficult to read.

4 Add distilled water to the mark on the tube, put the lid on and shake the container vigorously for about a minute. Leave the contents to settle.

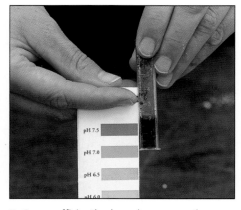

5 Once sufficiently cleared, compare the colour with those on the chart, choosing the one that most closely matches that of the solution.

If you find your soil is too acid for the plants you want to grow, you can reduce the acidity by adding lime some weeks before planting.

TAKING A NUTRIENT TEST

1 Place a small sample of the soil into the test tube up to the mark on the side.

2 Add a test solution (in this case one for nitrogen) up to the mark on the test tube.

3 Filter the solution to remove soil particles and leave just a liquid solution.

4 Decant the resulting filtered solution into another container for the final stage of the nutrient test.

5 Add a small amount of indicator powder. This will react with the solution and enable a colour reading to be taken.

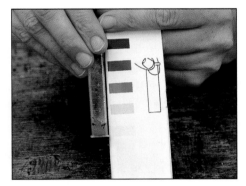

6 Shake for about 10 seconds and compare with the chart. Here, the reading indicates that a nitrogen-rich fertilizer will benefit this soil.

Loam soils These soils tend to contain a balanced mixture of clay, sand and silt, providing the perfect conditions for plant growth: free-draining but moisture-retentive and fertile. They warm up quickly in spring and do not dry out too much in summer. This is the type of soil to which most gardeners aspire.

Acid or alkaline?

The other factor you need to know when choosing plants for your garden is how acid or alkaline your soil is. This is measured on a pH scale ranging from 1 to 14, although the extremes are rarely encountered. The mid-point (7) is neutral and anything higher is progressively more alkaline, while anything lower is progressively more acid. Most plants prefer a pH of about 6.5,

slightly on the acid side of neutral. Some plants, rhododendrons and camellias, for example, need acid soil, of 5.5–6 pH, while others, such as philadelphus, need more alkaline conditions.

Testing your soil

Many people garden successfully without ever testing their soil, but they are probably fortunate in gardening on ground that is not deficient in nutrients, is neither too acid nor too alkaline, and receives plenty of nutrients as part of normal cultivation. If plants don't seem to be growing well, take a soil test. Professional soil testing is the most accurate for nutrients, but you can get a reasonable idea of the major nutrients in your soil with simple indicator kits. Testing for pH is

quick and effective. Bear in mind that kits vary from one manufacturer to another, so always follow the instructions if they are different from the advice given here.

IMPROVING SOIL FERTILITY

The fertility of the soil is much improved by the addition of organic material, but a quick boost can also be achieved by adding a proprietary fertilizer, spreading it over the surface and then raking it in.

Improving your soil

Fortunately, you don't need to know what type of soil you have to make improvements, because they all benefit from the addition of well-rotted organic matter. Unless you have a very peaty soil (which is already rich in organic matter) it is worth adding as much manure and garden compost as you can. All good gardeners make their own compost, because this is the best soil-improving material there is.

Adding organic matter

Organic matter can be dug into the soil or applied as a mulch and left for worms to take it down. It acts like a sponge in light, sandy soils, helping them retain moisture, while in clay soils it opens up the structure and improves drainage. It

will also improve the fertility of poor soils because it releases nutrients as it is broken down by soil-borne organisms. It is important that the organic matter is well-rotted before it is added to the soil; otherwise it will continue to break

down in the soil, using up valuable nitrogen in the process. Another way to add organic material is by growing green manures: nutritious, quick-growing crops that are sown on vacant ground and then dug in, to rot down in the soil.

SINGLE DIGGING

1 Divide the space in half lengthways. Mark the area with string. This avoids moving soil from one end of the plot to the other.

2 Take out a trench the depth and width of a single spade blade. Pile the soil at the end of the other half of the plot, as shown.

3 When you remove the next trench, throw the soil forward into the space left by the first. Digging is easier if you first 'cut' a slice with the spade right across the plot.

4 Push the spade in parallel to the end of the trench, taking a slice of soil about 15–20cm (6–8in) deep. Larger bites may be too heavy to lift comfortably.

5 Loosen the soil by pulling back on the handle, while aiming to keep the bite of soil on the spade. Keeping the spade upright places less strain on your back.

6 Flick the soil over with the wrist, inverting the clod of earth so that the top is buried. Lift the weight with your knees, not your back.

7 When the end of the plot is reached, fill the trench with the soil you took from the first row of the return strip.

8 Finally, fill the trench left when all the digging has been completed with the soil put on one side from the initial excavation.

When to dig

If you have a vegetable plot or other large area of ground that requires digging, this is a good time of year to do it. If the soil is a heavy clay, leaving it rough-dug over the winter will allow the action of frost and the weather to help break down large clods. This will make it easier to rake level and to produce a seedbed of tilth, a fine, crumbly soil in spring. You may prefer to leave digging a light, sandy soil until spring, because this type of soil tends to become flattened and compacted by winter rain if dug too early. New weed growth may also be a problem by spring and can be dealt with at the same time.

How to dig

Recently cultivated soil or small areas between plants can be dug most easily using a garden fork. Push in the fork to the full length of its tines and turn over the soil, breaking down any clods as you go. Incorporate well-rotted organic matter, or lay it on the surface as a mulch for soil-borne organisms such as earthworms to do the work for you. Vacant ground is probably best dug over with a spade. There are three main methods to choose from: simple, single and double digging – although there are many variations of each.

Simple digging is a quick and easy way of cultivating lighter soils. The

Green manures

Broad (fava) beans	nitrogen fixing
Italian ryegrass	quick growing
Lupins	nitrogen fixing
Mustard	quick growing
Phacelia	quick growing
Red clover	nitrogen fixing
Winter tare	nitrogen fixing

DOUBLE DIGGING

1 Divide the plot up in the same way as described for single digging, and deal with the soil from the end of each strip in the same way. But this time make the trenches about 40cm (16in) wide and 25cm (10in) deep.

2 Spread a generous layer of well-rotted manure or garden compost – or other bulky organic material that will retain moisture and add humus – over the bottom of the trench.

3 Fork this thick layer of manure or organic material into the bottom of the trench. A fork is better than a spade because it will penetrate the harder lower layer more easily and will mix the material into the soil better.

4 Move the garden line to the next position, maintaining the same 40cm (16in) spacing, or thereabouts. Cut and slice the soil and throw it forward as before, but take several bites per strip, so that the volume of soil isn't too heavy.

blade of the spade is pushed into the ground vertically and the handle is eased back to loosen the soil. The spade is turned and lifted in one motion to invert the spadeful of soil in the same hole it came from. This is a useful way of burying organic matter laid on the surface.

On heavier soils, single digging (see opposite) is a better technique for incorporating organic matter into the surface layer of the soil, and is likely to do more good for short-rooted plants than burying it deeply. However, for certain deep-rooted crops, such as runner beans, or to break up neglected ground, double digging (see above) can be useful.

ROTAVATING

In larger gardens with heavy soil, a rotavator (rototiller) will break down the soil into a fine tilth. Even a small one saves a lot of time, especially if the soil is too dry to break down with a rake.

Bringing on forced bulbs

Whether your bulbs flower during midwinter, or on any particular date, depends partly on whether you used prepared bulbs in the first place. However, flowering also depends on how cold you keep the bulbs and at what point you bring them out from their resting place into the light and warmth, about 10°C (50°F). After a week or two in these conditions, they can then be moved into their final flowering positions.

Treating bulbs for forcing

It is essential that bulbs placed into plunge beds in autumn are protected from mice and squirrels by covering them with a sheet of chicken wire. Bring in bulbs when they are at the right stage of growth. Hyacinths are the first to show and should be brought into a warmer environment when the flower buds are clearly visible. Forced daffodils should be moved indoors when their leaves are 5–10cm (2–4in) high. Crocuses and tulips should be left until you

can see colour in the breaking flower buds. For longer lasting displays, keep forced bulbs in a cool room in the house and water as necessary. Use hyacinths and hippeastrums (amaryllis) to decorate warmer rooms, because they are more tolerant of higher temperatures.

You can also advance the development of bulbs planted in the garden by covering them with cloches during early winter. They will be ready for cutting several weeks before the rest of the bulbs in the garden.

When flowering is over

It is not worth trying to grow the same hardy bulbs indoors for a second year. Forcing hardy bulbs to flower indoors drains their reserves and the results are almost always disappointing a second time. But there is no need to discard them. Plant them in the garden, where they should gradually recover over a few seasons. If you plan to keep your bulbs for growing in the garden, deadhead them as soon as the display is over. This will avoid energy being wasted on seed production. Do not plant directly into the garden, but acclimatize them gradually by

After forcing, plant out the bulbs so they can gradually recover and provide many years of colourful displays.

placing them in a coldframe or other cool but protected place. Regular watering and a dose of liquid feed will help them recover. In spring, plant the bulbs out in a border or other spot where they can be left undisturbed to grow as a natural group. Some types of bulb may not produce flowers the following season, but probably will do so in subsequent years.

Simple ideas like this single hyacinth and co-ordinated primula often have the most impact.

BRING ON FORCED BULBS

1 Check bowls of bulbs that have been plunged outdoors in beds of sand, peat or grit (to keep them cool and dark while roots develop). When they reach the right stage of development bring them indoors.

2 To protect the bulbs from slugs and other pests, the bowl of planted bulbs can also be put inside a plastic bag before being plunged in the bed outdoors. Open the bag carefully to check their progress.

Keeping hippeastrums

The houseplants popularly but wrongly known as amaryllis are specially treated by the supplier to flower six to eight weeks after they are planted. Many hippeastrums are also sold in flower during the winter. You should be able to keep them so that they flower another year if you follow the advice below. However, they will revert to their normal flowering period of late winter. Cut the flower stalks close to their point of origin once the flowers fade. Keep watered, and feed occasionally. From late spring onwards keep in a greenhouse or conservatory if possible. If you don't have a greenhouse or conservatory, stand the plant outside for the summer. Let the foliage die down in late summer or autumn, then keep the bulbs dry. Start into growth again in late autumn or early winter by gradually increasing watering.

Repotting hippeastrums

Every three or four years, repot using fresh compost – taking care not to disturb the roots. Mix grit into the compost to improve drainage. Replace the surface layer of compost that doesn't contain any roots with fresh each year.

Hippeastrums are specially treated by the supplier to flower in just six to eight weeks after planting, so plant one now for Christmas.

3 If you have kept bulbs in a cool, dark place indoors, such as in a cupboard or loft, check these periodically too. Bring them into the light when the shoots are 2.5–5cm (1–2in) tall.

4 If you sow grass seed on the surface as soon as you bring the bulbs into the light, you should have an attractive carpet of grass by the time they flower to set off the flower display beautifully.

5 Just before the bulbs come into full flower, cut the grass with scissors to a height of about 2.5–5cm (1–2in), to make it look even and neat. Take care not to damage the leaves or flower stems.

Warming up the soil

In the vegetable garden, start warming up the soil with cloches or floating mulches to get your vegetables off to an early start. Although most early vegetables are not sown until early spring, you need to have your cloches in position several weeks before you plan to sow. This effectively lengthens the growing season and provides early crops for the table.

Using a coldframe

If your coldframe is not packed with overwintering plants, make use of it now for early vegetable crops. Radishes and turnips are among the crops that grow quickly and mature early in a coldframe, but you can also try forcing varieties of carrot. Some varieties of lettuce also do well. Dig over the ground in the frame, working in as much organic material as possible. Well-rotted farmyard manure that has been put through a sieve is useful for enriching the soil for these early crops. Do not apply powerful artificial fertilizers at this time. Rake the soil level, and make shallow drills with your rake or a hoe. You can sow the seeds broadcast (scattered randomly), but this makes weeding and thinning more difficult. Sow the

Sow early peas and beans now in containers to get them off to a flying start.

seeds thinly, then rake the soil back over the drills. Water thoroughly, then keep the frame closed until the seeds germinate. Once they are through, ventilate on mild days, but keep closed, and if possible insulated, at night, especially when frost is forecast.

Prepare for beans and celery

You can grow a satisfactory crop of beans without taking special steps to improve the soil and achieve a fairly respectable crop of self-blanching celery by planting on ground that has not been specially enriched. But if you want an especially heavy and impressive crop, it is worth preparing the trench thoroughly first.

Take out a trench 25–30cm (10–12in) deep and 60cm (2ft) wide for runner beans, or 38cm (15in) wide for celery. Heap the soil to one side or both sides of the trench. Add as much well-rotted manure or garden compost as you can spare. This will add some nutrients and improve the structure and moisture-holding capacity of the soil. Fork the manure or compost into the soil at the bottom of the trench – don't leave it as a layer. Finally, rake the excavated soil back into the trench.

Early peas and beans

Peas and beans germinate readily in warm soil in early spring, but you can get them off to a flying start now by sowing in pots or in a length of gutter indoors (see below). This is also a useful technique for keeping sowings on schedule if you garden on heavy soil that is slow to warm up in spring, or if the weather is particularly cold or wet.

SOWING PEAS IN GUTTERING

1 A length of plastic guttering is ideal for starting off pea seeds early in the season. Block the ends and fill with soil.

2 Sow the seeds about 5–8cm (2–3in) apart, cover with soil, then keep warm and moist. Harden off the plants when ready to plant out.

3 Take out a drill with a draw hoe, and gradually slide the peas out of the gutter and into the row so that you do not disturb them.

WARMING A SEEDBED

1 Cloche designs vary considerably, but most can easily be made into long runs the length of the row. Make sure that they are butted close together and that plastic cloches are well anchored to the ground.

2 End pieces are essential for rigid cloches, otherwise they will just become a wind tunnel, which will be unsuitable for plants. Make sure they are fixed firmly in place with stakes or special clips.

3 Sheet plastic tunnel cloches are inexpensive to buy, and although they need to be re-covered after a few seasons, a replacement sheet is inexpensive. Fix the hoops first, then stretch the sheet over them.

4 Use the special fixing wires to hold the sheet in position so it does not blow away.

5 Secure the ends with sticks or pegs, pulling the plastic taut and fastening it down.

6 Heap a little soil over the edges to anchor the cloche and stop wind lifting the sides.

Well chitted potatoes have several short sturdy shoots and are ready for planting.

Chitting potato tubers

The technique known as chitting simply means encouraging the potato tubers to sprout before planting. It is useful if you want the tubers to get off to a quick start, as they will usually be through the ground a week or two before unchitted tubers. Maincrop potatoes can be treated in the same way but it is not really necessary. Place the tubers in a tray in a light position, perhaps by a window, where there is no risk of frost. The kind of long shoots that appear when potatoes have been stored in the dark for some time are no use – the shoots must be short and sturdy. Planting is easiest when they are about 2cm (¾in) long, which usually takes about six weeks.

Apply slow-acting fertilizers

Apply slow-acting fertilizers, such as bonemeal and proprietary controlled-release fertilizers, when the vegetable plot has been dug and levelled, prior to sowing from early spring onwards.

Controlled-release fertilizers release their nutrients only when the soil is warm enough for the plants to use them. Fertilizers should always be applied evenly and at the rate recommended by the manufacturer.

Divide the area into strips 1m (1yd) wide with string, and space canes at the same interval to form a square. Scatter the measured dose, then move the canes to form the next 1m (1yd) square down the row. Repeat until the whole area has been treated. Rake the fertilizer into the soil.

Making an early start

Get better displays earlier in the season by sowing tender bedding before the spring rush. A heated greenhouse or propagator will enable you to get plants ready for planting out as soon as the weather permits. Late winter is also an ideal time to pot up resting begonia tubers, if you have the heated growing space to keep them warm and safe until the threat of frosts has passed.

Sow early bedding

Late winter is a good time to sow the majority of frost-tender plants used for summer bedding if you have a heated greenhouse, although a few such as pelargoniums (bedding geraniums) and Semperflorens begonias, are best sown earlier to give them a long period of growth. Because you usually need quite a lot of each kind for bedding, it is normally best to sow the seeds in trays rather than pots. However, you may prefer to use pots for the more difficult seeds that need to be germinated in a propagator, as you can pack more in. Keeping the different varieties separate also allows you to treat them individually.

Early bedding plants, such as this lobelia, are worth sowing early if you have a reliably heated greenhouse and have the protected space to grow them on.

Sowing fine seeds

Very tiny seeds, such as lobelia and begonia, are difficult to handle and to spread evenly. Mix them with a small quantity of silver sand to provide greater bulk, then sprinkle between finger and thumb as you move your hand over the surface of the compost (soil mix). This not only allows you to scatter the seeds evenly but also enables you to see where they are.

Pricking out

Fill the seed trays with a compost recommended for seedlings. Level the surface, then firm it with your fingers or a pressing board. Prick out a seedling by loosening the soil and lifting up the plant by its seed leaves (the first ones that open, which usually look very different from the true leaves). Make a hole in the compost, deep enough to take most

START TUBERS INTO GROWTH

1 If you are growing your begonias as pot plants, start them off in small pots to save space in the early stages. Loosely fill the pots with a peat-based compost (soil mix), or alternative, intended for seeds or cuttings.

2 If the tubers have small shoots it will be obvious which is the top, otherwise it should be the side with a slight hollow. Lightly press the tuber into the compost. Put in a warm, light place and keep the compost moist.

3 If the begonias are intended for outdoors, perhaps in containers or baskets, start them off in trays instead of pots to save space.

SOWING BEDDING PLANTS

1 Fill a seed tray with seed-sowing compost (soil mix). All-purpose compost could inhibit germination or harm some seedlings. Strike the compost off level with the rim of the tray.

2 Use a presser board (a scrap of wood cut to the right size will usually do the job) to press the compost gently until it is firmed about 1cm (½in) below the rim.

3 Very large seeds can be spaced by hand, but most medium-sized seeds are easily scattered with a folded piece of stiff paper. Tap it with a finger as you move it over the surface.

4 Unless the packet advises not to cover the seeds (a few require light to germinate while others do better in light), cover them by sifting more of the seed compost over the top to provide an even layer.

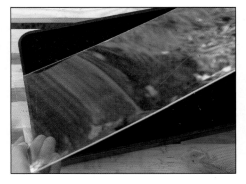

5 Unless you are placing the tray in a propagator, cover it with a sheet of glass, or place it in a plastic bag. Turn the glass over or the bag inside out regularly to prevent condensation drips.

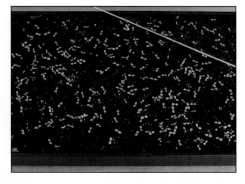

6 Remove any covering when the first seeds start to germinate. If you don't, the seedlings may succumb to disease. It may be possible to reduce the amount of warmth after germination, but good light is always essential.

Tuberous-rooted begonias can be started off in the greenhouse now for a prolonged summer display.

of the roots without curling them. Gently firm the compost round the roots. To help produce an evenly spaced box of plants, first prick out a row along the end and one side. When you have this spacing right, fill in the rest of the tray. The exact spacing will depend on the type of plant that you are pricking out. Large seeds need more space than small ones. You may find it more convenient to use a modular tray system. Although it is more expensive and takes up more room on the bench, it does makes spacing easier, and there is less root disturbance when the plants are eventually put in the garden.

Start off begonia and gloxinia tubers

Tuberous-rooted begonias can be grown as pot plants or in the garden and it is well worth starting them into growth now in the greenhouse. This way you will have well-developed plants to put in the garden that will flower much earlier than if the tubers were planted directly into the soil later on.

Gloxinias, which are suitable only for cultivation in the home or greenhouse, should also be started into growth now. If they are grown as pot plants you can plant them in their final 13–15cm (5–6in) pots. The hairy side is the one to press into the compost (soil mix).

Jobs in brief

No matter how experienced you are at gardening it is very easy to overlook something or forget to carry out an essential task at the correct time. Use the following checklists to help you plan ahead and if you require more details, turn to the relevant page within the book to find a complete description of each task often accompanied by step-by-step photographs. These seasonal checklists will also help you prioritize your gardening activities when time is short such as during the busy spring months. The exact timing of each garden task should not be determined by the calendar, but by the local weather and soil conditions in your garden. For example, you may have to delay early sowings and planting outside for several weeks if winter extends into spring or if you have heavy soil or garden on an exposed plot. Use a soil thermometer to check soil temperatures before you sow and plant and make sure that all plants are thoroughly hardened off before they are positioned outside.

A busy gardener needs to plan ahead to make best use of time, space and money available. The following checklists should help.

Mid-spring

The garden looks colourful again by this time of year, seedlings and cuttings are growing fast, and outdoor sowing and planting can begin in earnest. For many gardeners mid-spring is the most exciting as well as the busiest time of the year. This is often when priorities have to be decided if it isn't possible to keep up with all those urgent jobs. Plants sown or planted in late spring often catch up with those sown a month earlier if the weather happens to be unseasonably cold. Heavy showers are commonplace which can wash out outdoor sowings and emerging rows of seedlings, so it's important to have a stack of cloches to provide some temporary cover.

MID-SPRING JOBS IN BRIEF

The flower garden

- ☐ Stake herbaceous plants
- ☐ Create a mowing strip
- ☐ Sow wildflowers
- ☐ Make a new pond
- ☐ Make and plant a bog garden
- ☐ Make a pebble fountain
- ☐ Make and plant a rock garden
- ☐ Plant a hanging basket

The kitchen garden

- ☐ Choose the most suitable part of your garden for the vegetable plot and prepare the soil
- ☐ Start sowing vegetables without protection – many kinds can be sown from mid-spring onwards, so check the packets
- ☐ Improve areas of stony soil
- ☐ Plant potatoes
- ☐ Transplant cabbages and cauliflowers
- ☐ Protect crops against light frosts with newspaper or garden fleece
- ☐ Put cloches over strawberries if you want an early crop
- ☐ Protect crops against pests
- ☐ Plant a herb garden
- ☐ Make a herb wheel

The greenhouse and conservatory

- ☐ Sow tender vegetables such as outdoor tomatoes and runner beans to plant out later, and cucumbers for the greenhouse
- ☐ Harden off bedding plants by placing them in a coldframe, or similar, a week or two before planting out time

Support clump-forming perennials using proprietary hoops with adjustable legs. Stake tall flowering stems by tying them to a cane that is shorter than the eventual height of the plant and hidden from sight behind the stem.

Plant brassica seedlings with a trowel and firm the soil well. A convenient way to firm soil around the roots is to insert the blade of the trowel about 5cm (2in) away from the plant and press it firmly towards the roots.

Outdoor and greenhouse cucumbers can be sown now (top). Sweet corn is best raised in pots to plant out later (above), except in very mild regions. You can use ordinary pots, but many gardeners prefer to use peat pots.

PLANTS AT THEIR BEST

Forsythia (shrub)
Helleborus orientalis (herbaceous)
Hyacinthus (bulb)
Magnolia × *soulangiana* (tree)
Magnolia stellata (shrub)
Muscari armeniacum (bulb)
Narcissus (bulb)
Primula × *polyantha* (herbaceous)
Prunus 'Kwanzan' (tree)
Pulsatilla vulgaris (rock plant)
Ribes sanguineum (shrub)
Tulipa, various (bulb)

Dicentra formosa produces wonderful arching stems of pink heart-shaped flowers.

Full of spring cheer, *Narcissus* 'Carlton' produces glowing yellow trumpets.

Early Summer

The garden will be full of colour in early summer, and you should have time to relax a little and reap the rewards of all your efforts over the past few months. As well as enjoying abundant displays of flowers, you can begin harvesting early vegetable crops. There are still plenty of maintenance tasks, however: the lawn will be growing strongly, as will weeds, so these need to be kept under control. Many pests and diseases will be active at this time of year, too: keep a close eye out for any attacks, and whenever possible, take preventative action – such as putting up barriers – before any serious damage occurs.

EARLY SUMMER JOBS IN BRIEF

The flower garden
- ☐ Deadhead flowers
- ☐ Prune shrubs
- ☐ Renovate neglected shrubs
- ☐ Plant a window box
- ☐ Plant up tubs and patio pots

The kitchen garden
- ☐ Water vegetables
- ☐ Control weeds
- ☐ Plant potatoes
- ☐ Harvest vegetables such as beetroot (beets), lettuce and cabbage
- ☐ Prune fruit such as plums, cherries and apricots
- ☐ Care for soft fruit by layering blackberries and cutting back strawberries
- ☐ Sow French beans
- ☐ Take preventative measures against aphids on broad beans and root flies on cabbages, carrots and onions.

The greenhouse and conservatory
- ☐ Keep crops growing well by feeding and watering well
- ☐ Try biological pest control for greenhouse pests

Choose a tall or bold plant for the centre of a summer container and surround it with bushy plants with contrasting leaf shapes and complementary flower colour. (top). Water thoroughly after planting (above).

Regular maintenance, such as fertilizing and protecting from pests throughout the summer will ensure there will be plenty of vegetables, such as these runner beans to be harvested later on in the summer.

If tomato plants are supported by strings, loop the string around the top of the shoot when necessary. If it is supported by a vertical cane, use soft string wound twice around the stake and loop it loosely around the stem.

PLANTS AT THEIR BEST

Alchemilla mollis (herbaceous)
Allium (bulb)
Buddleja globosa (shrub)
Calendula (hardy annual)
Choisya tenata (shrub)
Cistus (shrub)
Clematis montana (climber)
Dianthus (perennial and biennial)
Dicentra (perennial)
Digitalis (biennial)
Genista (shrub)
Geranium (herbaceous)
Godetia (hardy annual)
Iris germanica hybrids (bulb)
Laburnum (tree)
Lupinus (herbaceous)
Malus (tree)

Herbaceous peonies make excellent specimen plants for the middle of a border in full sun or partial shade.

Sprawling *Geranium* 'Ann Folkard' produces a profusion of magenta flowers.

Late Summer

We can usually expect some hot, dry weather in late summer, and it's a good time to enjoy garden parties and barbecues, since there should be plenty to admire in the garden. The kitchen garden will be satisfyingly productive, too — a wide range of fruit and vegetables can be harvested, and there will usually be surpluses to give to friends or to preserve or store. Vegetables, containers and any newly planted specimens need diligent watering.

LATE SUMMER JOBS IN BRIEF

The flower garden
- [ ] Plant bulbs for spring
- [ ] Care for dahlias and chrysanthemums
- [ ] Trim hedges
- [ ] Trim groundcover to encourage the plants to grow more densely with fewer straggly stems
- [ ] Cut back shoots wherever reversion has begun

The kitchen garden
- [ ] Ripen and harvest onions
- [ ] Harvest other vegetables, such as aubergines (eggplant), courgettes (zucchini), French (green) beans, potatoes, sweet corn and turnips
- [ ] Choose a suitable way of storing vegetables
- [ ] Harvest fruit when it is in prime condition, taking care not to damage it as this will make it rot later on
- [ ] Choose a suitable way of storing fruit — freezing, storing in trays or cooking and preserving are some of the alternatives

The greenhouse and conservatory
- [ ] Sow spring-flowering pot plants
- [ ] Propagate pelargoniums and fuchsias
- [ ] Take leaf and semi-ripe cuttings
- [ ] Sow new seeds
- [ ] Plant hyacinth bulbs for early flowering under glass

Remove any kind of litter or rubbish that is lurking amongst the groundcover (top). Most groundcover will look better if it is trimmed back at least once a year (above).

As soon as the foliage of onions has turned a straw colour and is brittle, lift them with a fork and leave them on the surface for a few days to dry off. Lay with roots facing the sun.

Plant hyacinths by placing a layer of potting mixture in the container, then space the bulbs close together, but not touching (top). Pack more compost around the bulbs.

PLANTS AT THEIR BEST

Dahlia (bulb)
Erigeron (herbaceous)
Fuchsia (shrub)
Helenium (herbaceous)
Hibiscus syriacus (shrub)
Hydrangea (shrub)
Hypericum (shrub)
Lavatera (shrub)
Lilium (bulb)
Perovskia atriplicifolia (shrub)
Romneya (shrub)
Summer bedding
Verbascum (herbaceous)

Add a flamboyant touch to your late summer garden with the delicate paper petals of *Romneya coulteri*.

For robust reliability choose Rose of Sharon (*Hypericum* 'Hidcote') that bears golden blooms from midsummer onwards.

Early Autumn

The weather in early autumn is still warm enough to make outdoor gardening a comfortable experience, and although the vibrant flowers of summer may be gone, there are plenty of delights to be enjoyed in the form of bright berries and flaming foliage, not to mention late-flowering gems such as chrysanthemums and nerines. Apart from bulb planting, and protecting frost-tender plants, there are few really pressing jobs at this time of year. If you have extra time, it is worth getting ahead with tidying up the garden ready for winter.

EARLY AUTUMN JOBS IN BRIEF

The flower garden
- [ ] Clear summer bedding
- [ ] Lift and store gladioli and other tender bulbs, corms and tubers
- [ ] Plant lilies for the summer
- [ ] Store garden canes – extend their life by cleaning and preserving them, and storing in a dry place rather than leaving them exposed in the garden
- [ ] Remove thatch and moss from the lawn.
- [ ] Feed and weed the lawn
- [ ] Collect leaves, keeping those shed by deciduous trees and shrubs as they make good leafmould once rotted down
- [ ] Make any necessary lawn repairs
- [ ] Plant bulbs for a spring-flowering window box
- [ ] Plant early spring containers

The kitchen garden
- [ ] Protect outdoor tomatoes with cloches or fleece to extend their season and ripen more fruit
- [ ] Place cloches over lettuces and other low-growing vegetables
- [ ] Cut down asparagus haulms and apply a mulch
- [ ] Plant garlic
- [ ] Store vegetables

The greenhouse and conservatory
- [ ] Bring in pot plants from garden
- [ ] Use up spare bulbs left over from border planting outside to use for boosting indoor displays
- [ ] Remove greenhouse shading, clean off shading wash, remove blinds or nets
- [ ] Sow hardy annuals and perennials for planting out in the garden

Tender bulbs, such as gladioli, should be lifted now and stored in a frost-free place. Loosen the soil with a spade or fork before attempting to lift the plants.

Lift potatoes with a fork once the foliage has died down (top). Leave the tubers on the surface for a couple of hours so that the skins dry off and harden. Sort the potatoes before storing them. Grade them into four sizes: very small, small, medium and large (above).

Tender pot plants that have been put outside for the summer need to be brought indoors now before the first frost. Always check for pests and diseases (top). Wipe the pot clean with a damp cloth so that it does not make a mess indoors (above).

PLANTS AT THEIR BEST

Anemone x hybrida (herbaceous)
Aster novae-angliae (herbaceous)
Aster novi-belgii (herbaceous)
Chrysanthemum, early flowering garden
   type (herbaceous)
Dahlia
Hibiscus syriacus (shrub)
Hydrangea (shrub)
Lavatera (shrub)
Nerine bowdenii (bulb)
Pyracantha, berries (shrub)
Rudbeckia (herbaceous)
Sedum spectabile (herbaceous)
Solidago (herbaceous)
Sorbus, berries (tree)
Sternbergia lutea (bulb)

Chrysanthemum 'Primrose Allouise' is an outdoor variety that bears its superb blooms during early autumn.

Ice plant, *Sedum spectabile*, is a valuable late source of nectar for butterflies and bees.

Mid-autumn

The weather is unpredictable at this time of year, and it's crucial to keep an eye on the forecasts and take action whenever necessary to protect vulnerable plants. Fallen leaves will be plentiful, and these should be cleared away regularly, especially from the lawn, delicate small plants, and from the pond. Small quantities of leaves can be added to the compost heap, but they tend to rot down more slowly than other waste so don't add too many.

MID-AUTUMN JOBS IN BRIEF

The flower garden
- [ ] Naturalize bulbs in grass and under the canopy of trees
- [ ] Save tender bulbs for next year
- [ ] Plant new shrubs and hedges
- [ ] Prune rambling roses
- [ ] Cover the pond with fine-mesh netting to prevent leaves falling into it, or alternatively use a fish net or rake to remove the leaves regularly
- [ ] Make leafmould from fallen leaves
- [ ] Protect pond pumps
- [ ] Overwinter tender aquatics
- [ ] Protect tender plants in containers by moving them into the greenhouse or conservatory where they can be kept frost-free
- [ ] Protect permanent containers, raising them off the ground by standing them on small blocks
- [ ] Protect plants from the cold by wrapping pots in bubble wrap or covering plants with horticultural fleece

The kitchen garden
- [ ] Pot up herbs for winter use
- [ ] Use cloches or coldframes to protect Swiss chard
- [ ] Cut back globe artichokes
- [ ] Harvest leeks
- [ ] Add organic material such as well-rotted garden compost or farmyard manure

The greenhouse and conservatory
- [ ] Insulate the greenhouse with thermal screens made of clear plastic or special translucent fabrics
- [ ] Buy a heater – it is best to get one that is thermostatically controlled if you have an electricity supply to your greenhouse
- [ ] Overwinter pelargoniums
- [ ] Overwinter tender fuchsias

Prepare your pond for winter by clearing fallen leaves as well as overgrown submerged oxygenating plants, that will clog the pond.

Chives respond well to lifting for an extended season. Lift a small clump complete with rootball and soil to pot up.

Cut down heating costs in your greenhouse over winter by putting up insulation. Always insulate the ventilators separately.

The striking plum-coloured foliage of *Berberis thunbergii* f *atropurpurea* turns brilliant shades of red at this time of the year.

Japanese anemones give a reliable display of elegant blooms throughout the autumn.

PLANTS AT THEIR BEST

Acer, colourful foliage (tree/shrub)
Anemone x *Hybrida* (herbaceous)
Aster novi-belgii (herbaceous)
Berberis, colourful foliage and berries (shrub)
Fothergilla, colourful foliage (shrub)
Liriope muscari (herbaceous)
Parthenocissus, colourful foliage (climber)
Pernettya, berries (shrub)
Pyracantha, berries (shrub)
Schizostylis coccinea (herbaceous)

Late Autumn

It's important to protect vulnerable plants now, before winter sets in. Any that haven't already been moved to a frost-free place, or covered with a suitable protection, should be attended to as necessary. Now is the perfect time to plant deciduous shrubs and trees – bare-rooted specimens are now available, and container-grown plants, though they can be planted at any time, are best planted now. The soil is still warm, and should stay moist.

LATE AUTUMN JOBS IN BRIEF

The flower garden
- ☐ Lift and protect chrysanthemums
- ☐ Pot up winter aconites
- ☐ Overwinter chrysanthemums
- ☐ Weed and apply a generous amount of mulch to beds
- ☐ Lift tender perennials and pot them up or overwinter them in boxes somewhere frost-free
- ☐ Cut back dying foliage on herbaceous perennials
- ☐ Plant trees, and stake them if they are tall
- ☐ Take hardwood shrub cuttings
- ☐ Protect vulnerable shrubs for winter
- ☐ Protect newly planted evergreens from wind damage
- ☐ Cover alpines that need protection from winter wet with a pane of glass

The kitchen garden
- ☐ Plan a soft fruit garden – a sunny site that is sheltered from cold winds is ideal
- ☐ Plant bush fruit
- ☐ Support cane fruit
- ☐ Prune apples and pears
- ☐ Renovate neglected trees
- ☐ Prune blackcurrants, gooseberries and raspberries

The greenhouse and conservatory
- ☐ Scrub down all surfaces and the floor with a suitable diluted disinfectant
- ☐ Clean empty pots and seed trays using the disinfectant
- ☐ Protect permanent plants that can't be removed with a sheet of plastic while cleaning
- ☐ Except with winter-flowering plants that are still in strong, active growth, gradually give plants less water. Most will then tolerate low temperatures better and disease should be less of a problem

Insert three stout canes or stakes at equal distances around the plant being protected, then wrap a plastic sheet or several layers of garden fleece around the edge. Peg down the bottom and staple the sides together.

Most trees can be planted at any time of the year but they will establish more quickly if planted in the autumn as this is when the soil is moist and still warm. Bare-root trees are only available when dormant.

Diseases are easily carried over from one plant to another on old pots and seed trays. When you have time between now and spring, wash them all using a suitable garden disinfectant, scrubbing the inside aswell as the outside.

PLANTS AT THEIR BEST

Acer, colourful foliage (tree/shrub)
Berberis, colourful foliage and berries
   (shrub)
Cotoneaster, berries (shrub)
Fothergilla, colourful foliage (shrub)
Gentiana sino-ornata (alpine)
Liriope muscari (herbaceous)
Pernettya, berries (shrub)
Pyracantha, berries (shrub)
Schizostylis coccinea (herbaceous)

The eye-catching kaffir lily offers a late splash
of colour when most other flowers are past
their best.

Japanese maples give brilliant displays of
colourful foliage in autumn.

Early Winter

Before the weather gets too cold, it's a good idea to spend some time tidying up the garden. You can see the garden framework clearly now, which should give you ideas for future improvements. If the garden looks really drab, think about which plants you can introduce to make it more appealing next winter: there are lots of wonderful berrying and winter-flowering plants to choose from. And if you don't know much about your soil, it may be useful to get a soil testing kit, so that you can make any necessary improvements before planting begins again.

EARLY WINTER JOBS IN BRIEF

The flower garden
- [ ] Check bulbs, corms and tubers in store
- [ ] Move trees and shrubs, making sure that the planting site has been prepared and the hole properly excavated

The kitchen garden
- [ ] Test your soil
- [ ] Apply lime to your soil if the test shows it is necessary
- [ ] Make a nutrient test
- [ ] Improve soil fertility by adding organic material or for a quick boost add a proprietary fertilizer
- [ ] Incorporate organic matter into the surface layer of the soil by single digging
- [ ] For certain deep-rooted crops, such as runner beans or to break up neglected ground double dig
- [ ] Break down heavy soil into a fine tilth using a rotavator

The greenhouse and conservatory
- [ ] Protect bulbs in plunge beds by covering them with a sheet of chicken wire
- [ ] Bring in forced bulbs when they are at the right stage of growth
- [ ] When flowering is over plant the bulbs in the garden

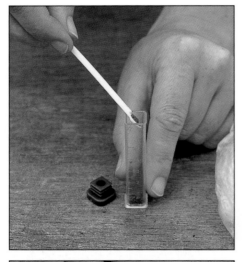

Use a simple kit to test your soil before adding plants to your garden. You can then take steps to alter the soil conditions if necessary before planting.

In larger gardens with heavy soil, a rotavator (rototiller) will break down the soil into a fine tilth. Even a small one saves time, especially if the soil is too dry to break down with a rake.

Check bulbs that have been plunged outside, bringing them inside when they reach the right stage of development (top). Gently open the bag to check their progress (above).

PLANTS AT THEIR BEST

Chimonanthus praecox (shrub)
Erica carnea (shrub)
Erica × *darleyensis* (shrub)
Hamamelis mollis (shrub)
Ilex, berries (shrub/tree)
Iris unguicularis (syn. *I. stylosa*)
    (herbaceous)
Jasminum nudiflorum (wall shrub)
Liriope muscari (herbaceous)
Mahonia bealei (shrub)
Mahonia 'Charity' (shrub)
Pernettya, berries (shrub)
Prunus × *subhirtella* 'Autumnalis' (tree)
Pyracantha, berries (shrub)
Sarcococca (shrub)
Viburnum × *bodnantense* (shrub)
Viburnum farreri (shrub)

Sweet box, *Sarcococca confusa*, bears fragrant white flowers in winter, followed by glossy black berries.

Ideal for any size garden, *Prunus* x *subhirtella* 'Autumnalis' will provide interest during mild spells all winter long.

Midwinter

If you made an early start with winter jobs like digging and tidying beds and borders, mid winter is a time mainly for indoor jobs like ordering seeds and plants, writing labels, and designing improvements for the year ahead.

These are not unimportant tasks, and by attending to them in good time you are more likely to make the right decisions and have everything ready for late winter and early spring when gardening begins again in earnest.

MIDWINTER JOBS IN BRIEF

The flower garden
☐ Protect winter hellebore flowers with a cloche or a piece of clear plastic stretched over wire hoops or a pane of glass supported on bricks
☐ Insulate coldframes for extra protection in the cold weather with sheets of expanded polystyrene (Styrofoam)
☐ Put a warm blanket or piece of old carpet over the coldframe at night but remember to remove it in the morning as the plants need light
☐ Prune conifers

The kitchen garden
☐ Force rhubarb
☐ Write labels in advance
☐ Force chicory
☐ Place cloches over the top of chicory and insulate on cold nights

The greenhouse and conservatory
☐ Take chrysanthemum cuttings
☐ Take root cuttings

Protect low-growing winter-flowering plants such as *Helleborus niger* with a cloche if you want perfect blooms to cut for indoors. The plant is hardy but the flowers tend to become splashed and damaged by the weather.

There are many ways to force rhubarb – make a frame from wire netting and fill with straw (top) or use a plastic dustbin (trash can) and cut the bottom out, using it the right way up with a lid on, or use it inverted without a lid.

Chrysanthemums that you potted up and brought indoors in autumn should have produced shoots by now, which you can use to take cuttings. Hormone rooting powder (top) may increase the success rate.

PLANTS AT THEIR BEST

Chimonanthus praecox (shrub)
Eranthis hyemalis (bulb)
Erica carnea (shrub)
Erica × darleyensis (shrub)
Galanthus nivalis (bulb)
Garrya elliptica (shrub)
Hamamelis mollis (shrub)
Iris unguicularis (syn. *I. Stylosa*)
　　(herbaceous)
Ilex, berries (tree/shrub)
Jasminum nudiflorum (wall shrub)
Lonicera fragrantissima (shrub)
Prunus × subhirtella 'Autumnalis' (tree)
Sarcococca (shrub)
Viburnum × bodnantense (shrub)
Viburnum farreri (syn. *V. fragrans*)
　　(shrub)
Viburnum tinus (shrub)

Eranthis hyemalis will light up the border under the bare branches of trees and shrubs.

Winter heathers provide much-needed and long-lasting colour during the coldest months.

Late Winter

There still aren't many pressing tasks in the garden, but you can enjoy the sight of the emerging bulbs and early-flowering shrubs. Some sowings can be made in the greenhouse or in progagators, but don't be in a hurry to sow or plant outdoors – seeds sown later will usually overtake the early-sown plants, which will struggle in cold conditions. You can start warming areas of ground in the vegetable garden by covering it with cloches or fleece.

LATE WINTER JOBS IN BRIEF

The flower garden
- ☐ Service your mower or have it done professionally
- ☐ Order seeds, bulbs and plants for the coming season
- ☐ Insulate the coldframe for extra protection against the coldest weather
- ☐ Tidy up the rock garden, and apply fresh stone chippings where necessary
- ☐ Check labels on shrubs and border plants and renew them if you think it is necessary

The kitchen garden
- ☐ Finish winter digging
- ☐ Apply slow-acting fertilizers when the vegetable plot has been dug and levelled
- ☐ Force rhubarb
- ☐ Start warming up the soil with cloches or floating mulches to get vegetables off to a good start
- ☐ Sow peas and beans in pots or in a length of gutter indoors
- ☐ Sow early crops in coldframes or beneath cloches
- ☐ Prepare runner bean and celery trenches
- ☐ Chit 'seed' potatoes (small tubers) of early varieties

The greenhouse and conservatory
- ☐ Sow bedding plants
- ☐ Start tubers into growth
- ☐ Sow seeds of bedding plants and pot plants
- ☐ Prick out seedlings sown earlier
- ☐ Start off begonia and gloxinia tubers
- ☐ Make sure glass is clean so that the plants receive plenty of light

Very large seeds can be spaced by hand, but most medium-sized seeds are easily scattered with a folded piece of stiff paper. Tap it with a finger as you move it over the surface.

Cloche designs vary considerably, but most can be easily made into long runs the length of the row. Make sure that they are butted close together and are well anchored.

Tuberous begonias can be planted now. Make sure you plant them the right way up – if there are no shoots, the top will be the side with a slight hollow.

PLANTS AT THEIR BEST

Crocus (bulb)
Daphne mezereum (shrub)
Eranthis hyemalis (bulb)
Erica carnea (shrub)
Erica × *darleyensis* (shrub)
Galanthus nivalis (bulb)
Garrya elliptica (shrub)
Helleborus niger (herbaceous)
Helleborus orientalis (herbaceous)
Iris reticulata (bulb)
Iris unguicularis (syn. *I. stylosa*)
    (herbaceous)
Jasminum nudiflorum (wall shrub)
Muscari armeniacum (bulb)
Prunus cerasifera (tree)
Prunus × *subirtella* 'Autumnalis' (tree)
Sarcococca (shrub)
Viburnum × *bodnantense* (shrub)
Viburnum tinus (shrub)

Viburnum tinus flowers are produced
all winter.

Create a carpet of dainty nodding snowdrops,
Galanthus nivalis.

Viburnum bodnantense bears fragrant clusters
of pink flowers.

Glossary of terms

Annual A plant that grows from seed, flowers, sets seed and dies in one year.

Aquatic A plant that lives in water: it can be completely submerged, floating or live with its roots in the water.

Bare-root A plant sold with no soil or compost around the roots. They are dug up from the nursery field and are ready for planting in the dormant season.

Bedding plant A plant that is raised for use in a temporary garden display; spring, summer and winter types are available.

Biennial A plant that grows from seed to form a small plant in the first year and flowers and sets seed in the following year.

Biological control The use of a pest's natural enemies to control its numbers in the garden or greenhouse.

Bog garden An area of ground that remains permanently wet and is used to grow bog plants that thrive in such conditions.

Capillary matting An absorbent material that holds a lot of water on which containers are placed and from which they can draw all the moisture they need.

Certified stock Plants that have been inspected and declared free of specific pests and diseases. They can be used as stock plants for propagation material.

Chit A technique used to encourage a potato tuber to begin to sprout before planting.

Cloche A small structure made from glass, clear plastic or polythene that is used to warm small areas of soil or protect vulnerable plants.

Compost (soil mix) A mixture used for growing plants in containers. It can be loam-based or peat-based. Peat-free versions are now available based on coir, composted bark or other organic waste material.

Compost, garden A material that has been produced from the decomposition of organic waste material in a compost bin or heap. Useful as a soil improver or planting mixture.

Cordon A trained form of tree or bush with a main stem, vertical or at an angle, and with sideshoots shortened to form fruiting spurs.

Crop covers Various porous materials used to protect plants or crops. Horticultural fleece protects plants from frost and flying insect pests; insect-proof mesh is a well-ventilated fabric, ideal for keeping out insects throughout the summer, but offers no frost protection.

Cultivate To prepare the land and soil for growing crops.

Damping down Wetting surfaces in a greenhouse to raise air humidity and to help keep temperatures down.

Deadhead To remove spent flowers to tidy the display, prevent the formation of seeds and improve future flowering.

Earth (hill) up To draw up soil around a plant forming a mound. Potatoes are earthed up to protect new shoots from frost and to prevent tubers from being exposed to light.

Tulips and double daisies

Espalier A trained form of tree or bush where the main stem is vertical and pairs of sideshoots are at a set spacing and trained out horizontally.

Fan A trained form of tree or bush where the main stem is vertical and pairs of sideshoots are pruned at set spacing and trained out either side to form a fan shape.

Fleece *see* Crop covers

Grafted plant A plant that has been attached on to the rootstock of another variety. Trees, especially fruit trees, are often grafted on to dwarfing rootstocks, while ornamental plants may be grafted on to a more vigorous variety.

Groundcover plants These are densely growing, mat-forming plants that can be used to cover the ground with foliage to prevent weeds germinating.

Hardening-off A method of gradually weaning a plant from the conditions inside to those outside without causing a check to growth.

Hardiness The amount of cold a type of plant is able to withstand. Hardy plants can tolerate frost; half-hardy and tender plants cannot.

Herbaceous plants Plants that produce sappy, green, non-woody growth. Herbaceous perennials die down in winter, but re-grow from basal shoots the following spring.

Horticultural fleece *see* Crop covers.

Humus The organic residue of decayed organic matter found in soil. It improves soil fertility.

Insect-proof mesh *see* crop covers.

Leafmould A material that has been produced from the decomposition of leaves in a leaf bin or heap. Useful as a soil improver or planting mixture.

Manure A bulky organic animal waste that is rotted down and used to improve soil structure and fertility.

Mulch A material that is laid on the surface of the soil to prevent moisture loss through evaporation and suppress weed growth. A mulch can be loose and organic, such as composted bark or garden compost, loose and inorganic, such as gravel, or a fabric, such as mulch matting or landscape fabric.

Perennial A plant that lives for more than two years. The term is usually applied to a hardy non-woody plant (*see* Herbaceous). A tender perennial is a non-woody plant that cannot tolerate frost.

Pricking out The spacing of seedlings while still small so that they have room to develop and grow on.

Rootball A mass of roots and compost that holds together when a plant is removed from its container.

Runner A horizontal shoot that spreads out from the plant, roots and forms another plant.

Slow-release fertilizer A specially coated inorganic fertilizer that releases its nutrients slowly.

Sucker A shoot that arises from the roots underground. The term is usually applied to shoots from the rootstock of a grafted plant that has different characteristics to the ornamental variety.

Transplanting The transfer of seedlings or young plants from a nursery bed where they were sown to their final growing position.

Windbreak A hedge, fence, wall or fabric that is used to filter the wind and therefore reduce the damage that it may cause.

Index

Pick strawberries when they are fully coloured.

Lupins usually only need staking in exposed positions.

A perfect specimen of Swiss chard.

Position winter pansies in a sheltered spot.

Any size garden can accommodate some fruit.

Insulating snow can prevent winter damage.

Acknowledgements

The publisher would like to thank Peter McHoy for his permission to use the following photographs: p48 all pics, p98 all pics, p99 all bottom pics, p149tr, tc, cr, cl, p168t, cl, cr, bl, br, p169c, p215bl, bc, br, p196t, p208br, bc, p209 bl, bc, br, p244br, cr, p256.

Photography: Peter Anderson, Jonathan Buckley, Sarah Cuttle, Paul Forrester, John Freeman, Michelle Garrett, Jacqui Hurit, Debbie Patterson and Steven Wooster.